TRADITIONAL FOOD
IN THE SOUTH PENNINES

Traditional Food
in the South Pennines:
Calderdale and Haworth

by

Peter Brears

Hebden Bridge
Hebden Bridge Local History Society, 2022
Occasional Publication No.12

Published by
Hebden Bridge Local History Society
The Birchcliffe Centre
Birchcliffe Road
Hebden Bridge
HX7 8DG
www.hebdenbridgehistory.org.uk

ISBN: 978-0-9933920-7-8

Front cover: *Emily Brontë watches her sister Charlotte cut up the meat for hash at Haworth Parsonage in the 1830s, but not as attentively as their cat 'Tiger' and dog 'Keeper'.*
Back cover: *Oxenhope's Sawood Wesleyans enjoying their walk buns after their Whitsunday walk to Old Town.*

Contents

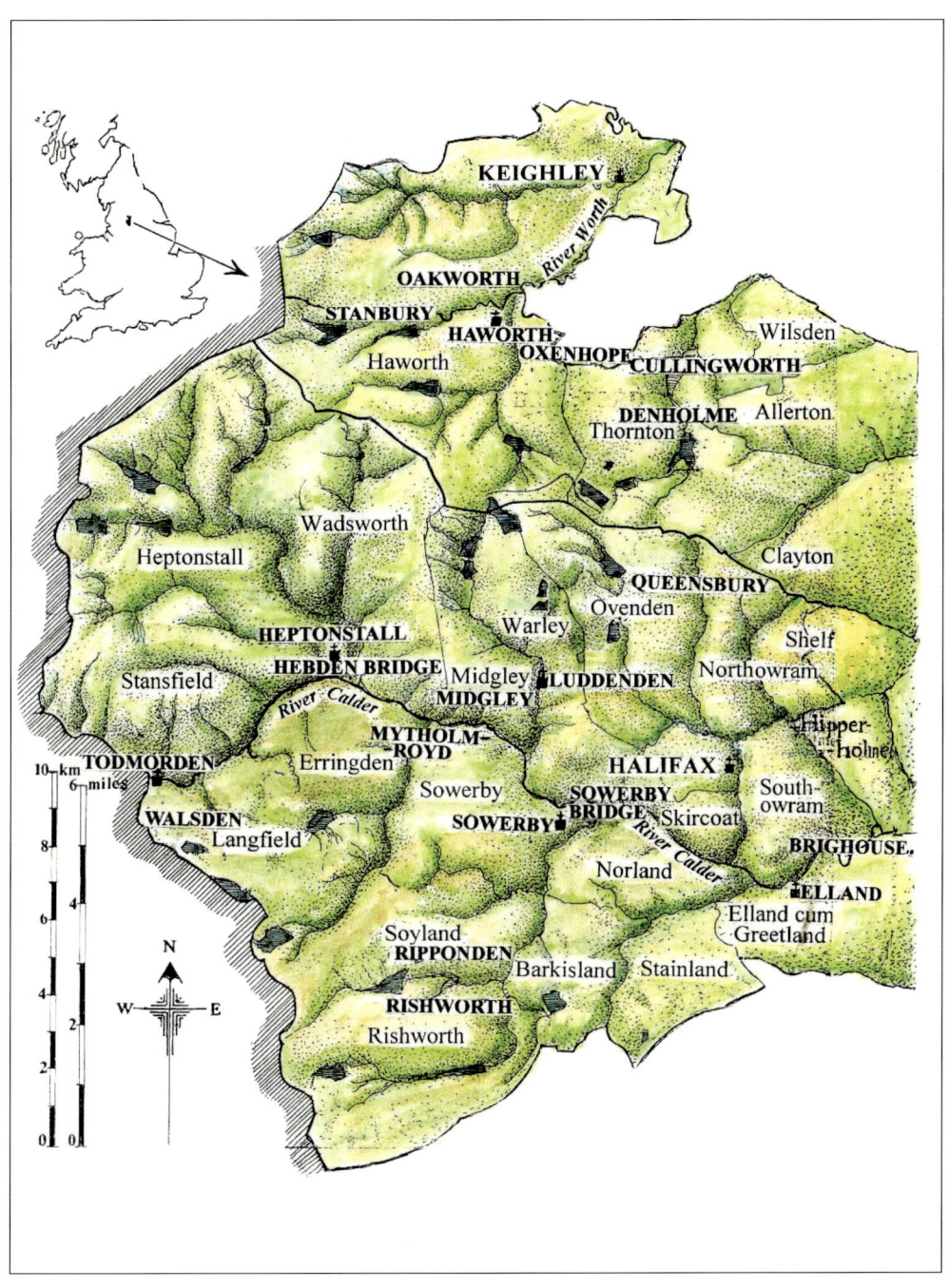

The Calderdale and Haworth area of the South Pennines

ACKNOWLEDGEMENTS

I would like to express my sincere thanks to the staff of Calderdale Libraries, both in the Central Library and its branches, for all their help in making their resources readily available to me over the last few years. In addition, Mr Stephen Wood of Haworth, Mr Tony Chadwick of Joseph Dobson & Sons of Elland, and the West family of Keighley, along with many others I have talked to in Calderdale since I first worked at Shibden Hall in 1970, have all provided welcome comments and information. The works of earlier writers have been invaluable, particularly the great W.B. Crump's *The Little Hill Farm: Calder Valley* of 1949, the insufficiently valued *Memory Lane* series compiled by Calderdale Libraries 1987-1992 and Shirley Kaye's *Yorkshire Cookery* written for the *Halifax Courier* in the 1970s. Although I know Calderdale's museum collections from personal experience, I also wish to express my thanks to Mrs Ann Dinsdale of the Brontë Parsonage Museum in Haworth and Ms Heather Millard of Cliffe Castle, Keighley, for access to their respective collections.

I am especially grateful to Mrs Susan Houghton (neé Foulds, formerly of Walsden) for her great help, friendship and ability to transform my longhand into neat, publishable typescript; and to Dr Nigel Smith for his singular care and attention to detail in editing and setting my text.

Peter Brears
Leeds, 2022

Measures and money

Money
1 penny (d). Smaller denominations are ½d (halfpenny) and ¼d (farthing)
1 shilling (s) = 12d
1 pound (£) = 20s

Conversion
1d = approx 0.417p
3d = 1.25p
6d = 2.5p
1s = 5p

Measures
Metric equivalents are given in the text

Temperatures
Both Celsius and Fahrenheit are given in the recipes

INTRODUCTION

For most communities cookery used to concentrate on putting just enough food on the table to satisfy hunger, but over the last fifty years it has grown into an extremely popular recreation. Eating out and photographing restaurant dishes, watching cookery programmes on the television and on-line, reading the food pages of newspapers and magazines, or buying some of the thousands of recipe books stocked in bookshops and charity shops, now entertains millions throughout the whole country. Given this abundance of readily available information, what is the point of yet another cookery book?

The current interest in food is based on ingredients, recipes and eating, but what a community grows, cooks and eats, and the role that meals play in society, opens up much more fascinating and revealing aspects of human life. Factors such as physical and social environments, centuries-old traditions, the state of the economy and trade, occupations and new technologies, have always influenced what, when and how we ate throughout countless ages. This book demonstrates this by concentrating on a small but significant patch of Yorkshire's South Pennines and on its working people during their progress from the hill-farming/handloom weaving period around 1800 through to industrialisation by the 1920s.

This is a particularly interesting area, for there are few parts of Britain where the interaction of a rugged landscape and its past generations of inhabitants is so clearly, and to Northerners, so beautifully demonstrated. Not only that, but its textile trade fostered an exceptionally vocal community. As Charles Dibdin discovered in 1788, 'Halifax is said to be the most musical spot, for its size, in the kingdom', the same trait enabling its workers to set down their memories in prose and verse while most of those elsewhere remained largely mute.[1] In this way their memories still provide rare first-hand insights into every aspect of the food and everyday life of the past. In addition, the area's church- and chapel-going housewives published hundreds of their personal recipes in fund-raising booklets, these giving the name and locality of each contributor. In the following pages many of these recipes have been rewritten in modern form for modern use, but their ingredients and methods remain accurately authentic. Most are admirably practical, wholesome and economical,

---

[1] *Halifax Courier* 5 July 1856.

1

producing dishes that make the best of their ingredients and natural flavours, well worth trying today as a contrast to take-aways or frozen meals. It has to be admitted, however, that a few fall below today's expectations, since they come from days when life was hard and ingredients were prohibitively expensive.

For those who don't know this area, a brief introduction is necessary. It is essentially a seventeen-mile stretch of hill country running eastwards from the Lancashire border from around Todmorden. From the valley bottoms at around 400 feet OD, steep hillsides rise up to wild bleak moorland at some 1,500 feet. Most of its pre-industrial farms and settlements are scattered around the 600-1000 feet contours. Here the moors provided rough grazing for cattle and sheep as well as peat for fuel, while stone-walled fields served as meadows, pastures and arable for growing oats, barley and rye, with smaller plots for vegetables. Even so, its people had to rely on a dual economy with the textile industry to earn their keep. The local lifestyle had already become well-established by the early medieval period, with many of its aspects continuing virtually unchanged through to the early twentieth century. It was one of the few areas where a medieval family could have walked into their farm six hundred years later (if this were possible!) and have been able to recognise, name and use most of its implements and cook its foods. The livestock, fields and crops would have been improved and extended, but porridge was still being boiled in its 'kilp pans', first mentioned in 1425, or posnets (1327) and food cooked on bakestones (1198) over a chafer or 'chaumin dish' (1395).

From the late eighteenth century the industrialisation of the textile industry brought enormous social and physical changes to the area, drawing workers into its new water- and steam-powered mills where cotton was turned into fabrics such as corduroy, and wool into worsteds and carpets. New local engineering factories made their textile machinery, as well as enormous mill engines and all kinds of machine tools, while new roads, canals and railways were constructed to bring in the coal and raw materials and carry away the finished products. As a result, the previously rural valley bottoms became a hive of industry, new terraced houses being built on every convenient space, and even one on top of another where hills were particularly steep. This produced the area's characteristic split personality, with the populous riverside communities, commercial centres and utilities frequently appearing as little more than an insignificant wooded gully when viewed from parts of the moorland 'tops'. Among their mutual benefits, the industrial community now had ready access to the fresh meat, poultry, eggs, milk and butter produced in the hill farms, while the hill farmers had not far to go to enjoy all the advantages of modern urban life. However, life here was rarely idyllic, both groups frequently having to struggle against adverse physical and economic environments in order to put food on the table and stave off starvation. Those who failed to do so frequently faced a miserable death and pauper's grave.

The purpose of this book is to tell the stories of the people of the Upper Calder Valley (Calderdale since 1974) and Haworth through the food they produced, bought and cooked to support their various ways of life, and to make their recipes available to all who wish to experience them for themselves. By doing this it hopes to supplement the wealth of outstanding local history studies produced by past and present generations that enrich our knowledge and appreciation of this remarkable area. Of these, William Bunting Crump's *The Little Hill Farm* of 1949 and Shirley Kaye's *Yorkshire Cookery* of the 1970s, though both out of print, remain essential reading.

Figure 1: *There are hundreds of little hill farms in the South Pennines, some still operating, while others now lie in ruins. For over 150 years they have been typified by a single example, Top Withins or 'Wuthering Heights' appropriately close to the 1500 feet border between Calderdale and Haworth.*

Finally, the inclusion of Haworth within Calderdale here needs some explanation, since they lie in separate local authorities, ancient parishes, and manors, and at opposite sides of miles of bleak uninhabitable moorland. However, they shared the same environment and industries and were occupied by the same light-haired, light-hazel/grey eyed people who had lived here for at least a thousand years.[2]   Haworth always looked towards Halifax and Calderdale rather than Bradford for its cultural and economic needs. From round 1700, if not earlier, Haworth weavers had carried their pieces to the Halifax cloth markets, some taking rooms in its great Piece Hall when it opened in 1775. They were still doing this in the mid-nineteenth century, when Alice Ickeringill, the Feather brothers and others were doing the same, and James Horsfall was taking his combed wool over the tops to Calverts' mill in Wainstalls.[3] Similarly Betty Sunderland was making the twelve-mile walk to Halifax with her butter and eggs every Wednesday in 1905, returning laden with groceries.[4]   Despite now being marketed as two separate tourist destinations, Calderdale and Haworth have far more similarities than differences and so have been treated together in this study, which, it is hoped, will be of interest to both communities and their numerous visitors.

Peter Brears

---

[2] J. Beddoe and J.H. Rowe, 'The ethnology of West Yorkshire', *Yorkshire Archaeological Journal*, 1907, 19, pp.31-60 & Table 3.

[3] M. Hartley and J. Ingilby, *Life and tradition in West Yorkshire*, London, J.M. Dent, 1976, p.19; W. Turner, *A spring-time saunter: round and about Bronte land*, Halifax, Halifax Courier, 1913, p.50.

[4] Turner, *A spring-time saunter*, pp.71-72.

CHAPTER 1

HARD TIMES

Up to the late eighteenth century most working families appear to have lived reasonably well, with locally grown oats, potatoes, beef, mutton, pork, milk and butter giving a plain and nutritious diet. As the Rev. John Watson stated in 1775, the poor had 'a constant supply of work, good wages, and plenty of the other necessaries of life, so that, so far as I know, not any country where, upon the whole, they live better.'[5]

Major problems were first experienced in the 1790s when disruption of trade caused by the Napoleonic wars and a series of bad harvests brought shortages and rising prices. In June 1797 there were riots in Halifax, during which farmers were robbed of their corn and butchers of their meat, Thomas Spencer and Mark Saltonstall, the ringleaders, being executed as a warning to others considering similar direct action.[6] By October 1799 oatmeal had reached 50s per 240 lb/108 kg pack, but it then rapidly doubled to 100s a pack before falling to 68s in 1802, which still caused real hardship. Flour, meanwhile, cost between 88s and 101s a pack, and potatoes 26s a basket.[7]

In 1812 oatmeal remained close to £5 a pack, well beyond the means of many of those who were in full-time work. Reporting on deaths caused by starvation, the Rev. John Taylor of Queensbury complained that 'There is not one in a hundred who even taste bread of oatmeal, or anything better than meal made of peas and beans. Nothing to feed their infants under a year old with [but] pottage made of bean meal.'[8] Barley was also substituted for oatmeal, its heavy texture and poor flavour being remembered with distaste forty years later, giving these years of hardship the title of 'Barley Time'.[9] They continued into the years after the Battle of Waterloo, Dorothy Wordsworth describing how, in 1817:

---

[5] J. Watson, *The history and antiquities of the parish of Halifax,* London, T. Lowndes, 1775. Republished Manchester, E.J. Morten, 1973, p.8.

[6] *Todmorden & Hebden Bridge Historical Almanack,* 1867, p.43.

[7] Ibid., p.87; Lonsdale Collection, *Newspaper cuttings,* Calderdale Libraries, Sowerby Bridge, vols.24, 64, 66.

[8] *Todmorden & Hebden Bridge Historical Almanack,* 1867, p.87.

[9] J. Crabtree, *A concise history of the parish and vicarage of Halifax,* Halifax, Hartley and Walker, 1836, p.150.

a great part of the population [around Halifax] is reduced to pauperism, a dreadful evil. Things cannot go on this way. For a time whole streets – men, women and children may be kept alive by public charity; but the consequences will be awful, if nothing can be manufactured.[10]

Things were just as bad in the mid-1820s, when the weavers and woolcombers could only earn about 6s a week and there were high levels of unemployment. Food and clothing were extremely scarce, some families having half naked children and not even a single blanket for their beds. Relief funds raised by local townships, sometimes by commissioning public works, together with donations from organisations such as the London Distressed Manufacturer's Relief Committee, provided much-needed help, but things were slow to improve.[11]

By the 1840s the price of oatmeal had fallen and trade had improved, bringing better diets. Most working families now appear to have had meals similar to those described by John Potterton, who was born in Ogden in 1829. Having wound pirns (bobbins) in his infancy, he began swinging a 7lb/3.1kg woolcomb by the time he was nine. At that time breakfasts were always of porridge and skimmed milk, while dinners at noon comprised

> a mixture made mostly of [oat] meal, and much like porridge, but called stir-about cooked in an iron dish. The mixture was quite stiff. When it had boiled long enough, a hole was made in the centre, into which bacon fat and treacle were poured. This iron dish was put on the table, each member of the family was given a spoon, and helped themselves out of the dish. No plates or table covers were used … those with the most voracious appetite getting the most. The most frequent complaint, however, was that one or other of the family was dipping in his or her spoon too liberally into the centre of the dish where the treacle and fat were.[12]

Those who were a little better off dined on lumps of bacon and beef boiled together with dumplings, or even spit-roasted beef with a Yorkshire pudding placed beneath to catch the dripping.

Tea, taken in the late afternoon, was of bread and butter if flour was affordable, or else oatcake and butter, although either bacon fat or suet was generally used as a butter substitute. Finally, later in the day, there was more porridge for

---

[10] W.B. Crump, 'Halifax Visitors Book, Vol.1', *Transactions of the Halifax Antiquarian Society*, 1937, pp.21-124.

[11] Lonsdale Collection, *Newspaper cuttings*, vol.8, p.25-26.

[12] Lonsdale Collection, *Newspaper cuttings*, vol.31, p.139.

supper. Tea was far too expensive for everyday use, the cheapest being 5d a pound and coarse sugar around 7d or 8d, and so most people still relied on home-brewed beer as their everyday drink.[13]

After this brief interlude, depression returned in 1841-1842, when only a third of the male workers retained full employment, but recovered in the mid-1840s, only to go backwards again in 1847-1848.[14] During the years of these 'Hungry Forties' or 'Dear Flour Times' many approached starvation, as they remembered years later. William Barrett of Rishworth had

> mostly spoon-work, oatmeal and that sort of thing. There was nothing to make broth of. If they got a bit of cake [i.e. bread] on Sunday they thought they were clever.[15]

Joseph Greenwood on the hillside above Hebden Bridge had 'oatmeal porridge and skim milk for food with rarely a change during the week.'[16] At Midgley 'weavers got up at daybreak, started work, had a breakfast of porridge, or brown bread, sometimes a bit of bacon, then worked on to 8 pm or later.'[17]

During the typhus epidemic at Heptonstall Slack the mid-day meal was reduced to small pieces of suet fried and mashed into a partial pulp with water, salt and boiled potatoes. This was eaten with oatcake, even a small piece of bacon being considered extravagant. Teas and suppers were merely porridge, oatcakes and skimmed milk. The condition of the people here was comparable with those of Napoleon's troops retreating from Moscow.[18] Sixty years later some in Luddenden Dean were claiming that

> Fowk know nowt baat clammin' [starving] nah o' days. Eagh! Aw con remember flaar 8, 7, 6, 5 and 4 shillin' a stooan [14 lb/6.3 kg]. Bless yo'r heart! It's a wonder haa we lived at all![19]

Times were changing as the domestic textile industry began its long and slow

---

[13] Ibid.

[14] B. Jennings (ed.), *Pennine valley: a history of Upper Calderdale*, Otley, Smith Settle, 1994, pp.149-151.

[15] Lonsdale Collection, *Newspaper cuttings*, vol.25, p.120.

[16] Lonsdale Collection, *Newspaper cuttings*, vol.24, p.131.

[17] Lonsdale Collection, *Newspaper cuttings*, vol.5, p.111.

[18] R. Howard, *A history of the typhus of Heptonstall Slack*, Hebden Bridge, 1844, pp.55-57.

[19] Lonsdale Collection, *Newspaper cuttings*, vol.8, p.109.

decline, being replaced by mechanised production in the woollen and cotton mills. According to economic historians, the 1850s were relatively prosperous, but this was not the experience of many who remembered life at this time, especially in the handloom weaving communities. Between November 1850 and December 1853 trade was bad, the wages of local woolcombers falling 40 per cent. Joseph Normington of Haworth remembered breakfasts about this time being a bowl of water-porridge called 'Old Tom' eaten with skim milk at ½d a pint, with a bit of oatcake. For dinners the family had to make do with bits of suet fried or roasted with potatoes, any vegetables coming from their own garden. Just a scrap of meat was bought for Sundays. Anyone with the means to keep a pig was considered as being truly affluent.[20]

Sam Banks in the handloom weaving community of Portsmouth, Todmorden, was growing up on a little more than porridge morning, noon and night, week in, week out;

> we three boys lined up to have breakfast in t' Back Hoile [back kitchen]. There would be porridge with perhaps a little blue milk, ½d a quart. If we had no milk, then maybe a little treacle or a little butter and sugar to make it more palatable. Often we mixed the treacle with a little water to make it go further. No use complaining, that was our diet, morning, noon and night.[21]

Similarly Daniel Eastwood of Wadsworth recalled

> But that was a sight, when our work began,
> And porridge was made in a big kilp pan,
> Some water, some salt, and a handful of corn,
> For breakfast we had, each day, and at morn.
> It wasn't a lot that was given to each,
> Not hardly enough to silence our speech,
> For barley-pan scrapings was said in a tick,
> While others said 'Nay, let me have a lick',
> When dinner time came, t'was the same o'er again,
> Some water, some salt, and same kilp pan,
> And barley-pan scrapings, another would say,
> 'Thou had it at morn it's my turn today.[22]

As John Travis confirmed, porridge and skimmed milk was the sole diet for most families, the monotony only rarely broken with a red herring or a bit of

---

[20] M. Baumber, *A history of Haworth from the earliest times*, Lancaster, Carnegie, 2009, p.109.

[21] E. Savage (ed.), *Sam Banks: his life and times*, Todmorden, Todmorden Antiquarian Society, 1985, p.5. Blue milk is the local term for skimmed milk.

[22] S. Mellor (ed.), *Biographies, sketches, & rhymes by the Calder Valley Poets*, Halifax, Edward Mortimer, 1916, p.30.

bacon as broad and long as three fingers for dinner. Sometimes a crude parkin would be baked on a 'bakestone and chover', this forming a good dinner if it contained suet.[23]

Prosperity only returned in 1859, but there was little to indicate that the economic life of the valley was about to be plunged into a period of even greater distress. Along with neighbouring Lancashire, the cotton industry was thriving with four-fifths of its raw material being regularly imported from the southern states of America. At the outbreak of the Civil War, the northern states effectively blockaded the south in order to ruin its finances, with the result that the supply of cotton into England virtually ceased in 1861. By January 1862 the cotton famine had forced most cotton mills to go on short time. By September, of the 1790 cotton operatives in Hebden Bridge, 942 were out of work, 570 on greatly reduced hours, and only 278 on full time trying to manufacture textiles with inferior cotton from other parts of the world.

Many working families were now plunged into desperate poverty, the Poor Law Unions attempting to cope with over five times the usual demand for financial help. Relief Committees were set up to gather funds to support the unemployed, Halifax raising the huge sum of £6,177 for example, but they could never make up for the drift into debt and sale of household goods that many families had to witness in order to buy food to keep themselves alive.[24] Tickets were issued to the heads of families for basic supplies of flour, sugar and coal, but some men were reduced to going round with a handcart, singing and begging for loaves of bread and muffins.[25] For some, the lack of food proved fatal, a report of 17 September 1862 stating that May Howorth of Gauxholme had just died 'supposedly of starvation'.[26]

It was not until 1867-1868 that things returned to normal, but the textile trade and its dependent industries were still subject to uncertainty: a boom in 1873-1874, a downturn in 1876 and depression from 1879 up to the close of the nineteenth century.[27] Unemployment continued to be a real threat, as John Hartley recorded in verse:

---

[23] J. Travis, *Notes: (historical and biographical) mainly of Todmorden and district,* Rochdale, 1896, p.28.

[24] Jennings, *Pennine valley,* p.166.

[25] Savage, *Sam Banks: his life and times,* p.16.

[26] *Todmorden & Hebden Bridge Historical Almanack,* 1875.

[27] Jennings, *Pennine valley,* p.169

I mi pocket aw havn't a rap, [counterfeit ha'penny]
Nor a crust, nor a handful o' meil,
An' unless we can get it o'th strap [credit]
we mun pine, [starve] or mun beg, or else steal.[28]

One practical alternative was to pool resources, as the quarrymen did at Upper Edge, Elland, when severe frosts made work impossible:

People would take anything they had, a few vegetables, bits of meat, and put them in the communal wash-house [set pot] for a large pot of stew when times were hard.[29]

The years between the close of the nineteenth century and the outbreak of the First World War in 1914 appear to have been a golden age of working-class food and cookery. A wider variety of foodstuffs at affordable prices was being imported from all parts of the British Empire, and most people were in work. Coal was relatively cheap, and so most families had at least one baking day each week to produce their own bread and cakes. Cheap meat, much of it imported from Australia, New Zealand, North and South America, was available for hot pots, pies and roasts, while drying, salting and tinning, along with efficient railways, provided a good choice of both preserved and fresh fish. Cheap sugar, salt and vinegar meant that jams, bottled fruits, sauces and pickles could all be easily made in the home. Evidence of this prosperity appears in the cookery books published by churches, chapels and societies as a means of raising funds for their particular purposes, each recipe bearing the name, and often the address, of its contributor. Like all good traditional home cookery they contain nothing very complicated or expensive; in fact much is quite plain, but still full of flavour and satisfying bulk. Useful as they were for circulating practical recipes, John Hartley warned housewives that;

Readin' a cookery book willn't fill a chap's belly, an' hoppin' for better times will'nt improve trade. Langin' for a thing nobbut maks yo' feel th' want on it, but workin for a thing generally gets it.[30]

From 1914, with the outbreak of hostilities, both milk and wheat began to rise in price, but it was from 1917 that the effects of the German U-boats began to be felt more severely. The government was forced to add maize and barley meal to flour, and to establish local Food Control Committees to set prices for all

---

[28] J. Hartley, *The Halifax Original Illuminated Clock Almanack,* Halifax, 1869, p.41.

[29] Calderdale Libraries, *Memory lane: recollections of Elland,* Halifax, Calderdale Leisure Services, 1987, p.38.

[30] Hartley, *Clock almanack,* 1895, p.22.

meats, margarine, butter and tea. Their rules were so strictly enforced that one Hebden Bridge confectioner was prosecuted for putting dessicated coconut on four of his buns, while another who put 5 per cent of sugar in his scones, instead of leaving them unsweetened, was fined £2. Since all milk had to be sold directly to the public and butter considered an unacceptable luxury, local farmers were even banned from churning their own cream.[31]

There was a brief return to good times immediately after the war, but economic conditions then began to deteriorate again, with further depression and unemployment. As Mrs Farnell of Halifax remembered from 1922 when her husband was out of work, 'we often dined on mashed turnips and dry bread, with an occasional 1d herring as a treat.' For others 'most of our meals [were of] broth and dumplings.' Meanwhile Mrs Begley of Ovenden saw her mother

> make a dinner for 2d for five of us; a hapenyworth of damaged potatoes, the same of savoury duck [faggot] from the butcher's, with gravy if you took a basin, which together with the potatoes and water made a hash, which was followed by a halfpennyworth of bruised apples stewed.[32]

Some, unable to take the strain, threw themselves into the Hebble Brook from Halifax's North Bridge, while the lake in Shibden Park was made shallower to prevent suicides.

Those who remained in work tried to carry on as before, especially by having a roast on Sundays and making the left-overs from the joint last over the next three days. As one lady explained, 'We were posh! When other families in Todmorden were having bread and jam on Thursdays, we had Foulds' potted meat!' Those who were a little more well off fared rather better, however. As Victor Watson remembered at his home at Rosemary Farm, Siddal, in the 1920s, breakfasts were always of bread spread with dripping saved from the Sunday joint, and teas of bread spread with margarine and jam, but dinners changed from day to day:

Sunday: Yorkshire Pudding and gravy, followed by a 4-5lb/1.8-2.2kg roasted joint of sirloin, pork loin or lamb served with roast potatoes and vegetables, then a rice pudding baked in a dish the size of a washing up bowl.

High tea at late afternoon/early evening included ham and tinned salmon

---

[31] P. Thomas, *Hardship and hope: Hebden Royd and Todmorden during the First World War (1914-1918)*, [Hebden Bridge], 2016, pp.89-90, 92-95.

[32] Hartley and Ingilby, *Life and tradition in West Yorkshire*, pp.101-102; Calderdale Libraries, *Memory lane: recollections of Elland*, p.48.

sandwiches, fruit, jelly and cakes.

Monday: Bubble and squeak with cold meat, all from Sunday's dinner.

Tuesday: Hash made with the bones, some of the meat and vegetables from Sunday's dinner, all stewed together.

Wednesday: The last of the Sunday joint cut in pieces, mixed with 8 oz/225g shin beef if necessary, baked with sliced potatoes under a huge suet crust. Sometimes this was followed by a baked egg custard, as the oven would be hot.

Thursday: Fried liver and kidney served with boiled potatoes and cabbage, turnips or carrots.

Friday: Fried fish for 2d and chips 1d.

Saturday: A quick fry-up of bacon, egg, and sausages, since the house had to be cleaned and shopping, including buying the joint, to be done in Halifax.[33]

The Second World War, with its rationing, made sure that everyone had the same share of the available foods, but it was not until the mid-1950s that conditions slowly began to improve. Many of the grandmothers who had baked before the First World War, and the daughters they had taught, still cooked every day. However, many others now largely relied on shop-bought bread and bakery, the labour-saving advances of tinned, dried and frozen products, or on various take-away meals to feed their families, a great contrast to the meagre, boring porridge diet of their ancestors.

Work Food

One of the advantages of the domestic textile industry was that carding, spinning and weaving could all take place alongside everyday household activities, including child rearing, cleaning, laundry and, most importantly, the preparation of meals. In the 1840s there might be up to four looms working in the chamber of a handloom weaver's home, with children busily winding factory-spun yarn put onto the pirns (bobbins) to fill the shuttles with weft. It was a happy communal life when trade was good:

> young men and women would most heartily and charmingly join in the hymn singing, while the musical rhythm of the shuttles would keep time to the tune and the merry mood was kept up.[34]

Working time was flexible, so that fine days could be devoted to hunting, knurr-and-spell, billet matches or shooting. The start of each week was taken

---

[33] *Siddal: our memories, our history*, Halifax, Workers Educational Association, 1989, pp.13-14.

[34] Lonsdale Collection, *Newspaper cuttings*, vol.24, p.111-112, 134.

at a leisurely pace, 'the looms saying M-O-N-D-A-Y-T-U-E-S-D-A-Y', while towards the end it was 'Friday-Saturday' almost as fast as could be repeated in order to make up for lost time.[35] Work usually started as soon as there was sufficient daylight, a breakfast of porridge and a hot drink around 8 a.m., and a hot meal at noon followed by a resting time called a 'nooiningscaup'.[36] A further break with food similar to breakfast took place in the late afternoon/early evening after which weaving often continued to 8 p.m. or later. When particularly busy, a can of porridge might be kept hot in the adjacent bedclothes, ready for eating, or just hung at the side of the loom.

The introduction of factory production in large textile mills saw the end of this flexible family-centred lifestyle. Now everyone's daily timetable became strictly governed by the needs of the mill, with its closely controlled working hours. As there were no catering facilities in the mills, food had to be provided back in the family home, a real problem if it lay some distance away. This caused great hardship, as Sam Banks of Portsmouth, Todmorden, remembered from the mid-nineteenth century. Having started work as piecers in the cotton-spinning mills in the early morning, he and his two brothers had to rush home about 8 a.m. for their first meal of the day:

> We 'st line up at breakfast, would three,
> My brother Tom, an' me, an eawr Jack;
> T'would 'a done yo' good just to see
> 'Gobble up eawr porridge then hurry back,
> Th' time were short, just thirty minutes
> An' a mile theere an' back,
> An' we had to spin it.[37]

Once, when the porridge was not ready for them, they were scolded by their master as they returned late to the mill door, being told that they must tell their mother that *she* was to blame for their loss of earnings. Other mothers, those with large families, would carry a large tin of porridge and a single round leaden spoon to the mill, each child taking a spoonful in turn. Sometimes it was milk porridge, at others 'curdled cruddy' made with sour milk, but there were no complaints; all was wolfed down.

Most adults took their food to work wrapped up in a red spotted 'jock' handkerchief, 'jock' being the very localised term for food in general, and work

---

[35] Ibid., p.113.

[36] Watson, *The history and antiquities of the parish of Halifax,* p.543.

[37] Savage, *Sam Banks: his life and times,* p.20.

Figure 2. The great Victorian expansion of the textiles, engineering and confectionery industries filled the towns with huge factories, their smoke joining with that from thousands of workers' homes rapidly blackening the buildings and much of the landscape. The massive Dean Clough Mills could only be seen from Beacon Hill in Wakes Weeks when all the works closed down for maintenance.

food in particular.[38]   From around the 1850s through to the 1940s wives and mothers would pack up jock each evening ready for next morning. Mrs Tupman of Heptonstall remembered her mother 'putting up bread for breakfast and teacake sandwiches for dinner the night before, all arranged around the table for the different members of the family, and my father made us a hot drink before we set out.'[39] She often spread the bread with dripping, better known as 'mucky fat', this being a satisfying and richly-flavoured favourite, It was essential that such food was kept safe overnight, one lady from Midgley who kept it on her sideboard overnight finding it missing next morning; 'rats had eaten t' jock and t' handkerchief.'[40]

When cooked dinners were being made at home, extra quantities would be made to provide hot meals in the mills and factories. Describing a widespread practice, an apprentice at Pollitt and Wigzell's engineering works has described how:

---

[38] *Halifax Courier* 22 May 1897.

[39] Hartley & Ingilby, *Life and tradition in West Yorkshire*, p.45.

[40] Ibid., p.86.

Mother often gave me a bowl of meat and potato pie wrapped in a Paisley shawl, for my lunch. I put it on top of the boiler at work so it heated up in time for dinner. With the tea scalded by an apprentice boy, that made a real feast.[41]

If within walking distance, basins of hot food were placed on a red-spotted handkerchief that was knotted over the rim, and were taken along to the works at dinnertime.[42] As a boy, Donald Middleton of Sowerby Bridge was given this task, having to carry it along the towpath for his father at Washer Lane Dyeworks. Being scalding hot and burning his fingers, he decided to dunk it in the canal until cool enough to handle. His father's reaction was described as 'serious trouble', but was probably more vigorous than that term implies![43]

As a convenient alternative to home-made food, many preferred to buy it from a local shop, either as take-away sandwiches, pies and fish-and-chips or else eat in where seating was provided, as in some tripe and pie-and-pea shops or public houses. These were always more expensive however, particularly where there was the temptation of alcoholic drinks that could soon absorb wages.

Most of the food was eaten in the workplace sitting amongst the machinery, only the larger and more progressive employers providing separate facilities in the nineteenth century. The Akroyd's works dining room at their Copley Mills was set up in 1840, and at the Hawden's Kebroyd Mills in the late 1880s, but many mills failed to provide canteens until the 1940s. A good description of dinners at Holdsworth's Shaw Lodge Mills in Halifax was provided by Angus Reach in 1849:

> A sort of small cookshop is established near the furnace of one of the main steam engines, and thither every girl who pleases brings her dinner, ready cooked but disposed in a dish so as to allow it to be readily warmed up again. I stationed myself in the dinner-bar at noon, and so had an opportunity of seeing nearly 300 of the messes prepared, and they were handed out through a sort of buttery-hatch to each applicant as she shouted the number of her carding-machine, her spinning-frame, or her loom. The dinners consisted of a portion of baked meat with potatoes, and in a few instances mushrooms. A great number had coffee and tea in little flaggons. Altogether the dinners seemed substantial and nourishing.[44]

---

[41] Calderdale Libraries, *Memory lane: recollections of Sowerby Bridge,* Halifax, Calderdale Leisure Services, 1990 p.66.

[42] Calderdale Libraries, *Memory lane: recollections of Elland,* p.81.

[43] A. Blinman, *Sowerby Bridge: our memories, our history,* Sowerby Bridge, Workers Educational Association, 1988, p.10.

[44] Brears, P., *Traditional food in Yorkshire,* Totnes, Prospect Books, 2014, pp.57-58.

These dishes or bowls of meat and potatoes were often carried to the mill in baskets, as described by Bill o' th' Hoylus End:

> They are off in the morning right early
> With their baskets o' jock on their arms;
> The bell is ting-tanging, ting-tanging,
> As they enter the mill in a swarm.[45]

Figure 3. Mill children of 1814 carried their food in small baskets, while later millworkers used basins tied in jock handkerchiefs or shawls and had them warmed up over heating pipes or in the boiler house.

Workhouse Food

In the early nineteenth century those natives of the area who were too poor to maintain their homes and feed themselves were supported by a poor rate levied on those who owned property in their respective townships. Most of the funds controlled by the local overseer of the poor were paid in cash as 'outdoor relief' that allowed paupers to continue living in their own homes, but where their circumstances made this impossible, many townships set up workhouses where they could be housed and work communally. The way in which

---

[45] Bill o' th' Hoylus End [W. Wright], *Revised edition of poems,* Keighley, John Overend, 1891, p.149.

workhouses operated is clearly illustrated by taking Ovenden as a typical example. Here in 1836 the occupants grew much of their own food, raising crops of oats, potatoes, turnips, and probably beans and onions too, in their fields and garden. They kept pigs that produced the twenty-six stone of bacon and forty-eight pounds of lard in their kitchen chamber, and the seven cows that provided their milk and butter. Using these ingredients they made soft oatcakes and porridge from the oats, broths from the vegetables, roasts and grills from their meat and bacon, and also brewed their own beer. Other items such as sugar, tea, coffee, hops, treacle, rice, mustard, salt, pepper and currants were bought in to provide a wholesome and varied diet, with meat on three days of each week. This was essential to enable them to quarry and cut the paving blocks and weave the cloths that were sold off to help defray the costs of their keep. In this way some forty people shared a productive lifestyle almost identical to that they had experienced in their own homes, one which provided essential support to the vulnerable and kept distressed families together as economically as possible.[46]

In 1834 the Poor Law Amendment Act sought to sweep away this humane system of out-door relief and small township workhouses. In its place much larger Poor Law Unions controlled by Boards of Guardians were now to erect prison-like workhouses where all those who could not support themselves would be incarcerated, their families being broken up into segregated wards for men, women and children. Following the implementation of the Act in 1838, Guardians were appointed for two Unions in the Calder valley, one in Halifax to serve the lower and middle townships, and one in Todmorden for the six upper ones. Halifax Union Workhouse opened in 1841, but with the backing of John Fielden M.P., whose employees and their dependants numbered some 3,000, Todmorden folk decided that they would defy central government policy. To them it was totally unacceptable that people should be treated as criminals, locked up in 'Bastilles', and separated from their loved ones just because they had fallen on hard times. Using a variety of tactics, excellently described in Bernard Jennings' *Pennine Valley*, no workhouse was erected for Todmorden Union until 1879, forty-five years after the Act, a great tribute to the independent beliefs, abilities and tenacity of this Pennine community.[47]

---

[46] C.A. Wilson (ed.), *Food for the community: special diets for special groups*, Edinburgh, Edinburgh University Press, 1993, p.128; West Yorkshire Archive Service (Calderdale), *Schedule of goods etc at Ovenden workhouse 3 March 1836*, HAS:209 (59).

[47] Jennings, *Pennine valley*, pp.147-151

Those who found themselves in the Halifax Workhouse from 1841 had a very basic diet, one not so good as they had enjoyed at home when in full employment, but certainly better than when reduced to starvation. It comprised:

Breakfasts & suppers:
1½ pt/900 ml oatmeal porridge with ½ pt/300 ml skimmed milk

Dinners:

Sunday & Wednesday	2 pt/1.2 l soup, 5 oz/125 g bread
Monday, Thursday, Friday	1¾ lb/790 g lobscouse, 3 oz/75 g bread
Tuesday, Saturday	5 oz/125 g meat, 1¼ lb/560 g potatoes.[48]

Doss House Food

For those poor folk who were not absolutely destitute, but could not afford the high cost of a hotel, Halifax was served by a number of doss-houses. Officially known as 'common lodging houses', they were regularly inspected by both the police and the Mayor as chief magistrate in order to maintain minimal standards. Some offered just a couple of dozen closely packed bedplaces, others up to 114, the total for the town being around 400, their prices ranging from 3d to 6d a night, depending on the facilities provided. On entering, probably in the late afternoon and paying for the night, basic food could be purchased from the 'bar'. This might be 'as much bread and jam as any person with a normal appetite could dispose of at two meals' for 3d, with an extra free 1½ inch thick slice if requested. Bacon was also sold, ready to be fried in the communal pan 'on which the dirt and grease of ages had accumulated', while potatoes were boiled over the communal fire. Some doss-houses banned the boiling of potatoes between 5 and 8 p.m., since this would have prevented the majority from quickly cooking their bacon or mashing their packet of 'mixed' tea or cocoa and sugar for their teas.[49]

Sat around the communal tables everyone, however dirty, scruffy and objectionable, was a 'gentleman', as in 'ask that gentleman to pass the salt please?' However, no-one would ever ask for the use of the knife, even for a minute, since, unlike the forks and spoons provided by the proprietor, these were personal possessions, without which food would have to be eaten with the fingers. The tea leaves left after draining the teapot into the basin used for drinking might be passed on to allow someone else to 'bull the pot' by adding

---

[48] Ibid., p.150
[49] Ibid.

a fresh batch of boiling water.[50] 'Bulling' meant to abuse violently, shaking the leaves in the teapot to extract all remaining flavour.[51]

In order to experience the life of a tramp, the journalist Tom R. Hewart once walked into Halifax by way of Rochdale and Littleborough, finding himself freezing on the steps of the Old Cock in the early hours of a February morning, with one ankle badly sprained. On being discovered by a police constable, who first checked that he was not drunk, he was surprised to be revived with the constable's own breakfast of huge mutton sandwiches and doses of hot coffee. Such acts of random kindness were probably more common than we might imagine today.[52]

As this chapter has shown, obtaining food when times were hard posed a major problem for many of the local inhabitants, especially when trade was bad. However, one community happens to have done rather better than most others; those who lived in the little hill farms. As the primary producers of food, and well used to backbreaking work and hard living, they avoided the abject poverty of their industrialised neighbours. As one explained to Whiteley Turner, when describing the hungry years of the mid-nineteenth century:

> We lacked nowt as far as owt t' eat went, we'd five meals in' th' day: porridge mornin' an' neet, an' a basin o' skimmed milk to 'em, an' as mich 'avver breead es yo liked; an it _wor_ 'avver breead, that. Ther's nooan sich nah – ommost a quarter of an inch thick, an' when yo' steep't it i' th milk it swelled aght twice th' thickness, - yo' kno' the' were nooan adulteration then. We grew all es own mayl. Then we'd allus a for'noon drinkin' an' supper; plenty o' meyt an' taties, for we'd ooarshuns o' puttatoes an' never noan to buy.[53]

[50] Lonsdale Collection, *Newspaper cuttings*, vol.17 p.53; vol.27, p.120; *Halifax Evening Courier* 18 August 1908, 1 May 1912.

[51] Wright, *English dialect dictionary*, under 'Bullyrag'.,

[52] Lonsdale Collection, *Newspaper cuttings*, vol.16, p.58.

[53] Turner, *A spring-time saunter*, p.56.

Figure 4. *The occupants of Halifax doss houses could buy their bread and jam from the 'bar' along with bacon and potatoes to cook over the fire and tea to mash in the teapots. Plates, forks, basins and condiments were provided, but each 'gentleman' brought his own knife.*

CHAPTER 2

FUEL AND FIRES

In some townships there is plenty of turf earth, which when prepared
for fuel, by drying in the sun, is reckoned a wholesome firing ... where
the use of this prevails, pestilential disorders have been more rare, and
less fatal.[54]

Since most of the medieval settlements in the Calder Valley were set amid the
fertile fields flanking its sides, the most convenient and readily harvested fuel
was peat. Over the centuries sphagnum moss and cotton grass growing on the
poorly drained moors had transformed themselves into considerable depths of
soggy, dark-brown fibrous pulp known as peat or turf. All those having the
right of turbary could collect it free of charge, usually starting in late May or
June, when the moors were starting to dry out. The first process was to slice off
the top layer of growing vegetation into narrow strips called fleights, from the
Old English and Old Norse *fleaht*, meaning to flay or pare. This was done with
a fleight spade with a triangular horizontal blade, the resulting strips then
being dried for use as fuel, or else replaced over the exposed peat pits at the
end of each season to ensure their continuing growth. Four of the places where
they were cut include Fleight Hills on Wadsworth Moor and Haworth Moor,
Fleight Clough on Heptonstall Moor and Flappit (i.e. fleight-pit) Spring on
Cullingworth Moor.[55] In 1902 the farmer at High House Farm was still cutting
fleights on Midgley Moor, since 'they were very useful to keep the setpot hot
when boiling turnips, and they saved coal and retained their heat for a long
time.'[56]

Once the fleights had been removed, the peat could be cut vertically using a
wooden turf spade shod with an L-shaped iron blade to form slabs measuring
some 9 by 3 in/23 by 8 cm in section and over a foot/30 cm long. Their bottom
edges were usually cut free with an ordinary spade thrust horizontally into the
face of the peat pit. At this stage peats were heavy, soft and easily broken, so
that they were first laid out in parallel rows on the moor until firm enough to

---

[54] Watson, *The history and antiquities of the parish of Halifax*, p.2.

[55] Grid refs: SD 985333, SD 933308, SE 051366.

[56] *Leeds Mercury*, Supplement, 2 May 1902.

handle, then reared on edge, then into small stacks and larger stacks until they had shrunk and dried rock-hard in the sun and the wind. In July and early August the peats would be carried down to the houses, being stored in peat cotes (outhouses), porches or in stacks to fuel fires over the following year. All had to be gathered in by 12 August, when the grouse shooting season started.[57]

Figure 5. Peat digging started by stripping off the surface vegetation with a fleight spade (1. from Upper Saltonstall) after which peat spades (2 from Upper Saltonstall & 3 from James Jowett, Carr House, Cullingworth) were used to cut vertical slices ready for drying.

[57] W.B. Crump, *The little hill farm: Calder Valley*, London, Scrivener Press, 1949, p.45.

Although the steep sides of the valley and its tributary deans and cloughs were heavily wooded, there was never sufficient to provide a regular supply of firewood. At Stone Booth in Crimsworth Dean it took a coal strike to cause the felling of the Katie Tree for fuel. According to local tradition this ancient elm was named after the girl fought over by the two men commemorated at the double Abel Cross centuries ago.

The traditional form of kindling used to light fires was called colons, the woody stems of ling or heather left after burning off the moorlands. Some of the places where they were collected retain placenames such as Colin Hill, Manshead, Collin Moor Lane, Greetland, and Collon Flat, Midgley Moor.[58] They were first recorded here by the Rev. John Watson in 1775 as 'the stalk of furze bushes which remain after burning', but W.B. Crump found mill girls still collecting them on Warley Moor in 1901.[59] By this time wood was being brought into the area from elsewhere and sold by professional firewood manufacturers. They cut it into small 'chips', bound these into bundles with wire and sold them either individually or by the box of twenty. Men such as G.H. Braund of Halifax Road, Sowerby Bridge, used a hand barrow to hawk them around the local streets.[60] A further supply of good kindling came from the peat pits. In pre-historic times the moorlands had been woodland, remains of trees that once grew there being preserved within the peat for millennia. Some of this ancient birch, as found on Cock Hill, was 'rare an' gooid firewood … 'specially to stick under th' oven o' th' bakin' day.'[61]

Beacon Hill, the steep 400 feet high, west-facing scarp overlooking Halifax, represents the major outcrop of Coal Measures that extends northwards towards Denholme and Cullingworth, and south towards Huddersfield. Along its line and further to the east there were numerous coal mines, some being small 'day-holes' or drifts, such as James Lister sank in 1720 in 'Colepit Field' to the east of Shibden Hall, and other later ones with deep shafts from which the coal was raised first by horse gins, and later by steam engines.[62] The large area of the South Pennines to the west of Halifax was gritstone country devoid of coal, except for a few very narrow seams around its perimeter. On Stanbury

---

[58] Grid refs: SD 933197, SD 9903361, SE 093217, SE 012288.

[59] Watson, *The history and antiquities of the parish of Halifax*, p.2; Crump, *The little hill farm*, p.48.

[60] Personal communication from the late Miss Marie Hartley.

[61] Turner, *A spring-time saunter*, p.68.

[62] W.B. Trigg, 'The Halifax coalfield: Parts 1-2', *Transactions of the Halifax Antiquarian Society*, 1930, 117-158; Parts 3-4, 1931, 73-111; Part 5, 1932, 261-292.

Moor between Height and Sladen Beck, a dozen or more adits were worked up to the 1860s, while others lay in Coal Clough in the Burnley valley north of Cornholme.[63]

Figure 6. *Up to his death aged 90 in 1893, Abel Jowett of Sim Carr used his team of three donkeys to carry coal from Wilson Pit on the Leeds-Bradford Road to homes in Northowram, the Shibden valley and Southowram. Fuel for kindling fires might take the form of bundles of ready-chopped 'chips' of wood, as sold by Mr G.H. Braund of Sowerby Bridge, or as 'colons' or 'collins', the dry stems of heather left after burning a 'swidden' on the moors.*

[63] D. Thompson, *Stanbury: a Pennine country village,* Calgary, Two Margaret's Publications, 2002, pp.155-158; Wood, S. & Brears, P., *The real Wuthering Heights: the story of the Withins farms,* Stroud, Amberley, 2016, pp.67-69, 74-79; M. & F. Heywood and B.A. Jennings, *A history of Todmorden,* Otley, Smith Settle, 1996, p.10; Grid refs SD 998360, SD 904275.

As the textile industry drew in thousands of extra factory workers and turned from water to steam as its major source of power, the demand for cheap coal expanded rapidly. The opening of the Rochdale Canal between 1799-1804 may have helped a little, but it was the arrival of the Manchester and Leeds Railway through the Calder Valley in 1840, and the Worth Valley line in 1867, that made the real difference. Coal from the great collieries of the central West Riding could now deliver plentiful cheap supplies to the elevated staithes that still remain alongside most of the stations. Having dropped into the waiting heavily-built carts, great shire horses delivered the coal into the valley-bottom towns and the hillside settlements well into the mid-twentieth century.[64] This was a great improvement from the panniers made of interwoven broad oak strips that were slung on the sides of donkey teams that had been used for coal deliveries up to the 1890s.[65] Particularly for those living on the tops, it was essential to get in sufficient supplies every autumn to last through to the following spring, since snow, ice and freezing fog could make the steep roads virtually impassable.

Most of the area's smaller towns established gas works by the middle of the nineteenth century, but they were primarily used to provide street lighting. Gas stoves remained prohibitively expensive for most families up to the early twentieth century. However, if gas was available a single gas ring might supplement a coal-fired range, particularly in the summer months. Even if not using gas, those who lived near the gas works could benefit from their major by-product, coke. Around Gaol Lane and Well Lane in Halifax, boys collected it as it tumbled from the wagons, then carried it home to burn on their fires.[66]

Having obtained the fuel, the next task was to ignite it. Where peat was used, this was rarely necessary, since its smouldering embers could usually be revived each morning. Otherwise, a bed of dry sticks or heather colons, including the 'ling bob' (i.e. a bundle of ling) of the Halifax placename, was used until knots of rolled newspaper eventually took their place.[67] Once arranged on the hearth or in a grate, it was time to reach down the tinderbox. At John Potterton's home in Ogden in the 1830s, brass candlesticks, a candle snuffer to trim the wicks and a snuffer tray occupied the centre of the mantelpiece, while a tinderbox stood at one end. It appears to have been of the

---

[64] E. Greenwood, *Life on a Pennine farm,* Burnley, 1998, p.38.

[65] Calderdale Museum collection. No.1948-32; *Halifax Courier,* 14 July 1939.

[66] A. Porritt, *It happened here: third series,* Halifax, Weardale Press, 1969, p.89.

[67] Grid ref SE 069257.

usual form of a cylindrical tinplate box with a candlestick on its lid. Inside was a layer of tinder, pieces of white cotton cloth scorched brown at night, a piece of flint and a U-shaped piece of steel called a striker. In use, the flint was held in one hand over the open box, so that the striker over the knuckles could send sparks down onto the tinder, these being gently blown to produce a glow. At this point the hot tinder was touched with a wooden match, a six by quarter-inch splinter dipped in brimstone (sulphur) for half an inch at each end. Made by John Priestley of Boggart Brig, they sold at a penny a bundle, and were used to produce a good flame to light either a candle or a fire. John remembered the first matches being used in his home around 1844. These cost 6d for twenty and were considered to be an expensive luxury.[68]   In Elland in 1839 brimstone matches were selling at a halfpenny a bundle, with the first friction matches at 4d a box.[69]   Extra draught to blow the flames came from traditional heart-shaped bellows, although some were using wheel bellows in the mid-nineteenth century.[70]

Fireplaces, 'Choffers', Ovens & Ranges

Where peat or wood was burned, there was no need for any kind of grate, since they would burn steadily and economically on a flat stone hearth when simmering pots, boiling kettles and heating rooms. However, this did not focus the heat and scattered ash and embers. The local solution was to contain the fire in a small round firebasket called a choffer, chaumindish, or chauvindish.[71] Used in West Yorkshire from at least the fourteenth century, they had a conical iron fire basket tapering from about 8 in/20 cm at the rim to 6 in/15 cm at the base, the bottoms taking the form of parallel firebars.[72] To provide a firm footing, there were three wrought iron legs extending about 8 in/20 cm down to the floor, and rising above the rim to support cooking vessels placed on top. A wooden handle projecting to the side enabled them to be moved or to be held firmly when in use. Examples are found in local collections.[73] Very practical, they probably went out of use towards the close of the nineteenth century.

---

[68] Lonsdale Collection, *Newspaper cuttings*, vol.31, p.139.

[69] L. Hamerton, *Olde Eland,* Elland, Gledhill, 1901, p.180.

[70] Calderdale Museum collection, nos.151.4; 1929.60; 1930.165; 1933.87.

[71] Savage, *Sam Banks: his life and times,* p.4; J.H. Dixon, *Folklore with old things of the Brontës, of Bronte land and of 'thrums,* Harrogate, 1906, no.202; J. Wright, (ed.), *The English dialect dictionary*, 6 vols, Oxford, Oxford University Press, 1923, under 'Chauvindish'.

[72] Wood & Brears, The real Wuthering Heights, p.59-60.

[73] Calderdale Museums collection AH 708; 1969.121/30; 1934.46; 1963.175; Cliffe Castle, Keighley, 275, 613.

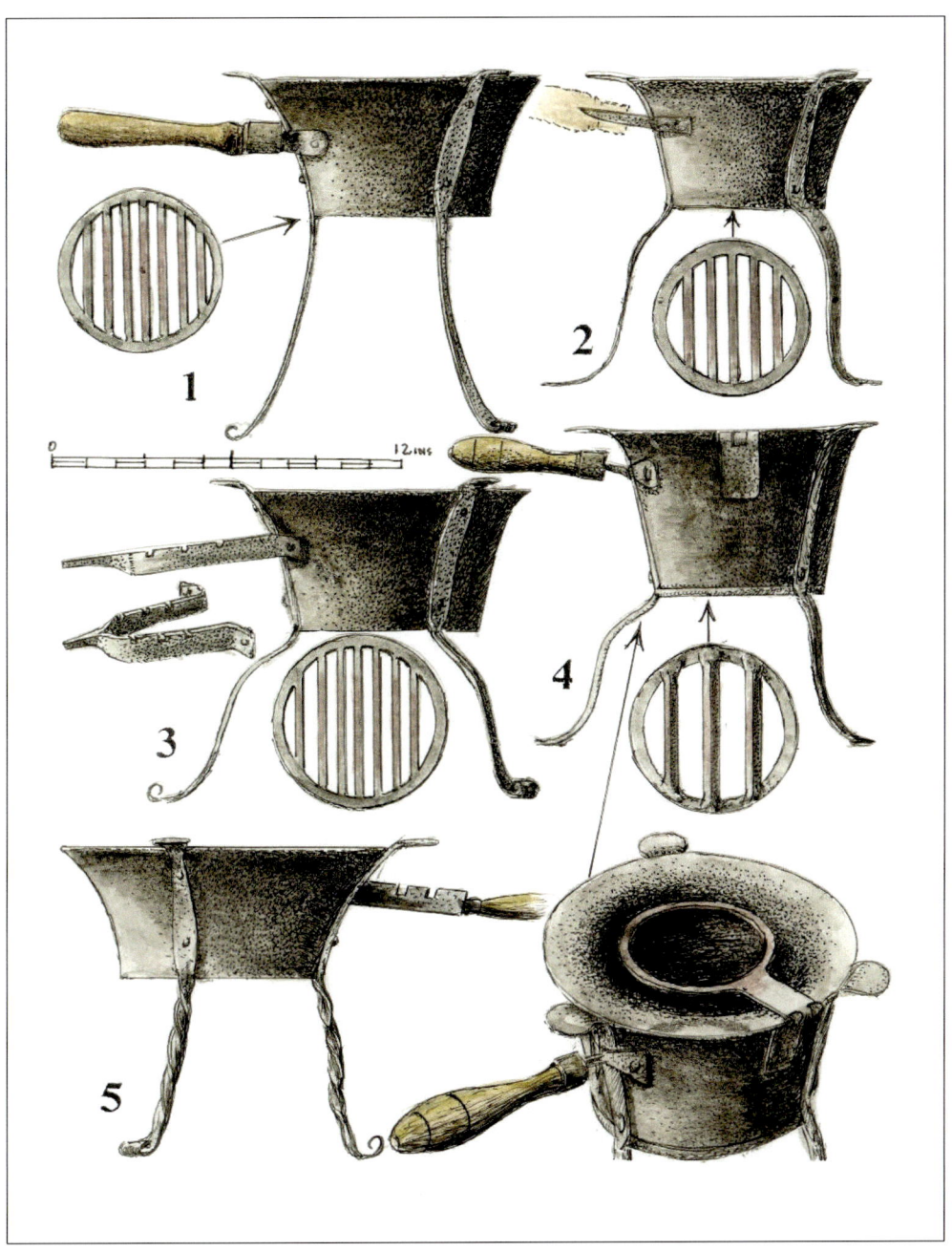

Figure 7. Between the fourteenth and nineteenth centuries much of the local cookery was carried out on portable peat-burning stones called 'choffers'. Of these shown here, No.1 was purchased for Bankfield Museum in 1909, and No.5 collected from Mary Sunderland of Top Withens by J.H. Dixon around 1900. The remainder are in the collection of Cliffe Castle, Keighley.

27

In use, pies or dishes of food were heated on these choffers, while in homes such as that of Sam Banks of Portsmouth, Todmorden, a bakestone was placed on top ready for baking oatcakes.[74] Bakestones were exactly what their name suggests; slabs of stone that were heated to serve as hotplates from the medieval period through to the early twentieth century. The earliest ones were quarried wherever there were outcrops of suitable rock as at Back Stone Hill, Todmorden.[75] By the seventeenth century the main centre of production had become concentrated on quarries at Delph, near Saddleworth, small ones about 18 in/45 cm square with rounded sides being carried into Calderdale by packhorse trains. In 1680 the Rev. Oliver Heywood of Coley saw an accident near Brighouse when a horse fell down with a large crash, for 'there was two bakestones on the horse that fell, which were mash't to pieces and the man made great lamentation for the breach of the Baking-stones.'[76] They were still being sold in the 1920s, a postcard in Cliffe Castle Museum reading 'Dear Madam, the price of the bakestone a foot square is 1s 9d. I would be pleased to oblige you with the same, yours respectfully, James Schofield'.[77]

These small bakestones were ideal for general small-scale bakery such as oatcakes, muffins, oven-cakes, suet cakes and pasties, but not large enough for the large, soft oatcakes that were increasingly popular from around the early eighteenth century. Much bigger bakestones were therefore installed as fixtures, their masonry bases incorporating an iron-doored firebox with ducts leading beneath the stone to a chimney. For this reason, they usually occupied one side of the recesses at the side of a main fireplace. At Walt Royd, Ovenden, Cornelius Ashworth helped Isaac Sharp when 'setting a Bakeing stone' in December 1785. It stood at the side of the chimney in the tall back kitchen or scullery where it was drawn by Arthur Comfort in the 1920s when it appeared to be in working order.[78]

In most parts of England where yeast-raised wheat loaves were everyday fare, many houses had a beehive-shaped masonry-lined oven built into the side of their kitchen fireplace. To use them a bundle of fast-burning hawthorn or

[74] Wood & Brears, *The real Wuthering Heights*, p.59; Savage, *Sam Banks: his life and times*, p.4.

[75] Grid ref SD936263.

[76] J. H. Turner, *The Rev. Oliver Heywood, 1630-1702: his autobiography, diaries, anecdote and event books*, vol.4, Bingley, 1835, p.20.

[77] Wood & Brears, *The real Wuthering Heights*, p.61.

[78] Crump, *The little hill farm,* p.31.

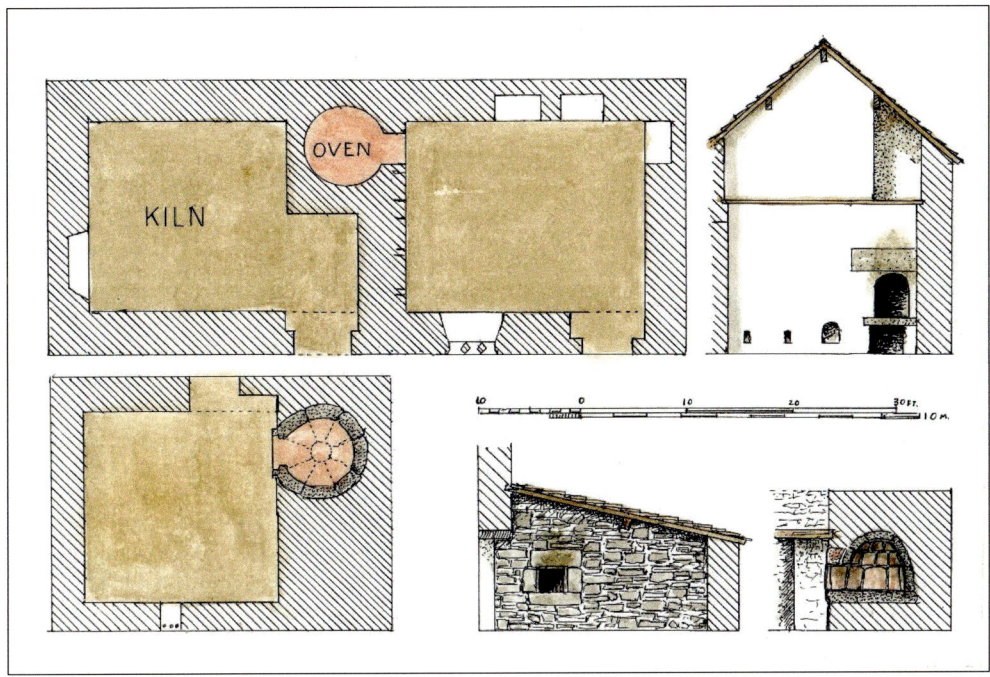

Figure 8. Since most families relied on oatcake, domed stone-lined ovens remained a rarity in this area. These examples are in a corn-drying/malt kiln by the side of Hebden Water in Hebden Bridge (above) and at Lane Ends Farm, Upper Saltonstall, at the head of Luddenden Dean.

similar wood was lit on the hearth and thrust into the back of the oven, its flames licking the underside of the domed roof before venting from the top of the oven doorway. Once the interior was really hot, the embers were raked out, the interior mopped with a wet rag called a maukin, the baking inserted and the door sealed up to keep in the heat. Most unusually, such ovens are extremely rare here; those at Top-o'-th' Hill, Kebroyd, Ripponden, Greystones in Warley, and a lost example at Hullen Edge, Norland, being the few recorded examples. A few more were located in outbuildings, such as at Lane Ends farm in Warley, Broadbottom in Wadsworth, Crawstone Hall in Greetland and in a corn drying/malting kiln at the side of Hebden Water in Hebden Bridge.[79] It would appear that firewood was so scarce and oatcake was so widely eaten in the Stuart and early Georgian South Pennines that there was little need for a

[79] C. Giles, *Rural houses of West Yorkshire 1400-1830*, London, HMSO, 1986, pp.221, 209; Crump, *The little hill farm*, p.44; Brears, *Traditional food in Yorkshire*, p.132; H.L. Roth, *The Yorkshire coiners and notes on old and prehistoric Halifax*, Halifax, F. King & Sons, 1906, pp.252-253.

bread oven in most households. There were probably a number in Halifax and the larger villages, however, in which professional bakers would bake both their own products and those brought in by the public in return for a small fee.

The main problems with this kind of oven were its intermittent nature, its reliance on wood and the burning embers and smoke it belched out. In the middle of the eighteenth century a completely new kind of oven was introduced here, one that was formed as an iron box set in masonry over its own fireplace, and closed by a hinged iron door. The Rev. John Lister had one of these installed in Shibden Hall in January 1750, his accounts describing a 'Perpetual Oven and setting £4 4s 0d, Smith work 9s, Lime 3s, bricks 1s, Plasterer's work and colouring 3s 5d' giving a total of £6 0 5d, a considerable sum at that date.[80] The name 'Perpetual Oven' indicates its main advantage of giving a continuous steady heat, but it could also burn peat or coal and its smoke ascended a flue rather than polluting the kitchen. The stone-flagged fronts of such ovens still remain in a number of houses in Halifax, showing where the firebox and ashpit were fixed beneath the oven.

As coal became more readily available, kitchen fires had to be provided with iron grates, since the fire required a good underdraught and only smouldered badly if burned on a flat hearth. The basic grate or 'range' had a number of horizontal wrought iron firebars across its front and base, the back and sides being of masonry. What would now be called hobs, the flat-topped, usually stone-faced blocks at each side of the range, were here known as hud- or hood-ends, since they stood beneath the ends of the former pyramid-shaped wattle-and-daub smoke hoods that had previously carried the fumes up to the chimney.[81]

For a number of years in the late Georgian period the kitchens in the larger houses had a number of separate cooking fixtures, each with its own fireplace. At Waltroyd in Wheatley, for example, Cornelius Ashworth installed a range, a boiling copper or 'pan' and a bakestone in 1785, adding an oven and a boiler in 1809.[82] Around this time the great iron foundries of Sheffield and Rotherham started to manufacture small coal-burning 'Yorkshire' ranges that had a central

---

[80] West Yorkshire Archive Service (Calderdale), Lister family: household bills, SH:3/B/1/1

[81] Wright, *English dialect dictionary,* under 'Hood', 8 & 9.

[82] R. Davies, A. Petford, J. Senior, *The Diaries of Cornelius Ashworth 1782-1816,* Hebden Bridge, Hebden Bridge Local History Society, 2011, pp.185, 241.

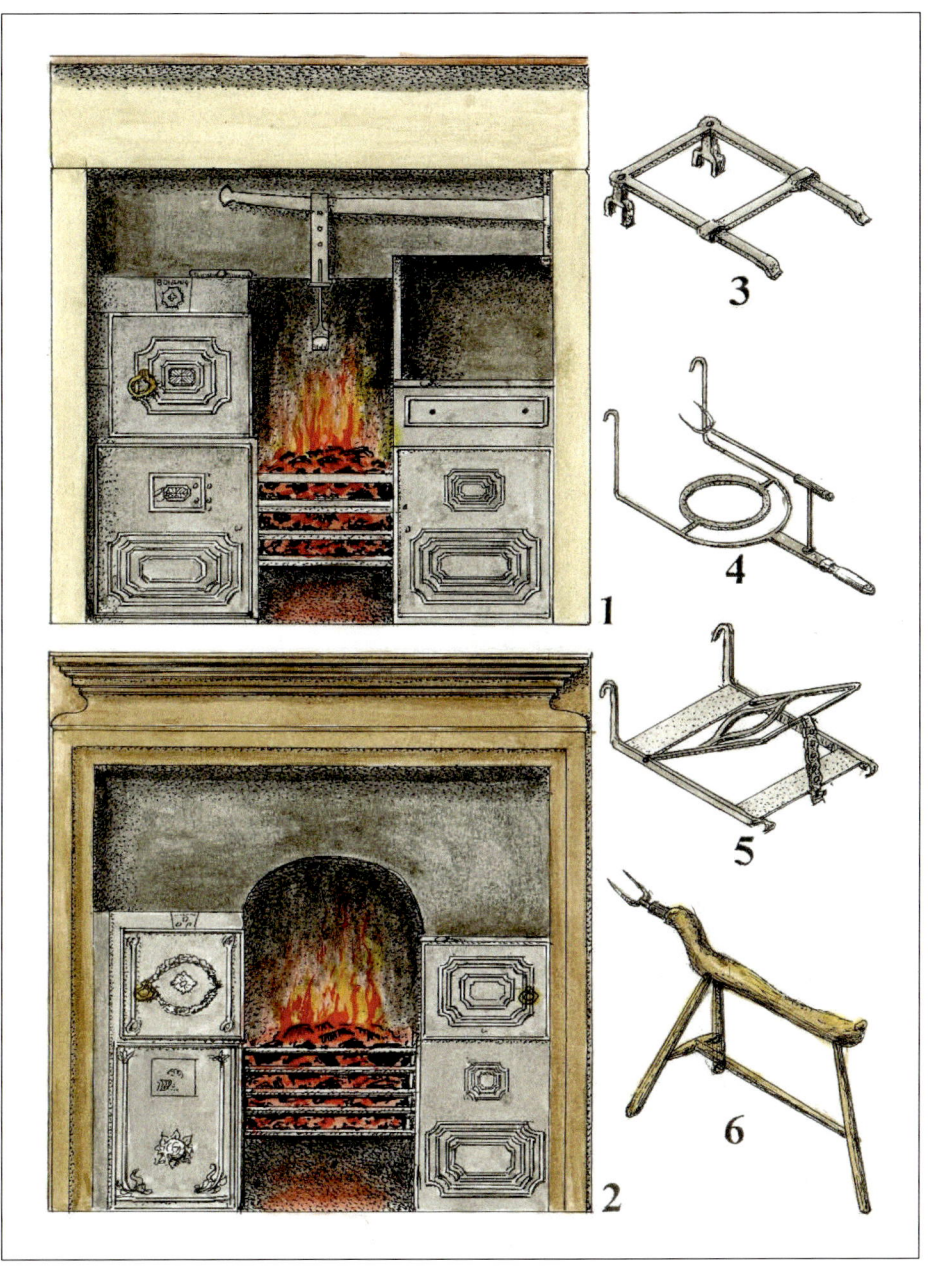

Figure 9. *Cast-iron cooking ranges were used here from the early nineteenth century, the earliest ones having an oven heated by a separate grate on one side and a boiler on the other. No.1 from a Haworth cottage, was made at the great Bowling Ironworks near Bradford, while 2 was formerly at Ponden Hall, Stanbury. The central fire could be bridged by a brandreth (3) to hold either a pan or bakestone, while the firebar toasters (4 & 5 from Haworth) hooked onto the top bar. Alternatively food might be held before the fire on a toasting bull (6 from Rastrick).*

31

Figure 10. *By the 1850s iron ovens were being heated by flues from the main fire, as seen in these Todmorden examples (1 & 2). No.2 was cheaper, lacking the decorative cast iron plates of No.1. Meat might be oven-baked in a dripping tin (3), grilled on a gridiron (4) over the fire or in a 'Dutch oven' (5 & 6) set before it. Prosperous households used a clockwork bottle jack (7) to rotate their joints before the fire, sometimes hanging it in a 'hastener' (8).*

coal-burning grate flanked by a perpetual oven at one side and a hob or side-boiler at the other. The Bowling Ironworks just six miles north-east of Halifax followed suit, and by the 1860s companies such as Samuel Crook and Thomas Milnes were making them in central Halifax.[83]

They began to be installed in smaller houses around the 1830s, and became standard fittings in the numerous terraces erected for the mill workers, soon becoming the very heart of every home. Heating the rooms, boiling water for drinks, baths, laundry, baking, boiling and toasting all manner of food, heating bricks and oven-plates to warm freezing beds in wintertime and irons for pressing clothes, made them the warm, glowing focus of family life. Their maintenance was a matter of great pride, the dark iron plates being black-leaded to perfection, while the bright fittings were polished to a silver-like sheen. Controlling their ovens demanded close attention, both in stoking the fire and operating the damper to achieve the required temperature while making the best of the current weather. When Eric Greenwood was living at Hartley Royd farm, high above Todmorden, cakes could only be baked on calm days, for the high winds made the oven so hot that only pastries could be attempted.[84] For those who could not afford a Yorkshire range, or where there was no convenient fireplace to house one, smaller portable 'American' stoves were ideal. Their smaller firebox usually heated a tiny oven and boiling rings, the smoke being carried away up an iron stove pipe.[85]

Yorkshire ranges remained in everyday use in many homes through to the years after the Second World War, often being supplemented by a gas ring where town gas was available along the bottom of the valleys. However, even though many housewives appreciated the quality of the bakery they produced, they were glad to see the end of the laborious carrying in of the coal, maintaining the fire, cleaning out the dust and ashes every morning, cleaning out the flues and blackleading every week, and the disruption of regular chimney-sweeping. As soon as clean, easily maintained and efficient gas and electric stoves and Agas became available they were quickly installed, making life much easier for everyone.

---

[83] *Halifax Historical Almanac* 1861, p.36; Hartley, *Clock Almanack,* 1867, pp.74, 85.

[84] Greenwood, *Life on a Pennine farm,* p.8.

[85] Turner, *A spring-time saunter,* p.6.

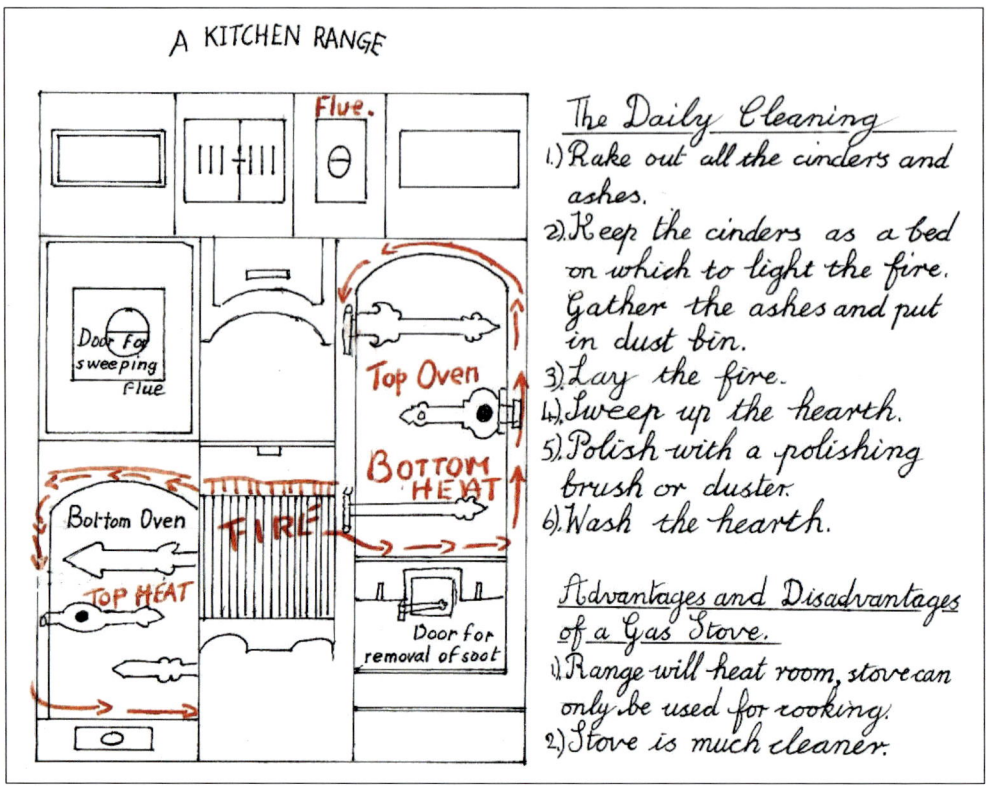

The handwritten content within the figure reads:

A KITCHEN RANGE

Flue.

Door for sweeping Flue

Top Oven

BOTTOM HEAT

Bottom Oven

FIRE

TOP HEAT

Door for removal of soot

The Daily Cleaning
1.) Rake out all the cinders and ashes.
2.) Keep the cinders as a bed on which to light the fire. Gather the ashes and put in dust bin.
3.) Lay the fire.
4.) Sweep up the hearth.
5.) Polish with a polishing brush or duster.
6.) Wash the hearth.

Advantages and Disadvantages of a Gas Stove.
1.) Range will heat room, stove can only be used for cooking.
2.) Stove is much cleaner.

Figure 11. Kitchen ranges only worked if they had all their flues cleaned out with coal-rakes and brushes once every week. The method was taught in schools, this being a page from the exercise book of 11-year-old Miss Dorothy Grimshaw at 'the Nashy', Todmorden's National School.

CHAPTER 3

OATS

Due to their ability to withstand thin soils and a wet and cold climate at altitudes often around the 1000-foot contour, oats were the most important crop in the area, virtually the whole population being dependent upon them for centuries. As Mrs Gaskell observed, 'what crops there are, on the patches of arable land, consist of pale hungry-looking grey-green oats'.[86] After being harvested in late summer, the grain was threshed out of the straw between August and January, and then taken to one of the local corn mills. Having been measured into 'strikes', a volume of two bushels or 2½ cubic feet, it was dried on a large square of horsehair cloth (later perforated ceramic tiles) over the gentle fire of a corn-drying kiln. This was the essential preparation for an initial coarse grinding that removed the husks and converted the grains into 'shilling', or groats. Next followed a second grinding, this time between coarse gritstone 'grey stones' to produce oatmeal. Advertisements for corn mills include details of these essential fittings, one from 1857 for the newly built Hebden Bridge Corn Mill describing its pair of shilling stones, two pairs of grey stones, and also four pairs of French burr stones for grinding wheat.[87]

The oatmeal that returned to the house in its 'meyl poke' was usually an unsorted mix of what is now sold as 'fine', 'medium' or 'pin-head' grades.[88] For storage it was packed down as solidly as possible into large chests called meal arks in the farms and larger houses, and probably into wooden tubs and pottery jars in smaller homes, as much air as possible being excluded to keep it in good condition for as long as a year or two. Its importance could not be over-estimated; without it the people would starve. As the population expanded during the nineteenth century, demand exceeded local supply. The 'miserable oats … some standing in shock [sheaves], … some still standing, and some yet nearly green' that William Cobbett saw here in September 1832 showed that a more certain source was essential.[89] Quantities therefore had to be imported, probably from the fertile Wolds of East Yorkshire, a task made easier once the canal and railway arrived.[90] It was only in the 1880s that the availability of

---

[86] E. Gaskell, *The life of Charlotte Brontë*, Originally published 1857, Harmondsworth, Penguin, 1975, p.55.

[87] Lonsdale Collection, *Newspaper cuttings*, vol.24, p.42.

[88] Savage, *Sam Banks: his life and times*, p.4.

[89] W. Cobbett, *Rural rides*, Vol.2, London, Dent, 1967, p.277.

[90] Crump, 'Halifax Visitors Book, Vol.1', p.92; *Leeds Mercury* 16 August 1800.

these oats, together with cheap imported wheat, allowed local farmers to concentrate on livestock and dairying rather than arable. This did not end the taste for porridge, oatcakes, parkins and other oatmeal bakery, however, these staples remaining very popular here for a further sixty years or more.

The local simile for having struck a good bargain was 'It's as good as meal in'th ark.'[91] With a full ark, there was absolute, re-assuring certainty of adequate food for the foreseeable future, much of it taking the form of porridge.

Porridge

For some families their sole food, year in year out, was porridge.

> 'we had porridge three times a day, only 2d for a 1 lb bag'.[92]
> 'porridge and milk three times a day'.[93]
> [He] 'lived chiefly on porridge'.[94]

Having porridge ready for mealtimes was one of the most important responsibilities of every housewife.

> Don't kal [chatter] abaht like monay a wan,
> Then have a broil, an' sweeat, an' run';
> Bud alas hev thi dinner done
> Withaht a moild [harassment]
> If its nobbut meil, lass set it on,
> An' hev it boiled.[95]

Today this would be considered dull, boring and miserable food, but past generations really appreciated it. Timmy Feather, last of the local handloom weavers, loved his few porridge; 'Eaah! iv'ry mornin', an thay'r t' best meeal et E get i' t' day'.[96] Meanwhile Elland folk didn't need doctors since 'the posnet was scarcely off the fire and they applied an oatmeal poultice inwardly every evening'.[97]

---

[91] Lonsdale Collection, *Newspaper cuttings*, vol.5, p.1.

[92] Calderdale Libraries, *Memory lane: recollections of Todmorden*, Halifax, Calderdale Leisure Services, 1988, p.49.

[93] Travis, *Notes: (historical and biographical)*, p.42.

[94] E. Southwart, *Brontë moors & villages from Thornton to Haworth*, London, John Lane, 1923, p.160.

[95] Bill o' th' Hoylus End [W. Wright], *Random rhymes & rambles*, Keighley, 1876, p.8.

[96] Turner, *A spring-time saunter*, pp.56, 132. Locally porridge was described by the plural term 'a few', rather than the alternative of 'some'.

[97] Hamerton, *Olde Eland*, p.3.

Figure 12. Porridge was the staple food here for centuries, the oatmeal being stirred into the water boiling in a posnet (1) or a kilp pan (2 from Haworth), using a wooden thible (3). Pewter spoons (4) cast from a mid-seventeenth-century mould over the next two hundred years, were used to scoop up mouthfuls of the porridge from the communal pan or dish, dip them into meas-pots (5) of skim milk, and then raise them up to the lips. Sometimes the porridge was sweetened with treacle that was stored warm and soft in a screw-topped treacle jar (6) on the mantlepiece.

The vessels in which the porridge was boiled were of two kinds. The kilp pan was a small cast-iron cauldron holding about a gallon (8 pts/4.8 l) that had a semi-circular handle called a 'kilp' or 'kelp' by which to hang it from a hook over the kitchen fire. (*kilpr* being the Old Norse for a handle). In contrast, the posnet was similar, but had three short legs and a projecting horizontal handle so that it could stand either amid the burning peats on the hearthstone or on the coals burning in the grate. The only other utensil was a thible, pronounced with a long 'i', a flat-sided wooden stirring-stick that was either home-made, or bought from shopkeepers such as Paul Greenwood of 24 Russell Street in Halifax.[98]

To make porridge, the oatmeal was gradually sprinkled into boiling water with one hand, while the whole mass was stirred with the thible in the other. This

---

[98] *Halifax Courier* 3 July 1897; *Halifax Historical Almanack*, Halifax, W. Stephenson, 1861, p.83, Calderdale Museums 2338 of 18/10/1918, 336-7 of 1902 & 1949.15.

process was not so easy as it sounds, as Emily Brontë described in her *Wuthering Heights* of 1847. Just as Joseph, the irascible old servant, was about to start making the porridge, Catherine decided to take over, crying

> "I'll make the porridge!" I removed the vessel out of his reach … Joseph beheld my style of cooking with growing indignation. "Thear!" he ejaculated, "Hareton, tha will'nt sup thy porridge tuh neeght; they'll be nowt bud lumps as big as maw nave [fist]. Thear agean! Aw'd fling in bowl un all, if al were yah! Thear, pale t' guilp [handle] off, un then yah'll hae don wi't. Bang, bang. It's marcy t'bottom isn't deaved.[99]

Porridge

For 2 people take 2 oz/50 g oatmeal and about 1 tsp salt. Today pin-head oatmeal is usually specified, but since unsieved meal would have been commonly used, a mix of fine, medium and pin-head is preferable.

Bring ¼ pt/150 ml water per person to the rapid boil with the salt, sprinkle in the oatmeal while stirring and simmer for 10-15 minutes, stirring regularly and adding a little more water if too thick. Cook for up to 30 minutes if using pin-head meal.

[An easier method of making porridge is to cover the pan as soon as it has come to the boil, wrap it in thick towels and leave for about 15 minutes before re-heating and stirring, repeating this until the porridge has cooked. This saves the long period of stirring, and may explain why some people left their hot porridge insulated in their bedclothes ready for eating on return home from work.]

The porridge was served communally, either in the vessel it had been cooked in or poured into a dish and placed in the middle of the table. Each person took a spoonful and dipped it into their meos-pot (mug) of milk that had been filled from a communal jug before raising it to the lips.[100] Back in *Wuthering Heights* Catherine had been appalled when Hareton seized their gallon pitcher of new milk, and slavered into it as he drank directly from its rim instead of using a mug in the accepted manner. Protesting that she could not take milk with her porridge after it had been so befouled, she was informed that he was 'every bit as wollsome' as she was, and should not be so conceited![101]

---

[99] E. Brontë, *Wuthering Heights,* 1847. Reprinted London, Everyman's Library, 1991, p.161-162

[100] Brears, *Traditional food in Yorkshire*, pp.100-101; Savage, *Sam Banks: his life and times*, p.5.

[101] Brontë, *Wuthering Heights*, p.162.

Sometimes the porridge might be eaten with a little butter and sugar, or black treacle. The treacle was collected from a grocery shop, where the counter staff would run off a quantity from a large barrel into the customer's own container. This might be an ordinary pottery jar, but some families had transfer-printed factory-made treacle pots with screw lids to exclude both dust and insects. These stood on the mantelpiece in order to keep their contents warm and soft, ready for use. When times were hard the treacle was watered down to make it go further.[102]

Oatmeal was also used to absorb the fats and flavours of fried bacon, converting them into tasty dishes that broke up the monotony of never-ending porridge. They included:

Waff[103]

1 tbs bacon fat or dripping
4 tsp medium oatmeal
pinch of salt
¼ pt/150 ml milk
1 tsp sugar, treacle or golden syrup

Melt the fat in the frying pan, stir in the oatmeal and salt for a few minutes over a gentle heat until all has been absorbed. Add the milk and continue stirring until the mixture thickens and comes away from the bottom of the pan. Serve hot with sugar, treacle or syrup.

Stirabout[104]

After bacon (preferably fatty dry-cured bacon) has been fried, stir in sufficient medium oatmeal to absorb the fat, sweeten with a little black treacle and serve hot with bacon.

Oatcake
Oatcake was second only to porridge in feeding the working communities. Its alternative name here was havercake, *hafre* being the Old Norse word for oats. It was made in a variety of ways, the simplest and oldest being:

---

[102] Savage, *Sam Banks: his life and times*, p.5.

[103] Savage, *Sam Banks: his life and times*, p.4; Travis, *Notes: (historical and biographical)*, p.118.

[104] Savage, *Sam Banks: his life and times*, p.5.

Oatcake[105]

8 oz/225 g fine or medium (or mixed fine and medium) oatmeal
½ tsp salt

Mix the salt into the oatmeal and stir in about 4-5 tbs cold water, just sufficient to form a lump of stiff dough. Press out on a meal-dusted board before rolling out as a ¼ in/6 cm thick round cake. Originally this was slid onto a bakestone and baked for 5-10 minutes on each side before being propped up before an open fire to cook/dry completely. Today it is best baked on a baking sheet at 180ºC/380ºF gas mark 4 for about 20 minutes, finally drying out for a day on a cooling tray.

Pieces of this kind of oatcake were simply broken off and eaten either plain or with cheese, dripping or some other spread. They were also used to thicken liquids. Mr Watson of Slade, Warley Moor, remembered how 'when yo' steep't it i' th milk it swelled aght twice th' thickness!'[106] Scalded with hot water or broth, they formed a quick and satisfying dish called browis.

Browis: Hebden Bridge

It was prepared in this way. Hot water was poured over oatcake in a bowl. It was allowed to stand for a short time and then the water squeezed out. The oatcake was then fried in deep fat and eaten hot.[107]

Later crisp oatcakes were much thinner and lighter, their recipes including flour, fat and baking powder.

Oatcakes: Mrs Kaye[108]

8 oz/225 g fine or medium oatmeal
1½ oz/35 g flour
½ tsp salt
½ tsp bicarbonate of soda
1 tbs melted lard

---

[105] See Brears, *Traditional food in Yorkshire* for further recipes.

[106] Turner, *A spring-time saunter*, p.56.

[107] Bedford, H., *Manuscript notebooks*, Leeds University, Brotherton Library Special Collections MS 432/4, p.97.

[108] Anon., *159 recipes from good kitchens*, Sowerby Bridge, 1914.

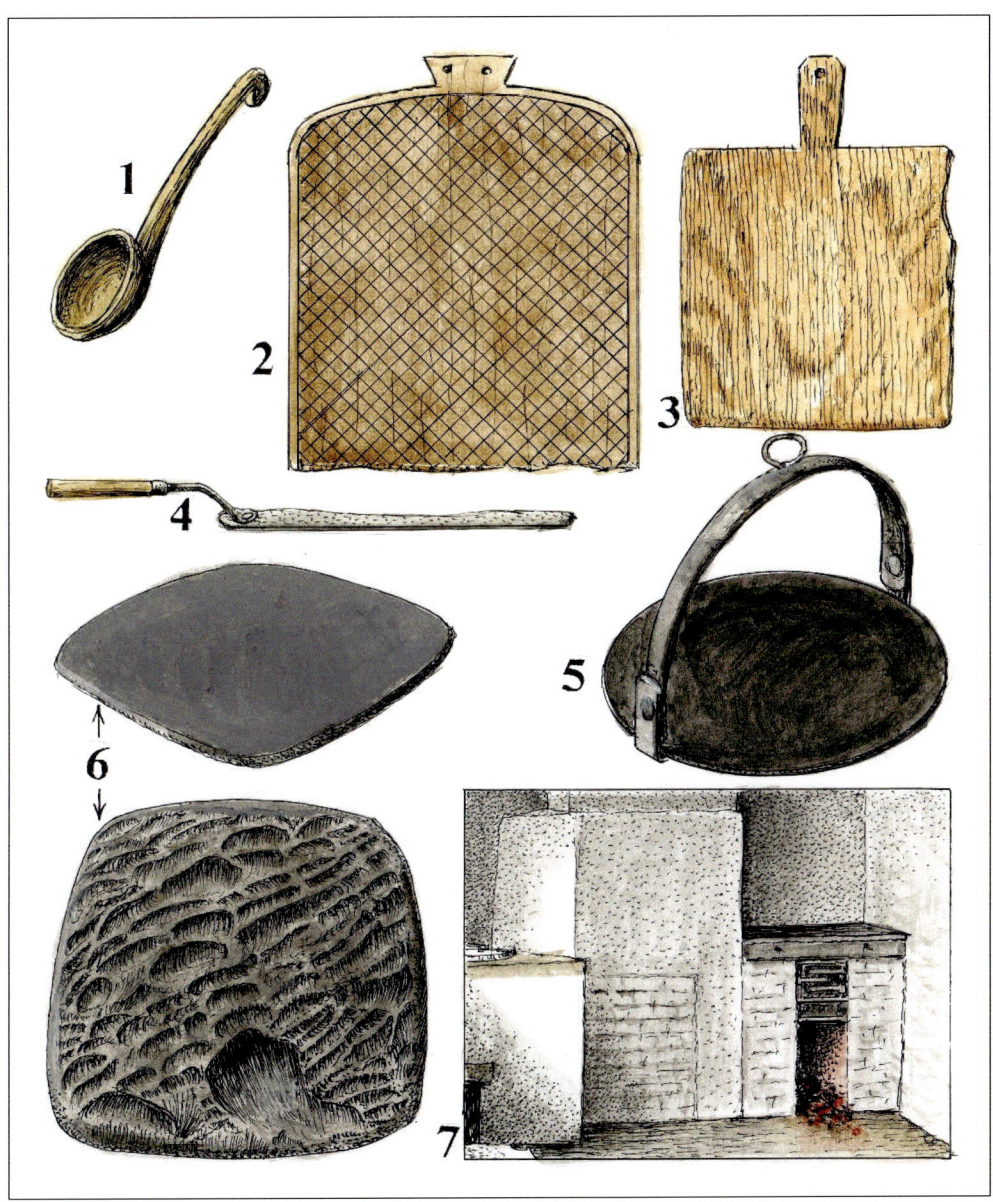

Figure 13. *To bake soft oatcakes, the batter was scooped up in a wooden ladle (1), poured onto an oatmeal-scattered riddling board or bakbrade (2 from Lane Ends Farm, Upper Saltonstall), slid onto a flannel covered spittle (3 used by Miss Hodgson, Castle Fields, Rastrick), and thrown onto a hot bakestone, from where the finished cake was removed using an oatcake knife (4 also from Lane Ends Farm). Iron girdles (5) were in common use, but many preferred the gentle heat of a stone bakestone (6) placed over the fire. Some farmhouses used built-in bakestones, as at Waltroyd in Wheatley (7 right).*

Mix the dry ingredients. Melt the lard in ¼ pt/150 ml hot water, and mix into the oatmeal with a knife. Place the dough onto a board dusted with fine oatmeal and rapidly roll out as thin as possible, rubbing in dry oatmeal onto the upper surface. Cut into quarter-rounds and, using a piece of stiff card as a support, transfer to a bakestone/griddle or to an oven sheet for baking at 180ºC/350ºF gas mark 4 for about 20 minutes.

Requiring only a bakestone, frying pan or oven and very basic skills, this thick, crisp oatcake was easily made but fell out of use during the later nineteenth century, being replaced by larger, thinner yeast-raised oatcakes locally called havercakes. The appearance of 'backbreads', implements solely used for making them, in local probate inventories show that they were being baked here before the 1690s.[109] Some housewives might have made their own havercakes, but most appear to have bought them from a professional or semi-professional baker who had the essential skills and equipment. Mary Brearley of Upper Slack, Luddenden Dean, was remembered as a maker, probably using the following traditional method.[110]

Havercake

1 lb/450 g fine oatmeal sieved from the 'fine' or 'medium' oatmeal (and not rolled oats) sold in shops
1 pt/600 ml tepid water or fresh (not cultured) buttermilk
1 tsp dried yeast (formerly yeasts left in the 'nakit')
½ tsp salt

The oatmeal was sprinkled onto the water in a coopered tub called a 'nakit' (i.e. knead-kit) and stirred in with the hand and forearm to form a smooth batter. After standing overnight in a warm place to ferment, a wooden ladle-full was poured onto a layer of fine oatmeal sprinkled onto the diagonally scored surface of a 18 in/45 cm square wooden 'backbread'. This was then held in both hands and swirled around to enlarge the pool of batter, the fine, dry oatmeal acting as a lubricant. By tilting the backbread towards its chamfered lower edge, the pool was slid on to a piece of flannel resting on a flat square board with a handle to one side, this being

[109] M. Crawford and S. Richardson, *Erringden, Langfield and Stansfield probate records, 1688-1700,* Hebden Bridge, Hebden Bridge Local History Society, 2015, p.37.
[110] Turner, *A spring-time saunter,* p.40.

called a 'spittle'. Then standing beside the bakestone and using a motion similar to serving a ball in tennis, the oatmeal pool was hurled off the spittle at an angle of 45º, so that it formed a long oval as it hit the hot surface. Only a few millimetres in thickness, it took only a few minutes to bake to firmness, when the edges began to curl away from the bakestone. At this stage a long, flat knife with a cranked handle was used to free the havercake and flick it over to briefly cook the other side. Now resembling a long oval piece of pale chamois wash-leather, the cakes were wrapped in white cloths and put into large wicker baskets ready for sale.

This was the method used by professional oatcake/havercake bakers such as Fred Suthers of 61 Walton Fold at the bottom of Cross Stone Road and Jackson's of Lumb's Buildings, Halifax Road in Todmorden, Willie Forton at Low Side, Stanbury and his sons in Ovenden, the Feather family in Haworth and E. Bailey of Cross Roads.[111] Some of them invested in one of the large cast-iron machines patented by Joseph Wright of Briggate, Shipley, in 1861.[112] His 'reeling' device set the backbread in a tray mounted on an eccentric shaft in order to rapidly spread the batter into a large round puddle. From here, the batter was slid onto the continuous canvas belt of a trolley that, running on rails and propelled by a long lever, threw the batter onto the hottest of two coal or coke-fired hotplates. Having cooked on one side, a long knife with a cranked handle was used to free it from the first hotplate and flip it over onto the cooler second hotplate to finish off. The last of the Yorkshire oatcake bakers was Mr Leslie Feather of Haworth who retired in 1975 when Mr John Ogden, the curator of Keighley's Cliffe Castle Museum, was able to rescue perhaps the only surviving example of a Joseph Wright hotplate/bakestone along with every other utensil used in the bakery. These remain dismantled and stored by the Bradford Museum service, but fortunately a complete photographic record of Mr and Mrs Feather using them in 1975 was made by those great social historians, Misses Marie Hartley and Joan Ingilby.[113]

Today it is expected that machine-made products will produce uniform results, but this was never true of earlier technologies in which the operator's skill

---

[111] Bedford, *Manuscript notebooks*, MS 432/4, p.52; J. Craven, *A Brontë moorland village*, Keighley, Rydal Press, 1907, p.14. Kelly's Directory of the West Riding of Yorkshire 1901.

[112] Brears, *Traditional food in Yorkshire*, pp.118-119.

[113] Hartley and Ingilby, *Life and tradition in West Yorkshire*, plates 98-102.

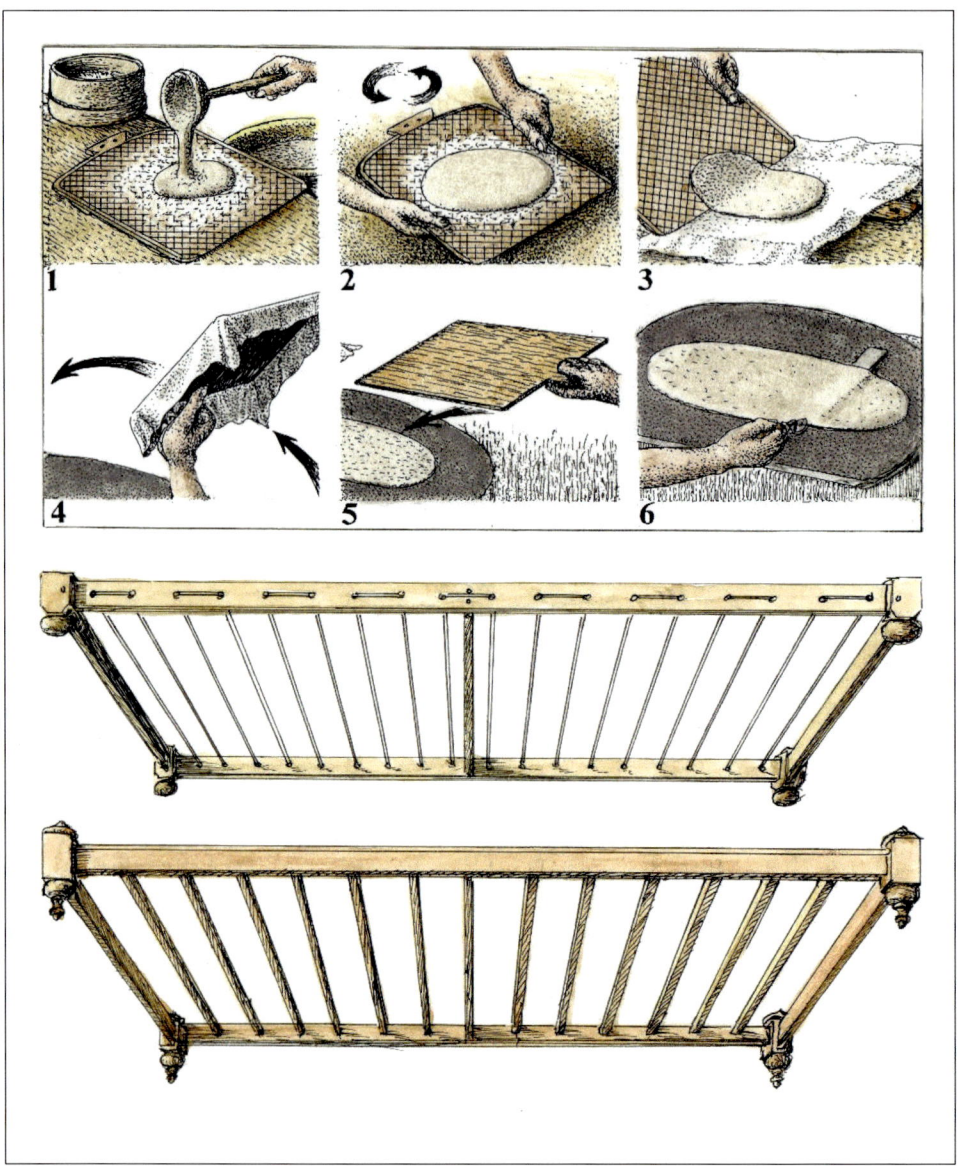

Figure 14. Making an oatcake proceeded from 1 pouring to 2 reeling, 3 sliding onto the flannel on the spittle, 4-5 throwing and finally 6 removing for drying on a flake suspended from the ceiling above the hearth. The upper flake is from Ripponden, while the lower one was used by the Brontë sisters in Haworth Parsonage.

remained of paramount importance. This was certainly true of the oatcake machines. The Feathers' oatcakes and muffins were light, soft and delicious, as I remember from my days living in nearby Oakworth, but others fell far below these high standards. When Dr Henry Bedford bought one of Jackson's in

44

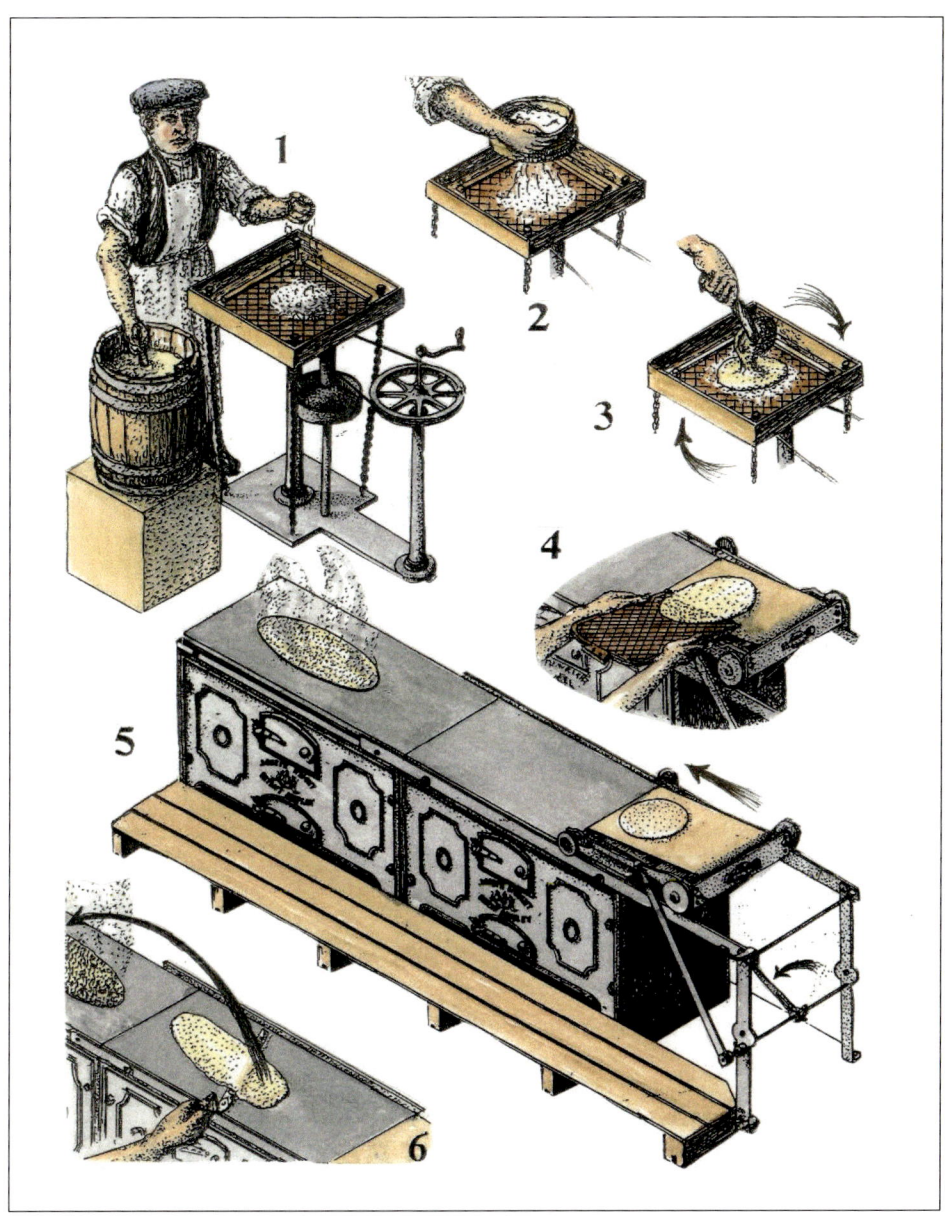

Figure 15. *Professional oatcake bakers rapidly adopted the mechanical riddling board, cake thrower and bakestone patented by Joseph Wright of Shipley in 1864. Having first sprinkled fine oatmeal on the riddling board either by hand (1) or through a sieve (2), a ladleful of the batter was poured on top and the board rotated to spread it out (3). The cake was then slid onto the canvas roller (4) which, on pulling the lever, threw it onto the hot bakestone (5), from where, after cooking, it was freed with a knife and flipped over onto the cooler end of the bakestone (6) to complete its baking. This example was used by Mr Leslie Feather of Haworth.*

45

Todmorden in 1941 he found it 'very thick and coarse and particles were visible which seemed to be bran. We were unable to eat it'.[114]

Some of the oatcakes/havercakes were sold directly to customers calling in either at the baker's own shop, or at one of the local shops he supplied. Large numbers were also hawked around the streets, being wrapped in clean white cloths within huge rectangular willow baskets carried over the arm.[115] Having been purchased, the customers hung them up to dry on a 'creel' or 'bread-flake' hanging from the ceiling immediately in front of the chimney breast.[116]

Some creels were of a thick, hairy string threaded through the holes drilled into horizontal boards at each side, as seen in photographs of Timmy Feather's cottage in Stanbury. Others were rectangular wooden frames enclosing a series of narrow square-sectioned rods, but whichever kind was used, the oatcakes were hung over two strings or bars, since they could crack if tightly creased over just a single one. Here, safe from the attention of children, pets or rodents, the oatcakes would dry out, being reached down by adults just as needed. Those without a creel sometimes used a hedge for the same purpose, if the weather was sunny.[117]

A favourite method of eating this havercake when soft was to roll it up 'with a layer of treacle between', Whiteley Turner relishing this treat since he claimed 'great faith in oats and syrup'.[118] However, butter, lard or dripping remained the more common spreads. When dried to crispness it was eaten with cold meats, the jellied beef brawn known as 'stew', cheese, sometimes with raw onions, or else crumbled up into hot water or stock to make browis or 'snap-and-rattle'.[119]

These oatcakes and havercakes enabled the people of the Calder Valley and Haworth to survive their harsh landscape and climate for countless generations. In the hungry years of the Napoleonic wars they had become the recognised emblem of the district, recruiting sergeants of the Duke of

[114] Bedford, *Manuscript notebooks*, MS 432/4, p.52.

[115] Ibid., p.97.

[116] Ibid., p.60'; Calderdale Libraries, *Memory lane: recollections of Todmorden*, pp.13, 58

[117] Bedford, *Manuscript notebooks*, MS 432/4, pp.60, 77.

[118] Turner, *A spring-time saunter*, p.40.

[119] Bedford, *Manuscript notebooks*, MS 432/4, p.97; Wright, *English dialect dictionary*, under 'Snap'

Wellington's Regiment carrying them on their sword-points bedecked with coloured ribbons and shouting 'Hey for t' havvercake lads!'[120] It is sad that, unlike Staffordshire and Derbyshire, they have gone out of production here, for they were greatly appreciated by many people, for whom there is no modern substitute.

Figure 16. *Oatcakes were such an important local food that one was beribboned and flourished on the sword of the Napoleonic recruiting sergeant of the Duke of Wellington's regiment, 'The Havercake Lads'.*

[120] Wright, *English dialect dictionary*, under 'Haver'.

Figure 17. In many late Victorian homes, a weekly baking day was devoted to making all the family's loaves, oven cakes, teacakes, cakes and pastries.

CHAPTER 4

DAILY BREAD

Due to the altitude and climate of its Pennine hill farms, the Calder Valley grew very little wheat, concentrating instead on oats and rye. As a result, the only bread eaten by most families in the eighteenth century appears to have been 'maslegen', a mixture of wheat and rye ground together.[121] Those who needed or preferred wheat, either to make size to dress warps for weaving, or for cookery, usually had to buy it from lowland farmers and dealers. In 1785, for example, Cornelius Ashworth of Wheatley bought a load of six bushels from Halifax, then having it ground into six stone (84 lb) of wholemeal that could be sieved into bran, meal and white flour after being carried to his home.[122] In the early nineteenth century dealers such as 'Old Wheehouse' sold corn at Todmorden's Thursday night market at the Royal George so that local grocers could obtain supplies and have them ground ready for sale in their shops.[123] So far as most local families were concerned, wheat was a very expensive commodity, white bread and pastries being considered rare luxuries. Oatcakes made from both locally grown and more distantly farmed oats remained the most important cereal food here long after the Napoleonic wars had finished in 1815.

However, from the 1830s to the 1840s, and particularly after local farmers stopped growing oats around the 1880s, the use of oatcake began to decline, being replaced by bread made of white wheat flour. This was bought from grocery shops, where it was scooped out of tubs into the customer's own 'flour poke', a stout white cotton or linen bag resembling a pillow-slip, that was then wrapped in a blue check cover, tied with a couple of knots, and carried home on top of the head.[124] As flour became the most important staple foodstuff, particularly after blight destroyed the potato crops, adulteration and profiteering became rampant.

---

[121] Watson, *The history and antiquities of the parish of Halifax*, p.542.

[122] Wright, *English dialect dictionary*, under 'Bushel'.

[123] Travis, *Notes: (historical and biographical)*, p.32.

[124] Calderdale Libraries, *Memory lane: recollections of Todmorden*, p.91; Calderdale Libraries, *Memory lane: recollections of Brighouse, Rastrick & Hipperholme*, Halifax, Calderdale Leisure Services, 1992, p.28.

Back in the hungry 1840s, a girl from the upper part of the Dean was sent down to Luddenden to buy flour for her family. Arriving at the shop, she and others were kept waiting for hours by the proprietor, who gave them 'spice' (sweets) to keep them happy. He only began to serve them when his son returned from Halifax with the news that flour had risen threepence a stone and had waved a white handkerchief or nappy out of the window to pass details of the rise on to shopkeepers in Midgley and Warley. As a result, this short-distance shopping trip took a full five hours and cost more than had been expected.[125]

Flour was in such great demand and relatively high in price, that some were tempted to steal it either for personal use or for sale to raise much-needed cash. In 1834 Mr Baines, who ran the corn mill at Brearley, saw three men removing sacks of his flour in the middle of the night, but they got away before he could catch them. He then found someone to act as a witness as he mixed tiny, marked paper punchings into his flour. When this too was stolen, he was able to recognise it in the house of one of the suspected thieves. As a result, three men stood trial at the summer sessions in Bradford, all being transported for seven years.[126] These incidents provide particularly useful evidence for showing when oatmeal and oatcakes began to be replaced by wheat flour and bread in many local working households.

The growing difficulties experienced in obtaining good, cheap flour led to the formation of organisations such as the Halifax Flour Society and the Todmorden Co-operative Society, both set up in 1847 to supply subscribers with pure flours at cost price. They proved highly successful, selling thousands of pounds of flour each year and erecting fine mills and warehouses, such as that just to the east of Halifax railway station, now part of the Nestlé factory. Their rise, combined with the demise of arable crops on the local hill-farms and the importation of cheap flour from America and Canada, saw the closure of most of the valley's small water-powered corn mills by the early years of the twentieth century.

Raising white breads with yeast had always been an uncertain process, largely depending on the skilful use of barm, the froth rising from fermenting beer. Stored in jars, it was unpredictable, causing silly folk to be called barmy or barm-pots. From the 1840s a new kind of compressed yeast with predictable results began to be imported from Dutch distilleries. Known as German yeast,

[125] Lonsdale Collection, *Newspaper cuttings*, vol.8, p.109.

[126] Turner, *A spring-time saunter*, p.57.

it rapidly became extremely popular, some 2,700 tons a year being imported into Hull by 1858, much being advertised by local grocers who weighed off as much as a housewife wanted from the soft, cream-coloured block.[127]   It had only to be beaten into a little warm water, perhaps with a little sugar, and kneaded into the flour to form a lightly raised dough, thus making it much easier to home-bake all the bread many households still might need.

About this period many households still relied on their bakestones and choffers, since coal-fired ranges with ovens remained prohibitively expensive. The only way to bake bread using a bakestone was to form it into flat loaves to be baked first on one side, and then on the other. The simplest method, used by wool-combers such as 'Old Sampson' of Luddenden Dean, was to mix a little salt and water into a handful of flour and form it into a cake called a 'dumb boy'. It was then cooked in a frying pan over the 'pot o' four' on which the woolcombers' combs were heated.[128] Such cakes were quick, cheap and easy to make, being good for filling stomachs when there was little else to eat.

Fatty cakes: Mrs E.M. Austin, Sowerby[129]

8 oz/225 g flour
pinch of salt
6 oz/150 g lard [or dripping]
a little milk

Rub the lard into the flour and salt, work in just sufficient milk to form a stiff dough, roll out ½ in/1 cm thick on a floured board, form into 3-4 in/7.5-10 cm rounds and bake either on both sides on a girdle, or at 200ºC/400ºF gas mark 6 for about 15 minutes.

In contrast, most families would roll pieces of their light, risen dough into a large flat round cake and bake it on their bakestone. When ranges were installed, the bottom of the iron oven performed the same purpose, these cakes then being called 'oven-bottom cakes' or just 'oven cakes', to distinguish them from loaves baked in tins.

---

127 Brears, *Traditional food in Yorkshire*, p.141; *Todmorden & Hebden Bridge Historical Almanac, 1876, p.44.*

128 Turner, *A spring-time saunter,* p.37.

129 S. Kaye, *Yorkshire cooking,* Halifax, Halifax Courier, 1969, p.200.

Thin cakes: Mrs Ambler, Elland, 1913[130]

4 oz/100 g risen bread dough
4 oz/100 g flour
4 oz/100 g lard
pinch of salt

Rub the lard into the flour and salt, knead into the dough, roll out into one large or several smaller rounds and bake for a few minutes on each side on a hot bakestone.

As J.H. Dixon noted in the early 1900s, 'Old Yorkshire people still think that no oven cake is equal to that off the stone, and this taste has no doubt come down from the time when an oven in a cottage was a thing unknown'.

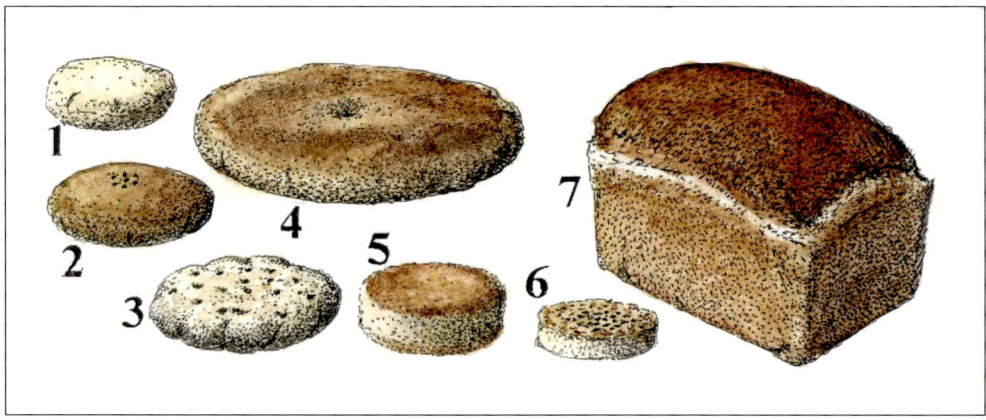

Figure 18. Traditional forms of bread including (1) fatty cake, (2) teacake, (3) suet cake. (4) oven-bottom cake, (5) muffin and (6) crumpet were all originally baked on bakestones, only (7) the tin-loaf, having to be baked in an oven.

Oven-bottom cakes: Mrs Cobb, Halifax[131]

1 lb/450 g risen bread dough
1 oz/25 g lard

Cut the lard into six small pieces and stick them anywhere deep into the top of the dough, fold some of the dough over the top to cover them, form into a round, flat cake about 10½ in/25 cm diameter, knuckle roughly level and prick a hole through the

---

[130] B. Leigh, *Book of golden recipes,* Leeds, 1913, p.35.

[131] Kaye, *Yorkshire cooking,* p.217.

centre, using a finger. Place on a greased baking sheet, lightly cover, keep in a warm place until risen, then bake at 200°C/400°F gas mark 6 for 20 minutes.

After baking they were either wrapped in a clean tea towel or propped on a doorstep or window-ledge to cool, although some couldn't wait so long, eating the delicious hot bread dripping with melted butter even when they knew it would give them heartburn. Oven-bottom cakes were ideal for everyday use, either cut through horizontally to make chunky sandwiches, or thinly sliced vertically for spreading with butter, dripping or jam.

The bakestone-and-chovver tradition of bakery probably established the continuing popularity of a number of other local breads, including teacakes, muffins, crumpets, and suet cakes. Compared to oven cakes, teacakes were smaller, lighter and richer, ideal for eating as sweet or savoury sandwiches, or split, toasted and buttered. They were made to three basic recipes:

Tea cakes: Mrs Smith & Mrs Brotherton, Oxenhope[132]

1 lb 4 oz/550 g strong white flour
½ tsp salt
1 tsp dried yeast
3 oz/75 g lard
1 egg, beaten
up to ½ pt/300 ml tepid milk

Mix the dry ingredients, rub in the lard, stir in the egg and sufficient milk to form a light dough. Turn out onto a floured board and knead for 10 minutes. Cover and leave in a warm place until doubled in size, then divide into 5 or 6 pieces, form each into a ball, roll flat, place on a greased baking sheet, leaving space for them to rise, cover, return to the warm until risen, then bake at 200°C/400°F gas mark 6 for about 15 minutes.

Currant teacakes: Mrs Edis, Haworth[133]

Follow the recipe above, adding 3 oz/75 g sugar and 4 oz/100 g currants.

---

[132] Oxenhope Church School Rebuilding Fund, *Recipe book,* Oxenhope, 1926; Hawksbridge Baptist Church, *A useful recipe book,* Oxenhope, [n.d.].

[133] Hawksbridge Baptist Church, *A useful recipe book,* Oxenhope, [n.d.].

Brown teacakes: Mrs Brumskill, Oxenhope[134]

8 oz/225 g strong wholemeal flour
2 oz/75 g strong white flour
½ tsp salt
1 tsp dried yeast
1 oz/25 g lard
about ¼ pt/150 ml tepid water

Follow the teacake recipe above.

Shorter in texture than teacakes, home-made suet cakes were popular around Todmorden, Haworth and Oxenhope.[135] They could be bought from Haworth bakers' shops up to the 1990s.

Suet cakes: Mrs Earnshaw, Oxenhope[136]

1 lb/450 g white flour
1 tsp dried yeast
¼ tsp salt
2 oz/50 g lard
8 oz/225 g suet
about ½ pt/300 ml tepid milk

Mix the yeast and salt into the flour, rub in the lard, stir in the suet, and mix with sufficient milk to form a dough. Knead 5 minutes, roll out ½ in/1.5 cm thick, cut into 6 in/15 cm rounds, place on a greased baking sheet, leave in a warm place until doubled in size then bake at 200ºC/400ºF gas mark 6 for about 15 minutes.

Currant suet cakes: Mrs Feather, Oxenhope[137]

Follow the recipe above, adding 2 oz/50 g lard and 4 oz/100 g currants. These cakes were sometimes toasted before an open fire for winter breakfasts.[138]

---

[134] Oxenhope Church, *Recipe book.*

[135] Savage, *Sam Banks: his life and times,* p.4.

[136] Oxenhope Church, *Recipe book.*

[137] Hawksbridge Baptist Church, *A useful recipe book.*

[138] Greenwood, *Life on a Pennine farm,* p.40.

Muffins

1 lb/450 g strong white flour
1 tsp salt
2 oz/50 g butter
1 tsp sugar
½ pt/300 ml warm milk & water
1 tsp dried yeast

Rub the butter into the flour, salt, sugar and yeast in a bowl, make a well in the centre, pour in the milk and water, mix together thoroughly to form a soft dough. Cover the bowl and leave to rise in a warm place for about half an hour, then divide into 8 pieces, mould into flattened balls on a floured board, or baking sheet, leaving space for them to expand, cover, and return to the warm until doubled in size. Bake either on a bakestone, first one side and then the other, until a pale brown, or in an oven at 190ºC/375ºF gas mark 5 for 15 minutes. To serve, cut through the crust halfway up the sides, toast on both sides, tear apart, thickly butter the torn insides, put back together and serve in a covered hot dish.

Pikelets/crumpets (1902): Mrs Marsden, Parkinson Lane, Halifax[139]

1 lb/450 g strong white flour
1 tsp dried yeast
pinch of salt
pinch grated nutmeg
1 egg, beaten
1 pt/600 ml tepid milk

Mix the dry ingredients, make a well in the centre, pour in the egg and milk, beat for 10-12 minutes, then cover the bowl with a cloth and leave in a warm place for about 2 hours to rise. Heat a girdle or thick-bottomed frying pan until a drop of water bubbles away in 3-4 seconds, or a sprinkling of flour browns in half a minute, then smear the surface with a little butter folded in a piece of cloth. Either ladle the batter onto the girdle in 5-6 inch pools for pikelets, or ½ in/12 cm deep into 4 inches round greased crumpet rings, and bake until the surface is covered in bubbles and has set firm. Then turn over to bake on the other side.

---

[139] Kaye, *Yorkshire cooking,* p.215.

These were then toasted on both sides and served hot spread with butter. Some also spread them with treacle, golden syrup, honey or jam.

Figure 19. Bread dough was first mixed, kneaded and left to rise in locally made pancheons (1) with white-slipped interiors, the yeast being stored in a barm-pot (2). Having been baked in either a stoneware loaf pot (3) or a tinplate loaf tin (4) the bread was kept clean, safe and humidified in a bread-crock (5).

From the 1840s to the 1850s all of these items, together with large tin-loaves, were increasingly baked in some of the cast-iron ovens now being installed into workers' homes. The developing popularity of wheat flour bakery created a demand for new products from the local potteries, especially for pancheons. These were large conical-sided mixing and kneading bowls up to around 2 ft/60 cm in diameter, the interiors of their red earthenware bodies being coated in white slip with a covering of glossy yellowish lead glaze. Frequently placed on a chair or stool, they were ideal for mixing and kneading the bread dough, as well as keeping it warm as it rose beneath a damp cloth when stood on the fender close to the kitchen fire. Further pots were now made for storing bread, the wide tops of their cylindrical or convex sides being provided with lids of unglazed earthenware or wood.

Now most families dedicated one weekday as their 'baking day'. Usually this was a Thursday, after the washing had been completed over the preceding days, and before the cleaning and preparations for the weekend were started on Friday. It was a day of hard, hot work, with the oven to be kept hot, the doughs kneaded and all the bakery completed before everyone returned from work or school. It was quite common for housewives to turn two stones (28 lb/12.7 kg) of flour into loaves, teacakes, currant cakes and oven-bottom cakes on their baking day, but on some farms there had to be four baking days using 112 lb/51 kg of flour every week.

Often starting at 6 a.m., and not finishing until early evening, this demanded an enormous input of time and energy, mixing, kneading, carrying in bucketfuls of coal to fuel the fire, and using nothing more than the bare hand or an elbow to judge when exactly the right oven temperature had been reached. It is little surprise to hear of occasional accidents. One Todmorden grandmother was startled by screams coming from her oven – the family's cat had sneaked in unseen. On opening the door 'it's fur was all frizzled up, but it jumped out and didn't seem badly hurt'.[140]

The main meal on a baking day often took advantage of the oven being hot, ideal for baking meat and potato pies or stews alongside the loaves and cakes. Alternatively, it had to be made of something quick and easy to prepare, such as liver and onions or sweetbreads.[141]

Devoting a whole day to baking became impossible for many women when they left their homes and families to work full-time in the textile mills. One solution was to cut out the laborious and time-consuming process of kneading and raising yeasted bakery and use the newly available chemical alternatives, bicarbonate of soda and cream of tartar. These had only to be mixed in with the usual ingredients to provide reliable and almost identical results. The bakery was just as light, but had a more cake-like texture, lacking the spongy elasticity and good flavour of yeasted doughs.

Soda bread[142]

1 lb/450 g flour

---

[140] Calderdale Libraries, *Memory lane: recollections of Todmorden*, p.5.

[141] Calderdale Libraries, *Memory lane: recollections of Elland*, p.35, 51; Calderdale Libraries, *Memory lane: recollections of Brighouse, Rastrick & Hipperholme*, p.33; *Siddal: our memories, our history*, Halifax, Workers Educational Association, 1989, pp.12-13.

[142] West family, *Manuscript recipe book*. Private collection, p.32.

½ tsp salt
2 tsp bicarbonate of soda
2 tsp cream of tartar
2 oz/50 g lard
about ½ pt/300 ml milk or buttermilk

Sift the dry ingredients together, rub in the lard, and mix to a soft dough adding the milk a little at a time. Put into a greased loaf tin and bake at 190ºC/375ºF gas mark 5 for about 45 minutes. [a loaf tin inverted over the loaf as it bakes helps the loaf to rise and remain moist}.

Milk cakes[143]

Use the recipe above, adding a beaten egg with the milk, divide the dough into 5 or 6 pieces, form them into balls, roll out as thin cakes, place on a greased baking sheet and bake at 190ºC/375ºF gas mark 5 for about 15 minutes.

Brown wholemeal bread had been eaten out of necessity from the 1840s but white bread was always the most fashionable and exclusive of breads.[144] For centuries it was reserved largely to the better-off and beyond the means of working folk, only becoming increasingly popular as the price of wheat fell dramatically during the course of the nineteenth century. In 1813 a quarter of 28 lb cost 120s (600p), in 1855 it had dropped to 74s 6d (373p), in 1873 it cost 58s 8d (243p) and in 1893 it was only 26s 4d (132p), less than a quarter of its price at the beginning of the century. Over the same period legislation had stopped the worst practices of adulteration, but from around the 1890s pioneering dietitians, such as the American Dr Sylvester Graham, had promoted the benefits of wholemeal breads that retained their natural bran and wheatgerm. As a result, many housewives began to bake it again for their families, some using yeast, and others bicarbonate of soda or baking powder since these gave good, quick, easy and reliable results.

Brown bread: Miss Dorothy Grimshaw, Todmorden[145]

8 oz/225 g strong wholemeal flour

---

[143] Ibid.

[144] Lonsdale Collection, *Newspaper cuttings*, vol.5, p.111.

[145] D. Grimshaw, *Manuscript exercise book*, written at Todmorden National School, 1933, Private collection.

8 oz/225 g plain flour
½ tsp salt
1 tsp sugar
1½ tsp dried yeast

Mix the dry ingredients and leave in a warm place for about an hour before mixing in about ½ pt/300 ml tepid water. Turn out onto a floured board and knead for 10 minutes, place in and bowl, cover, and leave in the warm until doubled in size. Knead it once more, put into a greased loaf tin and return to the warm until risen to the rim of the tin, then bake at 200°C/400°F gas mark 6 for about 40 minutes.

Meal cake: West Family[146]

8 oz/225 g wholemeal flour
8 oz/225 g plain flour
1 tsp salt
3 tsp bicarbonate of soda
2 oz/50 g butter
about ½ pt/300 ml milk and water

Sift the dry ingredients together, rub in the butter and mix in just sufficient liquid to form a soft dough. Put into a greased loaf tin and bake at 200°C/400°F gas mark 6 for about 45 minutes.

There was a strong tradition of home baking here, 'shop bought' being seen by some as second-rate, but this was probably more a matter of housewifely pride than reality. The practical advantages of buying the family's bread from a baker's or confectioner's shop included great savings in coal, time and trouble, and the ability to obtain fresh loaves etc. whenever required. Some bakers did without shops, their goods being distributed both to individual households, and to corner-shop groceries, for sale and local deliveries. In households where the wife and family were out at work all day, it was good to know that there would be freshly baked loaves and teacakes arriving at the door on the five weekday evenings. This was the after-school job of ten-year-old Wilfred Pickles, who earned a welcome 2s a week delivering bread around the streets of Halifax just before the First World War.[147]

---

[146] West family, *Manuscript recipe book*, p.25.

[147] W. Pickles, *Between you and me: the autobiography of Wilfred Pickles,* London, Werner Laurie, 1949, p.32.

Figure 20. *Around Walsden, Charles Foulds (1852-1935) and Young (1891-1948), his son, delivered bread from their family bakehouse using this flat cart and wicker hampers c.1900. Vernon (1917-2008), Charles' youngest grandson, and Young's son, had to get the horse, Dobbin, from fields up (Swinshud) Swineshead Road before he went to school. On leaving school he joined the family business, later (having learned to drive in WWII) introducing a van to deliver. The firm finally closed in the early 1960s.*
Personal communication, Mrs Susan Houghton, 2001.

CHAPTER 5

MEAT AND FISH

Many of the working families in Calderdale and Haworth had to spend long years subsisting on a largely vegetarian diet, their sole meat being bits of bacon or offal. Much of the beef, mutton, lamb and pork produced by the clothier hill farmers was for their own use, while that sent to market was unaffordable to those on the lowest wages. This situation became desperate as workers flocked into the mills and factories of the early to mid-nineteenth century, but then phenomenal improvements in transport and food preservation brought relief, enabling almost everyone to enjoy meat or fish meals on every day of the week.

Beef
With its hillside pastures, meadows and open grazing on the edges of the moors, this area supported herds of Shorthorn cattle from the early nineteenth century. These were supplemented by herds driven into the autumnal markets and fairs after fattening on the rich grasslands of Craven, ready to provide salt beef for use over the winter months. However, as the population increased more had to be brought in on the hoof for the cattle fairs at:

Elland	Third Monday in August.
Halifax	24 June and 1 November.
Hebden Bridge	Whit Monday & Friday after 11 October.
Todmorden	Thursday before Easter & 27 September.
Kebcote (on the Burnley-Heptonstall road above Todmorden)	At the end of April, and three weeks later.

The development of the railways in the 1840s gradually replaced the long-distance droving trade, while the opening of municipal cattle markets took over the business of the old fairs to give an efficient year-round supply to the ever-expanding mill towns.

While farmers would slaughter beasts to meet their own needs, others had to rely on joints sold by butchers attending the local markets. These included James Turner of Castle Naze and George Cockroft, butcher and manufacturer of Dobroyd, both described in a poem of 1801:

> There's Turner, the butcher, in liquor so big,
> He dare knock down an ox, yet's alarmed at a pig;

And George, at Dobroyd, who to deal is so keen,
He'll sell you fat beef, or a strong velveteen.[148]

Up to the 1820s it was customary for the parish clerk to stand near Todmorden's church gates after the Sunday service in order to inform the congregation which farmer or butcher would be slaughtering and at what price the beef would be sold. This was possible because butchers killed on Sundays, giving them a week to process the carcasses and hang the joints for the next weekend.[149] All those who could afford a joint would buy it on Saturday, ready for their Sunday dinners, many waiting until the evening when the butchers had to drop their prices or risk losing their perishable stock. If possible, the beef would then be roasted on Sunday morning.

Of all methods of cooking, roasting was always the most prestigious, since it required the tenderest of joints of meat, game or poultry, the most fuel, and careful attention from the cook. For this reason, a communal roast was often organised to celebrate some unusual event. Back in 1780, when the Black Pit where Hebden Water joins the Calder at Hebden Bridge had frozen solid, a large cock chicken had been roasted on the ice.[150] Later on, whole oxen would be roasted to mark special occasions, as for Brighouse's celebration of George V's Coronation on 10 May 1911. For this, the huge beast was mounted on a massive spit over a specially built hearth, a steam-powered traction engine slowly turning it from 9 a.m., the previous day through to 8 a.m., 23 hours being needed to ensure that it was thoroughly cooked. Then pieces of havercake dipped into the dripping were sold for a penny each, while 120 yard-long loaves were sliced up to make 3000 succulent beef sandwiches to serve the hundreds of people who had gathered here from the surrounding area.[151] Similar events were also organised at other settlements.[152]

In many early nineteenth-century homes roasting was virtually impossible where peat was the sole fuel, since it provided insufficient radiant heat. It was

---

[148] Dugdale, D., *Todmorden market: a 200 year snapshot of Todmorden life,* Todmorden, 2011, p.40.

[149] Calderdale Libraries, *Memory lane: recollections of Todmorden,* p.95.

[150] Antiquarian, *Sketches of old Hebden Bridge and its people.* 1882, p.15. Hebden Bridge Local History Society Archive MISC 50/4 S.

[151] Brighouse & District Local History Society, *What was happening in Brighouse 100 years ago,* Brighouse, 1992.

[152] Calderdale Libraries, *Memory lane: recollections of Brighouse, Rastrick & Hipperholme,* p.77.

only the arrival of cheap coal delivered by the new railways and the more widespread installation of coal-burning grates and cast-iron ranges in the mid-nineteenth century that made roasting before the fire available to most families. Even so, it remained beyond the means of the poorer members of the community. Only those who were better-off could afford the 10 lb/4.5 kg rib-joints of beef that cost around 7s/35p in 1860 to feed a family of six or eight people, along with the necessary equipment in the form of a vertical clockwork motor that was called a bottle-jack due to its shape. This was hung either from a bracket screwed onto the mantle shelf or from the top of a reflecting, tinplate screen called a hastener.[153] Joints suspended from its heavy flywheel rotated a few turns in one direction, then, after a click, a few turns in reverse, ensuring that the joint cooked evenly in front of the glowing coals. If the clicking stopped, so did the jack, having to be quickly wound up again to prevent the meat from being scorched on one side. As the fat melted and fell into a dripping pan placed beneath, it was regularly scooped up and basted over the joint to keep it moist and prevent it from drying out. This was well worth the trouble, for, being cooked in the open air before the fire, all its heavy, greasy fumes were carried away up the chimney, leaving a much finer flavoured and really tender joint.

Thinner pieces of meat in the form of steaks, chops or slices could also be roasted or toasted before the fire by being hung from a sharp-pronged fork mounted either on a trivet that hung from the firebar, or from a three-legged freestanding wooden 'toasting bull' or dog. Alternatively, a Dutch oven could be used, this being a shiny tinplate hood with a dripping tray at its base and a series of hooks from which to hang the steaks etc. These were ideal for quick snacks in cold weather, when slices of bacon or ham could be cooked crisp and vertical so that their fat and juices would fall on to a piece of bread set in the tray below, all to be combined in a delicious hot sandwich. This was preferable to using a grid-iron that hooked onto the top firebar and extended over the glowing coals in the grate, so letting the fat drop down and be wasted. Cooking by radiant heat probably gave the tastiest results, but it always took time and trouble. For this reason, most families found it more convenient to use their new ovens to bake their 'roasts' in baking tins they still called 'dripping tins', from their former use beneath the spit. Roasting was a relatively simple process, beef and poultry taking about 15-20 minutes per 1 lb/450 g + 20 minutes, lamb about 25 minutes per lb + 25 minutes and pork 30 minutes per lb + 30 minutes.

---

[153] Calderdale Museums, 1934.25 and 26; 1942.6/5; 1949.19.

The purpose of the Sunday roast was rarely to provide meat for Sunday dinner alone, for sufficient was usually bought for dinners for the next few days in the form of sliced cold meat, hash, pie, mince or rissoles. As one Sowerby Bridge lady explained, the remains had virtually run out by Thursday so they would 'have to stew the dishcloths after they'd wiped up all the drips.'[154] To make hash, the cooked meat was simply cut up into pieces and simmered with root vegetables in gravy or stock until all were tender. Other recipes for leftovers included:

Meat & potato pie: West Family[155]

1 lb/450 g leftover meat
1 tbs flour
1 tsp salt
½ tsp pepper
8-12 oz/225-350 g par-boiled potatoes
1 onion
½ pt/300 ml meat stock or gravy
Pastry made with 8 oz/225 g flour, ½ tsp baking powder, ¼ tsp salt and 3 oz/75 g lard with a few tablespoons of cold water

Cut the meat in pieces and slice the potatoes and onion, dust with the flour mixed with the salt and pepper, and layer with the gravy in a pie dish. Make the pastry by rubbing the lard into the dry ingredients and forming a stiff dough with a little cold water. Roll out on a floured board and use it to form the lid of the pie. Bake at 190ºC/375ºF gas mark 5 for 1 hour.

Cottage pie: Mrs A. Forton, Queensbury[156]

1 lb/450 g minced cooked meat
1 large onion, sliced
1 tbs lard or dripping
brown sauce, salt & pepper to taste
¼ pt/150 ml beef stock or water
2 lb/900 g mashed potatoes
1 oz/25 g margarine or butter

---

[154] Calderdale Libraries, *Memory lane: recollections of Sowerby Bridge*, p.14.

[155] West family, *Manuscript recipe book*, p.24

[156] Kaye, *Yorkshire cooking*, p.84.

Figure 21. *The introduction of cast-iron ovens enabled meat to be baked rather than boiled, grilled or fried. Now the local potters began to make stewpots (left) for hot-pots topped with a layer of sliced potato, tattie-pie pots (right) for meat and potato pies under a pastry crust, and baking dishes (centre) for cottage pies of mince under a layer of mashed potato.*

Fry the onions in the fat until golden, then stir in the meat, sauce, salt and pepper and water, and transfer to a pie dish. Spread the potatoes on top, roughen with a fork, dot with the margarine or butter, and bake at 190ºC/375ºF gas mark 5 for 40 minutes, until the top has browned.

Roasting beef was never the most economical method of cooking, since it used lots of fuel and caused the joints to shrink. For these reasons many preferred to simmer it over a gentle heat to save fuel and produce a quantity of good, nourishing broth. Before beef became readily available throughout the year, joints such as brisket and silverside were salted down for use throughout the winter months. Some might buy an old cow, share it between families, and then salt the joints before hanging them up to dry in their kitchens, ready for either boiling or cutting into rashers and frying like bacon.[157]

---

[157] Savage, *Sam Banks: his life and times,* p.5.

Wet pickle for beef

3-4 lb/1.25-1.75 kg rolled beef joint
1 lb 4 oz/560 g cooking salt
6 oz/150 g large-crystal sea salt
1 tbs saltpetre
[1½ oz/35 g brown sugar & 2 bay leaves, optional]

Rub the beef with 1 lb/450 g of the cooking salt for 10-15 minutes, then leave covered with the salt in a deep dish in a cool place for 24 hours. Meanwhile boil the remaining ingredients with 4 pt/1.8 l water, skin carefully, and leave until cold. Drain the meat, wipe dry, put into a stoneware jar, cover with the brine, and keep it submerged by placing a plate and a weight on top. Keep in a cool place for 5 weeks, checking it regularly, re-boiling, straining, cooling and replacing the brine should any trace of white appear.

This was subsequently soaked in cold water overnight, then put into a casserole of fresh water with:[158]

3 slices bacon
2 carrots
1 onion
1 bunch of savoury herbs
½ tsp mixed ground clove, allspice & mace
¼ tsp ground pepper

and baked at 180ºC/350ºF gas mark 4 for 4 hours. Leave to go cold in its liquid, remove and press between two plates and a heavy weight in a cool place overnight, then slice and serve cold.

Boiling a large piece of salt beef or a ham might precede some special event such as a funeral, a wedding, a feast or Christmas for which large numbers of people were expected. At other times only those who were rather better off would boil joints of beef and bacon together for their Sunday dinners, cooking big dumplings in the same pot.[159]

Rolled beef & broth: West Family[160]

4 lb/1.8 kg joint of brisket or silverside

---

[158] Kaye, *Yorkshire cooking*, p.77.

[159] Lonsdale Collection, *Newspaper cuttings*, vol.34, p.139.

[160] West family, *Manuscript recipe book*, p.1.

2 carrots
1 turnip
2 onions
2 oz/50 g pearl barley
1 tbs dried sage
1 tsp salt
½ tsp ground pepper

Trim and truss the joint, plunge into a large pan with 4 pt/2.4 l boiling water, skim off the scum, and simmer. Meanwhile peel and coarsely chop the vegetables and put the barley to soak in cold water. After simmering for 1¼ hours, add the vegetables, barley, sage, salt and pepper, and continue simmering for a further 40-50 minutes before serving.

Dumplings

6 oz/150 g flour
1 tsp baking powder
3 oz/75 g suet
pinch of salt

Sift the flour, baking powder and salt, mix in the suet, then a few tablespoons of cold water to produce a light dough. Break into pieces the size of a very small egg, roll into balls with flour-dusted hands and drop into the boiling stock 15-20 minutes before serving.

Beef cooked more quickly, and absorbed the flavours of other ingredients when it was cut into small pieces and stewed (perhaps with a cow heel for extra richness), baked in pies, or boiled in suet crust as a pudding or roly-poly. In homes where there was either no oven, or no need to fire up the oven, pies were made in pans hung over the fire or simmered on the hob. Here these were called pan-pies.

Pan pie: Mrs S. Robertshaw, Mytholmroyd[161]

8 oz/225 g cubed stewing beef (today most would use1 lb/450 g)
1 onion, chopped
½ oz/12 g lard
3 carrots, sliced

---

[161] Kaye, *Yorkshire cooking,* p.87.

2 leeks, chopped
2 tomatoes, chopped
½ tsp salt, pinch of pepper
Pastry made of 4 oz/100 g flour, ½ tsp salt, ¼ tsp baking powder, 2
oz/50 g suet & about 5 tbs cold water.

Fry the onions in half the lard until just starting to colour, and put into a deep 7 in/18 cm saucepan with the other vegetables. Dust the beef with flour, lightly fry in the remaining lard and put into the pan with ½ pt/300 ml cold water [or stock], and cover with the pastry rolled out to exactly fit inside. Cover and simmer for 1 hour. The crust may then be cut into segments in the pan, and served with the meat and vegetables.

Easy to make and very satisfying, pan-pies were coveted by hungry travellers. As one was cooking over the fire at the Cross Inn in Stanbury, two men came in and suggested to the landlady that they should all join in a prayer meeting. They then knelt down with their backs to the fire as one of the men prayed with all his might. Meanwhile the other grabbed the pan and ran off with it. Only after the prayers had finished did the landlady realise that she had been robbed![162]

The cheaper joints of beef were often the tastiest, but usually needed a longer cooking time or processing to make them tender. They were particularly popular when made into rolls, moulds or potted meats ready for mid-week meals or jock, one Todmorden butcher's wife boiling and hand-mincing 40 lb/18 kg a week in her own kitchen.[163]

Yorkshire roll: Mrs Broadhead, Sowerby Bridge[164]

12 oz/350 g steak
6 oz/150 g cooked fat bacon
4 oz/100 g fresh white breadcrumbs
½ tsp salt
pinch grated nutmeg
1 egg, beaten
browned breadcrumbs for coating

---

[162] Craven, *A Brontë moorland village*, p.122.

[163] Calderdale Libraries, *Memory lane: recollections of Todmorden*, p.71.

[164] Anon., *159 recipes from good kitchens*, p.25.

Finely mince the meats together and mix in the fresh breadcrumbs, salt, nutmeg and finally the egg, forming into a roll. Rinse a piece of fine cotton or muslin in cold water, wring and shake it out, dust one side with flour and shake off the surplus. Lay the roll on the floured side, roll up tightly, tying each end with a piece of string, put into a pan of boiling water and simmer for 2 hours. Remove from the water, leave until cold, then remove the cloth and roll in the browned breadcrumbs before slicing across.

Meat mould: Miss Wood, Rochdale Road[165]

1 lb/450 g lean steak
8 oz/225 g raw ham
1 tsp salt
⅛ tsp ground pepper
2 eggs, beaten

Mince the meats together, mix in the seasoning and pack into a greased basin or mould and cover with cooking foil pressed down around the rim [this is a replacement for the traditional greaseproof paper or cloth] and steam for 2 hours. It may be eaten hot but was usually left to be served cold.

Potted meat: Mrs Pedley, Oxenhope; Miss Pawson, Wadsworth House[166]

1 lb/450 g lean beef
6 oz/150 g lean ham
4 oz/100 g butter
1 tsp salt
¼ tsp ground pepper
pinch of mace (optional)

Cut the meat into small pieces, cover with water and simmer very gently for 2-3 hours until very tender. [This may be done in a double boiler or bain-marie]. Drain off and reserve the gravy, pass the meat through a mincer two or three times [or grind in a food processor] until very smooth, beat in the remaining ingredients with some of the gravy to make a firm paste and pack firmly into jars or dishes before covering with:

---

[165] Anon., *159 recipes from good kitchens*, p.26.

[166] Oxenhope Church, *Recipe book*; Hawksbridge Baptist Church, *A useful recipe book.*

Clarified butter

Melt the butter in a small saucepan and cook gently without allowing it to colour. Skim off the scum, pour through a piece of muslin into a bowl, allow to set, drain off the sediment, and re-melt the butter for pouring on to the potted meat. This will keep in a cellar or refrigerator for about a week.

Beef brawn: Mrs B. Hanson, Eldon Place, Halifax[167]

1 lb/450 g shin beef
1 cow heel [or 8 tsp powdered or 12 sheets gelatin]
¾ tsp salt
⅛ tsp ground pepper

Cut the beef and cow heel [if used] into small cubes, put into a jar with the salt, pepper and ½ pt/300 ml cold water, loosely cover, place in a deep pan of boiling water, cover, and simmer for 4 hours. Remove the bones and break up the meat with a fork. If using powdered gelatin, sprinkle it directly into the warm stock, but if using sheet gelatin, pre-soak in cold water for 5 minutes and drain, and stir in until completely dissolved. Mix the meat and stock together in a basin, then leave in a cold place overnight to set, before turning out and slicing thinly.

This was also known as pressed beef, potted beef, potted hough or stew, its combination of strands of tender beef set in rich, clear brown jelly being really delicious; it remains justifiably popular on the butcher's stalls at Todmorden and other local markets. Towards the end of the nineteenth century improved methods of preservation saw beef being imported in the form of frozen joints from the River Plate Meat Company etc., and as tins of corned beef, ideal for hashes, sandwiches and salads.

Local beef provided not only red meat, but also a plentiful supply of offal, from cow heels to tongues, tripe and bones. Tripe was particularly popular, local dressers converting it from a sloppy mess of green slime into sheets of pristine white ready-cooked 'seam', 'honeycomb', 'reed' etc. Tripe dressing appears to have been a diverse trade, some selling directly to the public, along with hot

---

[167] King Cross [Wesleyan] Circuit, *Recipes and quotations: souvenir of the British Empire bazaar*, Halifax, 1913, p.15.

pies and peas, mineral waters and ice cream, some selling to tripe dealers, and some offering either 'High-class [Pigeons] for Show or Flying purposes; also first-class Shooting Pigeons Always on hand and supplied at short notice' or their services as chimney sweeps.[168] Tripe could be eaten directly, seasoned with salt, pepper and vinegar either on their own or mixed with onions, or fried, boiled or stuffed.

Boiled tripe and onions[169]

1 lb/450 g tripe, in pieces
2 large onions, sliced
½ pt/300 ml milk
1 oz/25 g cornflour
1 oz/25 g butter
salt & pepper to taste

Barely cover the tripe and onions in water, simmer until tender, then drain. Mix the cornflour into the milk and add the butter and seasoning and simmer for 10-15 minutes. Serve hot with mashed potatoes and stir in the tripe.

Fried tripe and onions[170]

1 lb/450 g tripe, in pieces
2 onions, chopped small
1½ oz/35 g dripping
salt & pepper to taste

Fry the onions in the dripping until tender, add the tripe and fry, stirring occasionally for 10-15 minutes, then season to taste and serve hot.

The bones were used to make nourishing soups, by being chopped up and simmered for hours with a selection of vegetables. Served with dumplings or tattie hash, bone soups provided satisfying hot meals when times were hard.[171]

Bone soup: Mrs M. Crowe, Ovenden[172]

2 lb/900 g beef, pork or veal bones, all broken small

---

[168] *Todmorden & Hebden Bridge Historical Almanac,* 1896, p.142; 1897, p.100.

[169] Kaye, *Yorkshire cooking,* pp.187-189; Brears, *Traditional food in Yorkshire,* p.144.

[170] Brears, *Traditional food in Yorkshire,* p.144.

[171] Calderdale Libraries, *Memory lane: recollections of Elland,* p.48.

[172] Kaye, *Yorkshire cooking,* p.26.

1½ oz/35 g fat or dripping
2 sticks celery
2 carrots
1 onion
a little parsley and thyme
3 peppercorns
1 tbs sago
1 tsp salt

Fry the bones in the fat until well browned, add 3½ pt/2 l cold water and the salt, bring to the boil and skim carefully. Add the coarsely chopped vegetables, parsley, thyme, and peppercorns, cover and simmer for 4 hours. Skim, strain, return the soup to the pan. Sprinkle on the sago and simmer for a further 15 minutes before serving. [Today the sago may be replaced with short-grain rice].

Mutton and Lamb

The sheep traditionally bred in this area were usually of the Gritstone or Lonk breeds that were able to withstand life on the high moors and pastures of the local hill farms.[173] Like cattle, they were both home-killed for farming families, or sold to butchers attending the markets. Mutton from the older sheep was available throughout the year and provided the bulk of the meat used for roasts, hotpots and chops, the younger and more tender lamb being considered more of a luxury. Grass lamb suckled on ewes feeding on the first spring grass was available around April, May or June, while house lamb kept indoors around the farm and fed on hay and cow's milk was in season from October to December.[174]

Roast mutton came only second to beef as the Sunday roast of choice, and similarly appeared over the next few days as cold meat or hash. Writing from Belgium in 1843, Charlotte Brontë fondly remembered her life back in the Haworth Parsonage;

> in the kitchen, or in the back kitchen. I should like even to be cutting up the hash, with the clerk and some register people at the other table, and you [Emily] standing by, watching that I put enough flour, not too much pepper, and, above all, that I save the best pieces of the leg of mutton for Tiger and

---

[173] W.H. Long, *A survey of the agriculture of Yorkshire,* London, Royal Agricultural Society of England, 1969, pp.63-64.

[174] M.H. Ashton, C.A. Fletcher, & M. & F. Ingham, *The St Michael's recipe and quotation book,* Mytholmroyd, 1908, pp.3-4.

Keeper, the first of which personages would be jumping about the dish and carving-knife and the latter standing like a devouring flame on the kitchen floor. To complete the picture, Tabby blowing the fire, in order to boil the potatoes to a sort of vegetable glue[175]

The favourite way of cooking mutton here was as an Irish stew or hotpot:

Irish stew: West Family[176]

1 lb/450 g bits of mutton or scrag end
2 onions, coarsely chopped
1 tbs flour
salt & pepper to taste
2 lb/900 g potatoes

Mix the meat and onions in the bottom of a saucepan, sprinkle with the flour, salt and pepper and simmer with ¾ pt/450 ml water for 1 hour. Meanwhile boil the unpeeled potatoes for 10 minutes, drain, remove the skins, slice, arrange over the meat, cover, and continue stewing for a further 45 minutes. This version was cooked on the hob, without heating the oven, but for hotpots the ingredients were put into a covered stew-pot and baked at 170ºC/325ºF gas mark 3 for 2 hours, then a further 30 minutes at 200ºC/400ºF gas mark 6 with the lid off to brown the potatoes. Pickled red cabbage was the usual accompaniment.

Up to around the 1960s when wages began to improve, sheep's heads regularly appeared on local tables, as they had throughout previous centuries. Admittedly not the most beautiful of joints, they had the advantages of being cheap, flavoursome, and capable of producing meat for a number of meals. As Sam Banks remembered with pleasure, the heads his mother cooked for their family were 'a real meal which we relished'.[177] They also gave rise to some of the district's standard jokes:

> You must take the eyes out – they make it taste bitter.
> Mi mother never did!
> Whyever not?
> We were reight poor, so it had to see us thro' th' week!

---

175 Gaskell, *The life of Charlotte Brontë*, p.264.

176 West family, *Manuscript recipe book*, p.17; Grimshaw, *Manuscript recipe book.*

177 Savage, *Sam Banks: his life and times*, p.5.

One Sunday morning a Haworth woman had to leave her sheep's head simmering on the hob when she went off to church, leaving it in the care of her small son. All went well until it got too hot and boiled over, sending up clouds of steam and spouting the rich stock all over the fireplace. Unable to cope with this disaster, the boy ran to the church, opened the door and began to make urgent signs that he needed his mother to quickly return home. In the face of this humiliation in front of the congregation, she made emphatic signs for him to leave – but instead of doing this he loudly whispered for all to hear 'Stop winkin' your winkin's an' noddin' your noddin's, for t'sheep heead is tuppin' t' dumplins reight on to t' hearthstone![178]

Sheep's head

1 sheep's head
1 small turnip
1lb/450 g carrots
3 tbs pearl barley
1 stick celery
salt and pepper

Since each head was sold after the skin and wool had been removed, it was prepared in the home by singeing off any remaining strands, scraping clean, and chopping in two down the middle. After the eyes had been removed, along with the tongue and brains, it was soaked in salted water for about 8 hours before being covered with fresh water and simmered with the remaining ingredients for about 2½ hours. The head was then removed so that the meat could be stripped off, chopped, returned to the stock and served hot.

The tongue was poached separately in salted water for about 2 hours until the skin could be removed, then cooled and sliced thinly for sandwiches. The brains were skinned, soaked in cold water, tied in a muslin bag and hung half-way down the inside of a pan holding the sheep's head etc., its string being tied to the external pan handle. After simmering here for about 20 minutes they were then taken out and either mashed with a little vinegar to form brain sauce to be served with the head, or cooked with cream, butter and herbs for serving on toast.

---

[178] Southwart, *Brontë moors & villages*, p.101.

Pork

The old Yorkshire pig was big, weighing up to half a ton, but its flesh was coarse and flabby. From the 1840s Keighley became one of Britain's major pig breeding and feeding centres. Joseph Tuley, a weaver, and W.B. Wainman made such great improvements that their Yorkshire Large White breed swept the board at the Royal Show. For many years pig-keeping moved from being just the usual routine of having a few animals around the farmyard or backyard, into a popular passion. Keighley 'reserves its most touching sympathy for the pig' wrote one observer, while Bill o' th' Hoylus End described this new science as:

> Pigology
> If ivver yah go t' craw road tu Howorth fra Keethla, an sud happen ta drop inta Exleaheead, a village famus fer pig breedin', pig feeders, an' pig heyters, an' it sum 'appen to be on a Sundy – mack up into Stye Alley, an' yah'll find um assembled, sum skratchin', sum weshin', and some givin t' pig's meyl balls, wal uthers are amusin' thersell wi pig argiments an' pigology; an' sud yah meet wi Harry Chine, just ax him wat he'll tak fer a chig peek. [i.e. pig's cheek].[179]

Many of the farms kept a couple of sows, each producing a couple of litters each year, while factory-workers with access to a bit of land for a sty might have a sow or two mainly for their own consumption, but keeping a pig was always seen as a sign of comparative affluence. Their feed ranged from wheat offal, barley or oatmeal, and household scraps, along with any spare milk or buttermilk.[180]

Those who could not afford to keep a pig could still expect a share of one by leaving their potato peelings and similar waste food in bins by their back doors, from where they were collected by a local farmer. At Christmas time an appropriate joint would then be delivered in acknowledgement of their contribution. After the farmer who collected the swill from the home of John Nicholson, the Airedale poet, failed to produce the expected joint, he found the following note in the now empty swill bin;

> Thou villain, thou villain,
> Tha's tekken mi swillen,
> Tha's tekken mi thick, thin and fine.
> But tha's gone and neglected
> What was fully expected,
> Tha's sent nawther spare-rib nor chine.[181]

---

179 Bill o' th' Hoylus End [W. Wright], *Haworth, Cowanhead & Bogthorn Almanac*, Keighley, 1875, p.16.

180 Greenwood, *Life on a Pennine farm*, p.23.

181 *Bradford Telegraph & Argus* 1 September 1953.

Figure 22. Fine large white pigs such as (1) 'Parian Duchess' were first bred around Keighley in the 1840s. They were ideal for curing as ham, bacon or salt pork. After being scalded and scraped with an iron candlestick (2) the carcases were butchered, the hams being dry-salted in ham pans (3) and the pork wet-cured in pork-pots (4). The salt came in large blocks that had to be crushed and rolled (5) before being stored in either wooden 'salt-pies' (6 at the Brontë Parsonage) and local slipware 'salt kits' (7 made at Howcons Pottery, Halifax).

Pig killing could take place at any time of the year, but usually in the colder months. Traditionally a hog was slaughtered a few weeks before Christmas in order to provide extra food over the festive period.[182] Some performed the job themselves, while others employed their local pig-killer. Some, such as Todmorden's 'Tommy Dodd the Daisher' (dandy) appear to have taken their payment in kind, since it was 'noted that all the pigs he killed appeared to have thrived without needing livers as part of their anatomy'.[183] The first task was to catch the blood and keep it stirred until cold, ready for making black puddings, locally known as 'swines-blood pudding'. Usually small dice of fat, salt, pepper, herbs such as pennyroyal, sage and thyme and sometimes milk, breadcrumbs, cooked pearl barley or groats, would be mixed in before it was baked in shallow oven tins or basins, or simmered in skins.[184] Next, the carcase was scalded so that the round base of a sheet-iron candlestick could be used to scrape off all the hair, after which it was hung up, drawn, and left to cool ready for being cut up into joints.[185] The day usually ended with a communal meal called a Bedlam, where neighbours who had helped to feed the pigs with their potato peelings etc. were invited to dine on the liver, kidney and heart, all wrapped in the fatty membrane called a 'curtain' or caul and baked in the oven, accompanied by Yorkshire puddings.[186] Others served up blood puddings and 'craps', the crisp crackling left after rendering the lard in the oven, with slices of bread.[187] As the 'fry' of heart, lungs, liver and kidney was the most perishable, it had to be eaten first, perhaps being shared with neighbours who would return the favour when their pig was killed. In the Gibson family it formed the basis of a three-course meal:

Yorkshire fry[188]

1-1½lb/450-625 g heart, liver, kidney, sweetbread cut up with sliced

[182] Davies et al, *The Diaries of Cornelius Ashworth 1782-1816,* 12-13 December 1785; 29 November 1809; 23 November 1815.

[183] J. Holden, *A short history of Todmorden,* Manchester, Manchester University Press, 1912, p.69.

[184] H. Shackleton, 'Reminiscences of shopping in mid-twentieth century Midgley' in I. Bailey, D. Cant, A. Petford, & N. Smith, *Pennine perspectives: aspects of the history of Midgley,* Midgley, Midgley Books, 2007, p.305; Antiquarian, *Sketches of old Hebden Bridge* p.39; Greenwood, *Life on a Pennine farm,* p.25.

[185] Savage, *Sam Banks: his life and times,* p.5.

[186] Calderdale Libraries, *Memory lane: recollections of Sowerby Bridge,* p.88.

[187] Holden, *A short history of Todmorden,* p.5.

[188] Kaye, *Yorkshire cooking,* p.88.

stewing meat
1 lb/450 g onions, coarsely chopped
1 tsp each sage, thyme, marjoram
salt and pepper to taste

Put the ingredients into a covered casserole with 1½ pt/600-900 ml water and bake at 170°C/325°F gas mark 3 for 3 hours, then for the first course, drain off the stock and serve as gravy on a Yorkshire pudding. For the second course, serve the meat with baked jacket potatoes, and follow this with rice pudding and baked apples, all being cooked in the same hot oven.

The liver was often made into savoury ducks, these also being baked by butchers and also served hot with gravy at tripe shops and cheap eating houses.[189]

Savoury ducks[190]

8 oz/225 g each finely chopped pig liver, finely chopped onion, suet and fresh white breadcrumbs
1 tbs chopped sage
½ tsp salt
pinch cayenne pepper
2 small eggs, beaten
browned breadcrumbs

Fry all the dry ingredients except the browned breadcrumbs, mix in the egg, form into 2 in/5 cm balls, and roll each one in the browned breadcrumbs. Place side by side in a greased baking tin and bake at 180°C/350°F gas mark 4 for 30-40 minutes until cooked through and golden brown. Serve either immediately, or re-heated over the next couple of days with rich brown gravy.

The pig's trotters greatly enriched beef stews, while the head made succulent brawn.

Tasty brawn: Mrs F. Greenwood, Halifax[191]

½ a pig's head

---

[189] Calderdale Libraries, *Memory lane: recollections of Sowerby Bridge*, p.88.

[190] Brears, *Traditional food in Yorkshire*, p.160.

[191] King Cross [Wesleyan] Circuit, *Recipes and quotations*, p.15.

1 tbs salt
½ tsp each ground white pepper, mace & nutmeg

Wash the pig's head [available from some pork butchers and some markets, such as Leeds] and soak in cold water 1½ hours. Drain, put into a large pan, just cover with cold water, cover, bring to the boil, skim, and simmer for 1½ hours until the meat falls off the bone. Remove the head from the stock, take off all the edible meat, coarsely chop it and return to the stock, having discarded the skin, bones etc. Add the spices and simmer uncovered until reduced to half its volume. Stir it well, pour into bowls or dishes and leave in a cool place for a few hours, or overnight, to set firmly.

Butchers also used fresh pork to make polony, a paté-like sausage that was served cold, either with salad or pickles, or in sandwiches.

Polony[192]

1 lb/450 g each lean and fat pork
4 oz/100 g each rice or bread, rusk & salt
3 tsp ground white pepper
2 tsp each ground nutmeg & mace
½ tsp cayenne pepper

Finely chop the pork, scald and soak the rice until soft or soak the bread in cold water and press dry in a sieve. Mix in the remaining ingredients and mince together until smooth. Pack into a pig's windpipe (or roll 3 in/7.5 cm diameter in cling film) tie the ends, plunge into boiling water and simmer for 1 hour. Remove, allow to go cold, then slice as needed. Originally their skins were stained with a bright 'polony-red' dye to make them look as if they had been smoked, but these were later replaced by red plastic.

One of the favourite ways of cooking fresh pork was in crisp-crusted pies, their meat enclosed in a stiff savoury jelly. These were one of the specialities of the pork butchers that flourished here from the mid to late nineteenth century, being ideal for eating immediately, in the home, in the open air, or at a special 'pie and pea' supper.

---

[192] Brears, *Traditional food in Yorkshire*, p.160.

Pork pie: Miss K. Conway, Halifax[193]

Pastry: 1 lb/450 g flour
4 oz/100g lard
3 oz/75 g margarine
½ tsp salt
4 tbs water

Boil the fats in the water, pour in the dry ingredients and rapidly mix to form a dough. Use three-quarters to line a warmed and greased cake tin, and retain the rest to form the lid.

Filling: 1½ lb/675 g lean minced pork
1 tsp salt
½ tsp pepper
1 tsp sage

Mix all together and pack into the pastry crust. Use the remaining pastry to form a lid, dampening and sealing the edges. Cut two holes in the top and bake at 180ºC/350ºF gas mark 4 for 2½ hours, then fill with:

Stock: 2 pig's trotters simmered for 1½ hours in 1 pt/600 ml water and a pinch of salt [or 6 tsp powdered gelatin or 10 leaves soaked in ¼ pt/150 ml cold water, gently heated until dissolved], and seasoned with a little salt and ground white pepper.

Leave the pie to cool in its tin, and serve either cold or hot with mushy peas.

This left the pork joints to either be cooked from fresh or salted as ham or bacon. These required quantities of common salt, a slow-dissolving large-crystal sea salt called bay salt, saltpetre (potassium nitrate) and unrefined sugar now known as muscovado. Large blocks of common salt were bought from the salt-man who hawked them around the area following the age-old practice that gave its name to Salter Rake Gate in Walsden, and Salterhebble, and also from salt merchants based in the larger towns. The blocks then had to be beaten into a powder using a rolling pin and stored dry either in jars or a wooden salt-box with a sloping lid that hung conveniently at the warm fireside.[194] Salting often took place on a stone slab in a cool cellar, cheeks taking seven days, mild bacon twelve days, and hams eighteen days, before being brushed down and hung

---

[193] Kaye, *Yorkshire cooking*, p.174.

[194] Calderdale Libraries, *Memory lane: recollections of Sowerby Bridge*, p.33; Calderdale Libraries, *Memory lane: recollections of Brighouse, Rastrick & Hipperholme*, p.5.

up to dry.[195] Hams were often cured in large ham-shaped glazed earthenware pans made at the local potteries.

To cure hams: Lister Family, Shibden Hall[196]

1 large leg of pork
1 lb/450 g salt
1½ oz/35 g coarse sea salt
1½ oz/35 g saltpetre
8 oz/225 g muscovado sugar
1 pt/600 ml strong ale

Boil the salts and sugar in the ale until dissolved and leave until cold. Place the ham in a deep dish, pour the liquid over it and rub and turn the ham in it for 5-10 minutes each day for two weeks in a cool, dark place. Hang the ham up in a well-ventilated room for a further two weeks, then store and use as required.
[To boil a ham soak overnight in cold water, drain, put into a large pan of cold water, bring slowly to the boil and simmer gently for 20 minutes per lb/450 g. Allow to cool in the water, then peel off the skin and cover the surface with browned breadcrumbs.To bake the ham, soak overnight in cold water, drain, wipe dry, completely seal in a flour and water pastry crust or cooking foil and bake at 180ºC/350ºF gas mark 4 for 3-4 hours, until tender when tested with a sharp skewer, and leave to go cold before removing the crust.]

Ham was always considered to be a special treat, particularly for funerals, communal teas and excursions, when it would be thickly sliced to fill teacake or oven-cake sandwiches, or served with a salad. The advertisements in local almanacs regularly featured well-dried hams, boiling hams, and home-cured Cumberland and Westmorland hams suitable for these events. To many, the bacon cured from sides of pork was treated with similar respect when times were hard, scraps of it being the only meat that was both affordable and could be quickly fried using little fuel. Its importance to working families is clearly illustrated by the Todmorden name given to the bogey-man that parents invented to frighten children in to obedience – the 'Want Bacon'.[197] Bacon's combination of flavour and fat made it an ideal addition to starchy foods, as

---

[195] Greenwood, *Life on a Pennine farm*, pp.26-27.

[196] Brears, *Traditional food in Yorkshire*, p.165.

[197] Travis, *Notes: (historical and biographical)*, p.42.

when layered with potatoes in a casserole, put into a suet-crust roly-poly or into pastry.

Bacon & egg pie: Mrs D. Collins, Hove Edge, Brighouse[198]

3-4 rashers of bacon or thin ham
2-3 eggs
salt and pepper to taste
shortcrust pastry made with 14 oz/400 g flour, 7 oz/200 g lard and a pinch of salt

Cut the bacon or ham into small pieces, arrange over the bottom crust, add the eggs which may or may not be beaten beforehand and sprinkle with salt & pepper. Cover with the remaining pastry, seal the edges, prick the top with a fork and bake at 190ºC/375ºF gas mark 5 for 30 minutes. Serve either hot or cold.

When conditions improved bacon became the favourite food for breakfasts and quick fry-ups, sometimes with eggs, or as part of a Yorkshire sissup:

> My owd lass thowt shoo'd give 'em a reight Yorkshire sissup; soa shoo bowt some liver an' a cauf heart an' a bit o' bacon, an shoo smothered it wi' onions an' heearbs o' one sooart or another, an' when it coom on th' table it seant up sich a smell 'at one hauf o' th' fowk t' th' street had ther maaths watterin.[199]

Poultry

Unlike today, when chicken is one of the cheapest meats and most families can afford a turkey at Christmas, poultry remained an unaffordable luxury to many before the 1950s. Keeping hens was profitable, however, producing extra cash to farmers' wives and others who had access to a little land, even up to around the 1,300 foot contour. In Stanbury, for example, Timmy Feather the hand-loom weaver kept a flock of eighty, while up at Top Withins Ernest Roddie earned his living from his 150 hens in the 1920s.[200] The main income came from eggs and the hens that had stopped laying. These 'old boilers' that took hours of stewing to become tender, yet had good flavour, were often taken to market alive in baskets, only being killed when sold to a customer.[201] The rare inn name, *The Poultry Breeder's Arms*, at Lydgate demonstrates the trade's local

---

[198] Kaye, *Yorkshire cooking*, pp.176, 182.

[199] *Halifax Courier* 12 June 1897.

[200] Turner, *A spring-time saunter*, p.133; Wood & Brears, *The real Wuthering Heights*, p.47.

[201] Calderdale Libraries, *Memory lane: recollections of Todmorden*, p.41.

importance, but this increased enormously when, following the weavers' strike of 1906, Edgar and Ralph Thornber began to specialise in chicken breeding. By 1914 they were producing 2,000 to 3,000 chicks at Newhouse Farm, Mytholmroyd, this rising to 5,000 by 1928. Many others, especially Walter and Jack Lord at Hebden Bridge, followed suit, making Calderdale the country's major centre of chicken production, sales increasing to 5,000,000 by 1936.[202] Local farmers fed the chicks on mash, wheat and split peas, letting them run free-range in sheltered rough pastures, killing the cocks at eight weeks and hens at eighteen months for the meat trade.[203]

The recipes for cooking fowls were just the same as those used in other parts of the country, but there are two of local interest. Chicken moulds similar to boiled beef and ham rolls were made by beating butter, salt and pepper into the minced meat of a boiled chicken, pressing it into a mould, and coating it with a glaze made from the boiled-down carcase. To make a roast chicken go a long way after appearing on the table for a couple of days, the carcase was simmered for hours with a few slices of onion and a little salt to produce soup for the third day, after which milk and vegetable marrow were added and the carcase was re-boiled for the fourth day. As Mrs Hegginbottom of Friendly remembered 'I have known a good large chicken go on for eight days in this way and to be really good to the end'.[204]

The geese kept on the farms, some of whom enjoyed swimming in the Rochdale Canal, were usually kept for special celebrations, and so their recipes are given on pp.214-215.

Rabbit & Game
Before myxomatosis culled their numbers, rabbits flourished here, being taken with ferrets and nets to provide good hot dinners. Memories of 'Uncle Fred who caught rabbits for rabbit pies baked in a big green enamel bowl' were typical, but rabbits were also stewed, jugged like hares, served as a broth with dumplings or baked in an oven.[205] Their recipes are similar to those used elsewhere, except for:

---

202 Long, *A survey of the agriculture of Yorkshire*, p.107; D. Riley, 'When Derek's dad got the bird', *Milltown Memories*, 2004-2005, 10, pp.22-23.

203 Greenwood, *Life on a Pennine farm*, pp.28-29.

204 Kaye, *Yorkshire cooking*, pp.100-101.

205 Shackleton, 'Reminiscences of shopping' in Bailey et al, *Pennine perspectives*, p.305; Kaye, *Yorkshire cooking*, pp.101-102, 106.

Tasty rabbit: Mrs Whitwam, Halifax[206]

1 rabbit, cleaned and jointed
2 onions, peeled and sliced
1 oz/25 g dripping
salt and pepper

Fry the onions in the dripping until golden brown, then the pieces of rabbit until browned on both sides. Transfer the onions and rabbit into a stewpot or casserole, cover with water, cover and bake at 170ºC/325ºF gas mark 3 for about 2 hours until tender.

This might be accompanied by:

Onion dumplings: Mrs A. Forton, Queensbury[207]

Mix *8 oz/225 g flour, 4 oz/100 g suet, 4 oz/100g chopped onion, ½ tsp salt, a little pepper and sufficient milk* to form a stiff dough. Form into balls and add to the broth for its final 30 minutes.

Since much of the uplands here have long been preserved as grouse moors, it might be assumed that moor game was enjoyed by the local populace, but this was never the case. Gamekeepers were employed to prevent poaching. This was a dangerous job in the nineteenth century when large gangs disguised with blackened faces and old clothes, all armed with guns, muck-rakes, hay-forks, besoms and cudgels had to be fought off. Those who were caught received severe sentences, one local man being given six months in gaol, followed by another year unless he could find sureties of the huge sum of £20 to keep him from poaching over the next two years.[208]

Sauces

Many families preferred to make their own fresh sauces to accompany meat, rather than buying ready-made versions from the grocers. One exception was mustard, since this popular relish for beef, ham, bacon and black pudding could only be made from commercially-ground powder marketed nationally by companies such as Keen's of London or J. & J. Colman's of Norwich. This was instantly prepared by mixing a little with water, an eggcup frequently being used as a convenient mustard pot. Other fresh sauces included:

---

[206] King Cross [Wesleyan] Circuit, *Recipes and quotations,* p.21.

[207] Kaye, *Yorkshire cooking,* p.100.

[208] Turner, *A spring-time saunter,* pp.59-60.

Apple sauce [for pork, and locally for poultry too]

1 lb/450 g cooking apples
1 oz/25 g butter
1-2 tsp sugar

Peel, core and chop the apples, simmer in about 3 tablespoons of water for about 10 minutes until soft, and beat to a pulp. Stir in the butter and add sugar if the apples are too tart.

Bread sauce [for poultry]: West Family[209]

3 oz/75 g fresh white breadcrumbs
1 onion, peeled
2 cloves
8 peppercorns
¾ pt/450 ml milk
½ tsp salt
pinch ground white pepper

Cut the onion in two vertically, stick each half with a clove, and put into a pan with the peppercorns and milk and simmer, covered, for about 15 minutes until the onion is tender. Strain off the onion and peppercorns, stir in the crumbs, salt and pepper, and simmer, stirring occasionally for about 10 minutes.

Horse radish sauce [for beef]: Miss Fletcher, Red Acre House[210]

2 tbs freshly-grated horseradish root
1 tbs malt vinegar
1 tsp sugar
½ tsp made mustard
¼ pt/150 ml thick cream
½ tsp salt
pinch ground white pepper

Mix all together and serve with cold meats, or heat without boiling for hot meats.

Fish

Due to their steep gradients and numerous waterfalls, most of the small

---

[209] West family, *Manuscript recipe book*, p.8.

[210] Kaye, *Yorkshire cooking*, p.231.

streams that fall down the steep hills from the tops into the valleys produced no fish suitable for cooking. The upper reaches of the larger ones are frequently blocked by the dams that once powered corn and textile mills or currently provide drinking water for the surrounding towns and cities. It was a different situation in the larger streams and rivers, however, where salmon, trout and coarse fish thrived. In the early nineteenth century a landowner with fishing rights described how:

> the Calder was a brilliant fishing river. I could take my rod, or send my keeper, if a friend came unexpectedly to dinner, and have a salmon for him to a certainty.[211]

The leister or fish-spear from Stanbury given to Keighley Museum suggests that local poachers also enjoyed locally caught salmon![212]

By the 1860s this idyllic situation had changed beyond recognition, as a combination of dyes, soaps and chemicals from the mills and untreated sewage from the new valley-bottom communities poisoned and stained the water. In Halifax the Hebble Brook was so hot that it steamed, meanwhile constantly changing its colour. Since the area lay some seventy miles from the Yorkshire fishing towns and thirty-five from those of Lancashire, little fresh fish arrived here.[213] Salt cod was sometimes eaten but was not popular. Herrings were available, some brined and smoked as red herrings that weaving families grilled and served with bread and potatoes, while others were simply gutted, salted and packed into barrels at the ports.[214] Farmers in the Scammonden valley used to club together to buy these for use over the cold months of winter. To most people, fresh fish meant shellfish that was kept alive by being packed in wet seaweed throughout the course of its long journey from the sea. Carriers such as 'Old Surry' used either a horse or donkey to bring in pannier-loads over the 1,300 ft. pass from Bacup into Todmorden, while 'Old Sam Wilson' brought them up the valley from Halifax.[215]

This situation changed completely with the opening of the Lancashire and Yorkshire railway along Calderdale in 1841 and the linking lines to Scarborough, Hull and Whitby in 1845, 1846 and 1847 respectively. Now, for

---

[211] J. Parker, *Illustrated rambles from Hipperholme to Tong,* Bradford, Percy, Lund Humphries, 1904, p.349.

[212] Cliffe Castle Museum KLY 436.

[213] Hamerton, *Olde Eland,* p.93.

[214] Travis *Notes: (historical and biographical),* p.28.

[215] Ibid., pp.29, 35.

the first time, cheap, fresh sea-fish was available from the new fishmongers that rapidly set themselves up in every town. Much of it was simply boiled, baked or dusted in breadcrumbs or flour and fried to produce a good hot meal in a matter of minutes, while kippers were just grilled before the open fire. Local fish recipes tend to be quite plain:

Cod steaks: Mrs Grave, Burnley Road, Mytholmroyd[216]

2 cod steaks
8 oz/225 g tomatoes
1 slice onion
1 oz/25 g butter
1 tbs flour
½ pt/300 ml light stock
salt & pepper

Wash and dry the fish, season with salt and pepper and steam for 10-15 minutes. Meanwhile finely chop the onion and fry it in the butter until starting to turn golden. Mix the flour into the stock, stir into the onions, add the thinly sliced tomatoes and simmer very gently, stirring occasionally, for 15 minutes, then season to taste. Place the fish in a dish, pour the sauce over, and serve.

Any left-over fish was usually recycled in:

Fish cakes: Mytholmroyd[217]

8 oz/225 g cooked fish
5 oz/ 125 g mashed potato
½ tsp chopped parsley
pinch of ground mace
salt & pepper to taste
1 or 2 tbs milk
1 oz/25 g melted butter
1 egg, beaten
browned breadcrumbs
dripping for frying

Remove all skin and bones from the fish, and divide into flakes.

---

[216] Anon., *159 recipes from good kitchens*, p.8.

[217] Ashton et al, *The St Michael's recipe and quotation book*, p.8.

Mix the potato, parsley, mace, seasoning, milk and melted butter together, and work in the fish. Form into small cakes, brush or dip in the egg, coat with the breadcrumbs and fry on both sides in the dripping until heated through.

By the 1870s fried fish shops had arrived; their instant, trouble-free availability, fine flavour and texture combined with their hot, satisfying nourishment made them extremely popular. They were the first really well used take-away meal, ideal for families who only came together after long days in the mills and factories. In Halifax each shop had some 800-1000 regular customers by 1905-1909, even though most families still considered them something of an expensive luxury, only to be enjoyed once a week.[218]

Around 1920 a fish cost 2d, while 1d would buy a child's portion called a 'bit', a scoop of chips, fish pressed between two slices of potato called a 'cake' or 'sandwich', three or four slices of battered potato called 'collops', or some brown peas. There would also be requests for 'scraps', the drops of batter that fell from the fish as it was plunged into the boiling dripping, and then emerged as a delicious crunchy treat.[219] Whether taken home to be eaten from a warmed plate using a knife and fork, accompanied by tea and a breadcake, or sprinkled with salt and vinegar from the counter and eaten outdoors directly from their enclosing newspaper with greasy fingers, fish and chips were delicious. Their sole drawback was 'Devil up the Spout'. For this youths rolled up their greasy papers, stuffed them up cast-iron drainpipes and lit them with a match. This created a fiery organ-pipe effect of unearthly howls with flames spouting up above the gutters.[220]

One of the unforeseen advantages of the booming fish and chip trade was the manufacture of coal or gas-fired ranges in Halifax engineering factories. Those of Fred Whiteley of Victoria Street, Northgate, had stainless steel covers to their pans and hygienic tiled surfaces featuring fishing scenes.

Up to the latter years of the nineteenth century salmon remained a prestigious, but unaffordable luxury well beyond the means of most families. It then began to be imported in tins from North America, selling at 8d/3p a tin in 1896, so that

---

[218] J.K. Walton, *Fish and chips and the British working class 1870-1940*, Leicester, Leicester University Press, 1992, p.27.

[219] Hartley & Ingilby, *Life and tradition in West Yorkshire*, p.113.

[220] Calderdale Libraries, *Memory lane: recollections of Todmorden*, p.14.

Figure 23. Fish and chips were first fried in set-pots identical to those used to boil laundry, but these were soon replaced by hygienic and attractively designed coal- and gas-fired ranges, as made by Whiteley's in Halifax.

it could be served when entertaining friends or clergy at Sunday teas or similar occasions. From this time local cookery books provide recipes for salmon pies, moulds and rissoles in which breadcrumbs and eggs were used to double its bulk in order to make its purchase worthwhile.

Salmon mould: Miss J. Appleyard, Halifax[221]

1 lb/450 g tin of salmon
3 tbs fresh white breadcrumbs
2 tbs chopped fresh parsley
2 eggs, beaten
2 oz/50 m. melted butter
salt & pepper to taste

Remove all skin and bone from the salmon, chop up the fish, mix with the remaining ingredients and the liquid from the tin, pack into a buttered mould or basin, cover with greaseproof paper, and steam for 30-60 minutes until set. Serve hot with peas or cold with sliced cucumber or hard-boiled egg.

The cockles and mussels that had been brought into the area from around 1800 were still as popular as ever, whether fresh for boiling at home or pickled in jars and hawked around the public houses in the towns. Due to the development of steam trawlers, refrigeration and railways, fish was now available to all from the fishmongers' shops and the markets. Even so, the habit of buying it as late as possible on Saturday nights in order to get the best bargains still continued. As reported in Halifax in 1907, 'everything about fish rendered at 10.30 p.m. usually is perishable – save the aroma, and that haunts and caresses our nostrils still!'[222]

---

[221] Kaye, *Yorkshire cooking,* p.58.
[222] Lonsdale Collection, *Newspaper cuttings,* vol.15, p.28.

CHAPTER 6

VEGETABLES

Today a wide range of vegetables is readily available on market stalls, in shops and in supermarkets, some having been grown in the fertile fields of the eastern counties, and others imported from distant countries. There is an expectation that, especially with the benefits of freezing, most can be bought throughout the year, regardless of the season. In the past there was a total reliance on largely home-grown produce, recipe books often listing what could be had month by month as a guide and reminder to cooks and housewives. The first crop of each vegetable, such as green peas or new potatoes, was looked forward to with eager anticipation, for another year might pass before their tastes could next be enjoyed.

Beans	July - September
Broccoli	January - March
Brussels Sprouts	October - December
Cabbages	April - June.
Carrots	January - September
Cauliflowers	July - September
Celery	March - October
Leeks	March - October
Lettuces	July - September
Marrows	October - December
Onions	October - December
Parsnips	October - December
Peas	April - September
Savoys	January - March[223]

The hillside villages and farmsteads where most people lived until the nineteenth century were far from ideal for vegetable production due to the combination of thin acid soils, altitude and exposure. The best solution, just as in the Hebrides and Shetland, was to enclose a garden plot near the house within a drystone wall, as at Top Withins and similar hill farms. Their original crop was probably brassicas such as kale and cabbage, a close at Middle Withins being named 'Cabbage' back in 1620.[224] Potatoes were introduced in the eighteenth century, soon becoming an important part of the local diet.

---

[223] Ashton et al, *The St Michael's recipe and quotation book,* pp.3-4.

[224] Wood & Brears, *The real Wuthering Heights*, p.11.

Writing in 1801, Thomas Sutcliffe of Midgley was reporting that 'small as the quantity of potatoes appears, yet almost every farm grows more or less, many not more than two perches', meaning sixteen yards, probably only enough for the family's needs.[225] A few years later, in 1807-15, Cornelius Ashworth of Waltroyd was carefully noting the progress of his potato crops in his diary, setting them in April, hoeing in June and July, and digging them up in October; hopefully they were not 'fleuked' with holes, like those then being sold on Todmorden market.[226] As elsewhere, their blight would have caused scarcity in the 1840s, but their importance grew steadily as the use of oats declined, quantities being brought into the valley for sale so that they became the staple food here.

Figure 24. Having been boiled and drained, potatoes were left by the fire to become 'floury' before being mashed in their pan using a wooden masher (left, from Halifax, before 1904, right, used by the Whalley family of Denholme).

In 1844 the poorest families were dining on nothing more than boiled potatoes mashed with bits of fried suet.[227] When conditions improved they still formed an essential part of every main meal, either incorporated into meat and potato pies and fishcakes, or to be boiled, mashed or fried to accompany all manner of meats and fish. New potatoes might be boiled either in their skins or scraped, while old ones were usually peeled, boiled for about 15-20 minutes in salted

[225] N. Smith, Farming before the nineteenth century in Bailey et al, *Pennine perspectives*, p.53.

[226] Davies et al, *The Diaries of Cornelius Ashworth 1782-1816*, pp.54-55.

[227] Howard, *A history of the typhus of Heptonstall Slack*, pp.55-57.

water, drained, the lid put back on and then shaken and kept warm by the fire to develop a floury texture. This made them more absorbent to soak up gravy and juices on the plate. They were also cooked as:

Oatmeal potatoes: O. Bryan, Sowerby Bridge[228]

1 pan freshly boiled potatoes
½ oz/12 g dripping
2 oz/50 g fine oatmeal
2-3 oz/50-75 g minced cooked meat
salt & pepper

Drain the potatoes in their pan, add the dripping and shake over a gentle heat until it has melted. Sprinkle in the remaining ingredients and continue shaking, adding more dripping if needed, until the potatoes have turned a golden colour, then serve immediately.

Potato savoury: S.A. Blackburn, Halifax[229]

2 large potatoes, peeled and diced
½ oz/12 g butter
1tbs flour
½ pt/300 ml milk
½ tsp chopped parsley
½ tsp salt
pinch pepper
few drops raw onion juice
a few tbs browned breadcrumbs

Make a white sauce by melting the butter in a saucepan, stirring in the flour, salt and pepper, then the milk. Stir continuously until it has thickened, then pour a thin layer across the bottom of a baking dish. Fill the dish with layers of potatoes and sauce, seasoning each with salt, pepper, parsley and onion juice, finishing with a layer of sauce. Top with the breadcrumbs and bake at 180ºC/350ºF gas mark 4 for 30 minutes and serve hot.

The other really popular vegetable here was the onion, its savoury taste

---

[228] Kaye, *Yorkshire cooking,* p.185.
[229] Ibid., p.186.

sometimes giving it the title 'the poor man's beef.' It was included in stews, hot-pots and pies, as well as forming a complete meal by itself.

Stuffed onions: Mrs W.A. Laycock, Hopwood Lane, Halifax[230]

3 large onions
pinch of salt
2 oz/50 g cooked meat
2 tsp fresh parsley
1 oz/25 g butter
2 tbs fresh breadcrumbs
½ pt/300 ml brown gravy
1 tbs browned breadcrumbs

Peel the onions, cover with hot water and stew with the salt until par-boiled when tested with a skewer. Drain, cut in two top to bottom and remove some of the interior. Chop the removed onion finely with the parsley, mix in the fresh breadcrumbs, meat and a little of the gravy (or brown sauce) to form a stuffing. Pack this inside the onions, put into a fireproof dish, sprinkle with the browned breadcrumbs, cover with buttered paper [or cooking foil] and bake at 170ºC/325ºF gas mark 3 for about 30 minutes. Serve hot with the gravy, or with brown sauce.

One of the valley's characteristic vegetable dishes was onion pasty. This was usually made as a plate pie for family use. In Methodist circles at Sowerby Bridge it was tantamount to a declaration of love if a boy bought one for a girl, and squares cut from huge tray-baked versions formed part of every chapel supper. I first encountered them at the end of a lecture I had given in Hebden Bridge when new to the valley some fifty years ago. With a dry throat I sank my teeth into what looked like a square of luscious apple pasty, the taste of the savoury onions coming as a complete contrast to the anticipated cool sweetness!

Onion pasty[231]

2 large onions finely chopped, or boiled, peeled and sliced
1 oz/25 g butter
salt & pepper

---

[230] Brears, *Traditional food in Yorkshire,* p.148.

[231] Bedford, *Manuscript notebooks*, MS 432/4, p.38.

Pastry

12 oz/350 g flour
pinch of salt
6 oz/150 g lard

Rub the fat into the flour and salt until they resemble fine breadcrumbs. Sprinkle in 3-4 tablespoons of cold water and stir with a round-bladed knife until it forms into lumps. Knead these lightly to form a smooth pastry, cover, and leave to rest in a cool place for 30 minutes. Roll out on a floured board to make two rounds and use one to line a greased ovenproof plate. Spread with the onion, dot with the butter, sprinkle with salt and pepper, dampen the edges, and seal on the lid, pricking it with a fork. Bake at 180°C/350°F gas mark 4 for 40 minutes.

Cheese & onion pasty[232]

Make as above, filling it with 1 large onion boiled and sliced, 1 large potato, peeled, boiled and sliced, and 3 oz/75 g grated cheese.

Parsley pie: Mrs J. Breaks, Greetland[233]

1 large onion, finely chopped
2 tbs parsley, finely chopped
3 tbs grated cheese
1 egg, beaten
¼ pt/150 ml milk
salt & pepper

Make as above, spreading the onion first, then the parsley, followed by the cheese, and finally the egg beaten into the milk, salt and pepper.

Due to the seasonal nature of vegetables, there was a steady demand for dried versions, especially in the winter months. The most common were split peas and lentils that had to be soaked overnight before being boiled for hours. They were best when made with the stock from a cooked joint of bacon or ham.

---

[232] Ibid.

[233] Kaye, *Yorkshire cooking,* p.174.

95

Pea soup: West family[234]

8 oz/225 g yellow split peas
½ tsp bicarbonate of soda
1 small carrot
1 small turnip
1 large onion
2 tsp dried mint
4 tsp or 5 leaves gelatin
¾ tsp salt
⅛ tsp ground pepper

Soak the peas overnight with the bicarbonate of soda in 1½ pt/900 ml cold water. Next morning drain the peas, discarding the water, and put into a large pan with the diced vegetables, and 1½ pt of fresh water. Bring slowly to the boil, skim, cover and gently simmer for 3½ hours. Stir it vigorously [or blend] to produce a smooth mixture before straining it into a clean pan. Stir in the gelatin, having pre-soaked the sheets in cold water for 5 minutes, the mint, salt and pepper. Cook for a further 10 minutes, then serve hot.

Lentil soup: Mrs Ingham, Red Acre Farm[235]

4 oz/100 g lentils
[3 vegetable stock cubes]
1 carrot
1 turnip
1 onion
6 peppercorns
1 oz/25 g butter
1 oz/25 g rice flour
½ pt/300 ml milk or cream
salt and pepper to taste

Soak the lentils in cold water for 4 hours, drain, and put into a pan with the finely sliced vegetables, stock cubes, peppercorns and 2 pt/1.2 l cold water. Bring to the boil, cover and simmer for about 1 hour until everything is tender. Rub all through a sieve [or blend]

---

[234] West family, *Manuscript recipe book*, p.51.

[235] Ashton et al, *The St Michael's recipe and quotation book*, p.6.

into a clean pan. Melt the butter in another pan, mix in the rice flour, and stir in the milk little by little over a gentle heat until thickened, add the soup, return to the boil, season to taste and serve with toast.

As well as cooking garden vegetables, there was a long tradition here of gathering wild plants for food. One of them, tansy (*Tanecetum vulgare*) can often be found growing near old farmhouses. Its leaves and stalks have an exceedingly bitter taste – it really is horrible – but for centuries it was used to make a kind of omelette made at Easter-time to symbolise the bitter herbs eaten by the Jews at Passover. It also had a reputation as a herbal remedy, but today is considered poisonous.

There was a popular belief that everyone needed a good tonic of fresh green herbs every spring in order to 'clean the blood' after the long, dark months of winter, curing spots and pimples. The simplest way of doing this was to make nettle porridge.

Nettle porridge: Mrs S. Robertshaw, Mytholmroyd[236]

1 pt/600 ml young nettle shoots, gathered when about 2 in/5 cm tall
2-3 tbs fine oatmeal
about 1 tbs butter
salt & pepper to taste

Wash the nettles, shake them dry in a cloth, then plunge into 1 pt/600 ml boiling water and boil, uncovered, for about 10 minutes until tender. Scoop them out of the pan, chop them finely, and return to the pan with the oatmeal and butter. Boil again, season to taste, and eat with either oatcake or bread and butter.

This resembles the nettle haggis of Cumbria, where Easter Sunday was celebrated with a 'pudding' made from a variety of herbs and tender vegetables, particularly the bistort *polygonum* (now *Persica*) *bistorta*, there known as Eastermangiants. In the Upper Calder Valley the same plant grows in the lower fields, where it is still called either Passion-dock, or Easterledge, since it appears at Easter-time. Around Mytholmroyd, Midgley, Hebden Bridge and Heptonstall it was used as the main ingredient for a dish called dock pudding, even though no-one outside this area would ever recognise it as

---

[236] Kaye, *Yorkshire cooking*, p.192; Crump, *The little hill farm*, p.73.

a pudding. Something like the seaweed-based laverbread of coastal Wales, it is a thick green mixture to be fried with bacon and potatoes as a breakfast or supper dish. Each family had its own recipe, these being typical:

Dock pudding 1 (1954)[237]

1 lb/450 g dock leaves
1 lb/450 g young nettle leaves
2 onions, chopped finely
2-4 oz/50-100 g medium oatmeal
salt & pepper to taste

Wash the dock and nettle leaves thoroughly, rinse and remove their stalks, mince them with the onions, or place them directly into a saucepan, half-covering them with water with the salt and pepper, and boiling for about 10 minutes until tender. Stir in the oatmeal and continue stirring as it simmers gently and thickens over the next 15-20 minutes.

Dock pudding 2[238]

2 lb/900 g Passion dock leaves
8 oz/225 g nettles
2 large onions or two bunches of spring onions
1 tbs butter
1 handful oatmeal
salt & pepper to taste

[Follow the recipe above]

Dock pudding 3: Mrs Waterworth, Luddenden[239]

Passion dock leaves
tops of young nettles
Ladies Mantle (Alchemilla mollis), here known as Nine Nooks
Sorrel (Rumex acetosa) here known as Sweet Dock or Greensauce
spring onions, especially the green part

Mrs Waterworth sometimes served the Passion dock on its own as a fresh

---

[237] R. Stanton, 'Dock pudding', *Dalesman*, 1954, 16, p.41.
[238] Hartley & Ingilby, *Life and tradition in West Yorkshire*, p.112; Kaye, *Yorkshire cooking*, p.191.
[239] Crump, *The little hill farm*, p.73.

vegetable, or stewed it with these additional ingredients, keeping the mixture for frying with oatmeal to be eaten either on its own or with home-fed ham or bacon.

Other wild plants were collected as food. Good King Henry (*Chenopodium bonus-henricus*) that grew on the richer soils and around farmyards, its broad arrow-shaped leaves, being cooked like spinach.[240]

Good King Henry

1 lb/450 g Good King Henry
½ oz/12 g butter
salt & pepper

Wash the leaves, cut away and discard the stalks, put the leaves in a pan with a few tablespoons of water, cover, cook for about 10 minutes until tender, then drain and chop. Return to the pan with the butter, stir until re-heated, season and serve hot.

The young leaves of hawthorn shoots were nibbled as they were plucked from the bushes, particularly by children. Although the taste is completely different, they were always known as 'bread and cheese'. Meanwhile the Greater Golden Saxifrage (*Chrysoplenium oppositifolium*) that preferred acid soils was formerly 'used as a sallad early in the spring with cresses'.[241] The use of wild plants as food appears to have lingered longer here than in most other parts of England, probably due to the valley's general continuance of local customs combined with a shortage of home-grown green vegetables over many years.

Most vegetables were cooked in the home, the only exception being dried, green or brown peas that were sold in hot pea saloons, better known as 'pay 'oiles' in the towns. One standing next to the canal in Brighouse was operated by Edmund Stake, a local blacksmith who donned his flat cap and 'pinny' before serving his customers. The main feature of the shop was a large range on which simmered a large pot of brown peas and another of green peas, its shelf holding a tray of sausages in gravy. Those who wished to 'eat in' could help themselves to salt and vinegar before taking their white basin of peas to one of the well-scrubbed tables. There they drank off the liquid before eating the peas. Alternatively, they could have a sausage sandwiched into a teacake

---

[240] Ibid.

[241] Watson, *The history and antiquities of the parish of Halifax*, p.738.

called a 'muff' (short for muffin). Others brought their own jug to collect peas, sausages and gravy, Mr. Stake then

> covered it with a piece of paper that was folded round the top and fitted round the handles, keeping it all warm. As we took it home, we lifted up one side and drank the gravy. We thought mother wouldn't know what we'd done. But, of course, she soon found out.'[242]

Figure 25. Local 'pay 'oiles' provided green and brown peas, sausages in gravy and bread-cakes called muffins, either for eating around their well-scrubbed tables or to be carried home in the customers' own jugs.

---

[242] W.R. Mitchell, *By gum, life were sparse: memories of northern mill towns*, Originally published 1991, London, Warner, 1993, pp.134, 147.

CHAPTER 7

PUDDINGS: SWEET & SAVOURY

Due to their dependence on porridge, virtually every family had a kilp pot in which to boil not only this staple of their diet, but also equally substantial puddings.[243] Even so, boiled puddings were never as popular an everyday food here as they were in some other parts of this country. Instead, they tended to be restricted to family gatherings, perhaps for Sunday dinners, or for feasts and thumps. Their ingredients were usually quite basic, just oatmeal and suet sweetened with treacle or the later golden syrup, if to be served at the end of a meal.

Oatmeal pudding[244]

8 oz/225 g medium oatmeal
3 oz/75 g suet
4 oz/100 g golden syrup

Mix ¼ pt/150 ml cold water into the mixed oatmeal and suet and form the mixture into a ball. Take a 15 in/40 cm square of fine cotton or muslin, scald it, squeeze dry, shake out, lay flat, sprinkle with flour, and shake off the surplus. Place the pudding in the middle, gather the cloth around it and tie with string. Plunge into a deep pan of boiling water, cover and boil for 1½ hours, topping up with more boiling water as necessary. Turn the pudding out into a hot dish and serve with a jug of the syrup heated with a little water.

Since they lacked eggs, or any other raising agent, these puddings were heavy and stodgy, but some were far less palatable than others, as 'Nathan Hotchops' of Haworth and 'Sammy Slyman o' Wuthering Heights' described in local pamphlets. They refer to an event in Haworth at Christmastide around 1857, when a gang of mischievous characters decided to persuade John Appleyard of West Lane to make them a pudding for their suppers. Since neither the required ingredients nor skills were readily available, it eventually took the form of a solid lump of suet set in a mass of highly peppered dry bran, all

---

[243] See p.37.

[244] King Cross [Wesleyan] Circuit, *Recipes and quotations,* p.29.

enclosed in an old rusty nail-bag. An equally rusty old hammerhead was included to submerge it in its posnet as it boiled over the fire. At this stage the gang went off for a glass of ale at the White Lion, where the Keighley Band were playing in an upstairs room. Grasping the opportunity for some good sport with the Keighleyites, and with the full cooperation of the landlady, the band was invited to supper, a table below being set out in grand style with tablecloth, tableware and decanters, and Tom Kay clad in white apron and sleeves to act as a first-class waiter.

When the bandsmen had taken their places, Tom served out the pudding, with its accompanying mess of boiled pig potatoes (small or inferior potatoes), but those who tried it shot up and started 'boacoming (retching and vomiting) fit ta thraw their hearts up … By, lad tha sud a seen 'em; tha'll a laft fit to crack thee sides, hah do wish tha hed been thear!' Then:

> As suin az they could see ther way,
> Thay walk'd off hoam, ay, quickly;
> "By stars", sed Jim, "ther heaads ul swim,
> Fer they'll feel raither sickly!"

After feeding the remains of the pudding to John's pigs, the next task was to make sure that all in Keighley knew how their bandsmen had been made to look foolish. This was done so effectively that the pudding was still being written about ten years later.[245]

Other puddings were far more palatable, especially one made to celebrate the opening of the Worth Valley Railway in April 1867. The massive example had to serve over fifty people gathered at the Black Bull in Haworth. As Bill o' th' Hoylus End described, proper ingredients were now used, not 'that stuffment they gav the Keighley band!'

> For twelve stone of flour (3 lbs. to a man)
> Wur boiled I' ould Bingleechin's kah lickin pan,
> Wi' gert lumps o' suet 'at the cook had put in't
> 'At shane like a ginney just aht 'at' mint;
> Wi' knives made a' purpose to cut it i' rowls
> And the sauce were i' buckets and mighty big bowls.

After the parson had said grace, the pudding was then served:

---

[245] N. Hotchops, 'Keighley Pudding Eaters', *Keighley Visitor and General Advertiser*, Temperance Society, October 1858; January 1859; S. Slyman, *T' story o' th' pudding macking un eiting: a defence for Haworth*, Cullingworth, 1867.

Yo' should a seen Locker-taaners brandishin' their knives,
An' choppin' an' cutting thor wolloping shives [slices],
An' all on 'em shaatin they lik'd th' puddin' best,
Fer nowt wor like th' puddin' for standing th' test.'[246]

From the 1860s, as conditions began to improve, these puddings were largely replaced by richer, lighter ones that did away with the pudding cloths. Now the mixture contained raising agents such as baking powder and eggs, and were either gently steamed in greased pottery pudding basins, or baked in an oven.

Ginger pudding: Mrs A. Mitchell, Sowerby Bridge[247]

4 oz/100 g flour
3 oz/75 g suet
2 oz/50 g brown sugar
1 tsp ground ginger
½ tsp baking powder
 2 eggs, beaten
4 oz/100 g black treacle
a little milk

Mix the dry ingredients, make a well in the centre, drop in the eggs and treacle and mix together, adding a little milk if necessary to make a soft mixture. Put into a 1½ pt/900 ml greased basin and cover with a piece of greaseproof paper which has had one pleat folded across it, and another at right angles, and tie down around the rim. [Alternatively cover with a piece of kitchen foil pressed tightly around the rim]. Steam for two hours.

Other puddings used breadcrumbs, these giving a lighter texture and providing an economical way of using up stale bread.

Marmalade pudding: Mrs Spencer, Hollock Lee[248]

4 oz/100 g flour
4 oz/100 g freshly grated breadcrumbs
4 oz/100 g suet

---

[246] Bill o' th' Hoylus End [W. Wright], *Random rhymes & rambles,* pp.110, 114.

[247] Ashton et al, *The St Michael's recipe and quotation book,* p.12.

[248] Ibid., p.15.

4 oz/100 g sugar
4 oz/100 g marmalade
½ tsp bicarbonate of soda
1 egg, beaten
2 tbs milk

Follow the instructions above and steam for 3 hours.

The lightest and richest steamed puddings were also the most expensive, since they creamed butter with sugar and used more eggs, just as if making a cake.

Victoria jam pudding: Mrs Walton, Mytholmroyd[249]

2 eggs and their weight of butter and flour
2 tbs brown sugar
2 tbs raspberry jam
1 tsp bicarbonate of soda
2 tbs milk

Cream the butter and sugar, beat in the eggs, little by little, then the flour, the jam, and the bicarbonate of soda dissolved in a little milk. Put into a buttered 1½ pt/900 ml basin or mould, and cover and steam as described in the Ginger Pudding recipe, but for 1 hour.

When ovens became available, they made it possible to bake puddings by using similar recipes.

Railway pudding: Mrs B.T. Clegg, Mytholmroyd[250]

2 eggs, beaten
4 oz/100 g white sugar
3 oz/75 g flour
¼ tsp salt
1 tsp baking powder
1 tbs milk
1-2 tbs jam
sugar for sprinkling

Beat the sugar into the eggs, then add the flour followed by the

---

[249] Ibid., p.15.

[250] Ibid., p.16.

milk, the salt and the baking powder. Pour into a greased Yorkshire pudding tin and bake at 180ºC/350ºF gas mark 4 for 10 minutes. Allow to cool, split open, spread with the jam in between, replace the top part, sprinkle with sugar, cut into finger-sized lengths and serve.

Swiss pudding: Mrs J. Robinson, Mytholmroyd[251]

1 lb/450 g apples, peeled, cored and chopped
4 oz/100 g brown sugar
4 oz/100 g fresh grated breadcrumbs
2 oz/50 g suet
½ oz/12 g butter, melted

Stew the apples with very little water until tender, then stir in 3 oz/75 g of the sugar. Mix the remaining sugar with the breadcrumbs and suet. Put half of this mixture into a pie dish, cover with the apples, then the rest of the mixture, pour the butter on top and bake at 180ºC/350ºF gas mark 4 for about 30 minutes.

The steady heat of the coal fires that burned continuously in the Yorkshire ranges was ideal for cooking milk puddings made with macaroni, semolina, sago, tapioca and rice that were now being sold by groceries and Co-operative stores.

Rice pudding

2 oz/50 g short-grain rice
2 tbs sugar
1 pt/600 ml milk
knob of butter or margarine
grated nutmeg

Grease a 1½ pt/900 ml baking dish, add all but the nutmeg and stir together, sprinkle with nutmeg, and bake at 150ºC/300ºF gas mark 2 for about 30 minutes.
[for sago and tapioca use about 2 tbs and follow this recipe.]

As an extra treat, milk puddings sometimes had a spoonful of jam added to each serving.

---

[251] Ibid., p.16.

Barley pudding: Shibden Hall[252]

4 oz/100 g pearl barley
½ pt/300 ml milk
[1 oz/25 g butter]
2 tbs sugar

Bring the barley to the boil in 1 pt/450 ml water, half-cover the pan and simmer for 40 minutes, stirring it until all the water has been absorbed. Stir in the remaining ingredients, pour into a greased 1½ pt/900 ml baking dish and bake at 170°C/325°F gas mark 3 for 1½ hours.

Cold puddings

Long before homes had refrigerators and freezers, most families had a cellar, pantry or dairy in which cold, refreshing puddings could be kept cool for serving on hot summer days. Most homemade puddings were quite plain in comparison to the over-sweet and rich contents of the dessert aisles of modern supermarkets, since they had to make economical use of basic ingredients.

Rice mould with stewed prunes: West Family[253]

4 oz/100 g short-grain rice
1 pt/600 ml milk
½ tsp salt

Bring a large pan of water to the boil, pour in the rice, boil uncovered for ten minutes, then drain off the water. Add the milk and salt and stir over a gentle heat until all the milk has been absorbed and the rice has thickened. Turn into a freshly rinsed basin and set aside to cool before turning out onto a dish.

The prunes:
1 lb/450 g prunes (without stones)
4 oz/100 g sugar

Soak the prunes for 1 hour in 1 pt/600 ml cold water, add the sugar, and simmer gently for 1 hour [today most prunes are far softer than in the past, so the cooking time may be reduced]. When cold, either pour around the mould in its dish, or serve separately in their own bowl.

---

[252] West Yorkshire Archive Service (Calderdale), Lister family: household bills, SH:3/B/1/1
[253] West family, *Manuscript recipe book*, p.5.

Trifles were already popular around the late nineteenth century, particularly when companies, such as Goodall and Backhouse of Leeds, started to market packet jellies and packet custards, and sponge biscuits could be bought ready-made from local shops. The following 1908 version probably originated at the great Ben Rhydding Hydro just outside Ilkley, where prosperous Victorians flocked to take their spa treatments.

Ben Rhydding pudding: Mrs F. Greenwood, Sowerby Bridge[254]

1 lb/450 g apples
1 large sponge cake or a pack of trifle sponges
½ pt/300 ml whipping cream or thick custard
1 oz/25 g sugar

Peel, core and slice the apples, place in a saucepan with the sugar and a few tablespoons of water, cover, and cook slowly until tender, then leave to cool. Use slices of the cake or sponges to line a 1½ pt/900 ml dish or basin, fill with layers of apple and cake, finishing with a layer of cake. Pour the cream or custard on top and set aside in a cool place for a few hours before serving.

Rhubarb summer pudding[255]

1 lb/450 g rhubarb (forced is best)
5 oz/125 g sugar (more or less to taste)
6 -7 oz/150 -175 g crustless sliced bread

Trim the leaves off the rhubarb, cut into short lengths, layer with the sugar in a saucepan and leave for a few hours or overnight until syrup has formed, then simmer gently until tender but not pulped. Line a 1½ pt/900 ml basin with some of the bread, then use a pierced spoon to fill the interior with layers of rhubarb and bread, finishing with bread. Pour in sufficient of the remaining syrup to just cover the bread, press down lightly, leave for a few hours, turn out onto a dish and serve with cream or cold custard.

Probably the most unexpected cold pudding to be made by Calderdale families was the syllabub. Very popular in gentry households in the seventeenth and

---

[254] King Cross [Wesleyan] Circuit, *Recipes and quotations*, p.25; Ashton et al, *The St Michael's recipe and quotation book*, p.15.

[255] Calderdale Libraries, *Memory lane: recollections of Brighouse, Rastrick & Hipperholme*, p.55.

eighteenth centuries, it had then fallen out of fashion and become forgotten in most parts of England, but here it was still being made in the early twentieth century. Some descriptions of them as 'cream curdled with citrus juice' make them sound distinctly unattractive, although this is technically accurate. To those who have never tried them, they are probably best described as frothy, alcoholic lemon yogurts floating on a layer of sweet lemony wine. The following examples both include raw egg white. If this is considered unsuitable, sterilised egg white works just as well.

Syllabub: Mrs J. Reat, Illingworth[256]

¼ pt/150 ml sherry	2 tbs brandy
juice & pared zest of 1 lemon	1 egg white
½ pt/300 ml cream	2–4 oz/50–100 g sugar to taste

Soak the lemon zest in the sherry for a few hours (or overnight), remove the zest, add the remaining ingredients and whisk vigorously until a froth appears. Rinse a piece of muslin, lay it in a sieve and put in the froth as it rises. Finally divide the remaining liquid into six wine glasses, top with the froth and serve.

Rich syllabubs: Mrs M. Marsden, Parkinson Lane, Halifax[257]

1 pt/600 ml sherry or madeira	3 tbs brandy
juice & pared zest of 1 lemon	1 egg white
1 tbs redcurrant or blackcurrant jelly, (optional)	2–4 oz/50–100 g sugar to taste

Soak the lemon zest in the sherry overnight, then remove it. Stir in the juice, sugar and brandy and egg white, then whip vigorously to a froth. Spoon the froth into wine glasses as it rises, until all has been used, then set it in a cool place overnight. To produce contrasting colours, half the cream can be mixed with either redcurrant or blackcurrant jelly before being whipped separately. Leave in a cool place overnight, when the syllabub will separate into a stiff froth with a clear liquid beneath.

For those with gardens or allotments, fresh home-grown strawberries, black

---

[256] Kaye, *Yorkshire cooking,* p.158.

[257] Ibid., p.158.

currants, gooseberries or raspberries were a real seasonal treat when served with cream and a sprinkling of sugar. Everyone else had to wait until they appeared on market stalls or in greengrocers' shops, or gather what they could from the verges and moorlands. Even though some bilberries and blackberries might be nibbled raw, as they were being collected, they were usually eaten in a prepared form as tarts, pies and jams. In contrast, the hips and haws of the hawthorn were gathered and eaten raw by children around Walsden, probably as a means of satisfying their hunger. Some took them home, stewed them until soft, then removed the stones, chopped them up with butter and spread them on bread – an enormous amount of trouble for very little food. It gave Todmorden folk a feeling of superiority to chant about:

> Heps and hages and Hollin grubs [haws and holly-berry food],
> Are fit for naught, but Walsten cubs.
> Imeber and blager [blackberries] and other such prout
> For which lads and lasses in Torm'den shout.[258]

Wild tree fruits, including the crab apples, used to make sour verjuice and sloes for flavouring gin, were gathered, but it was never a good place for growing fruit. Only the larger houses planted their own orchards. Some grew bitter, cherry-sized wild plums called bullaces (*Prunus domestica*), the name Bullace Trees surviving in two farmhouses, one in Warley and another on Back Lane in Stanbury.

Due to the seasonal nature and relative scarcity of fresh fruit here, dried fruits provided a useful alternative. Prunes, dried apricots and apple rings could be bought throughout the year, only having to be soaked and gently simmered before serving either hot or cold. Tinned fruits only became affordable to most in the early twentieth century but were generally considered to be a real luxury served only at Sunday teas or when entertaining guests. They were always eaten with cream or evaporated milk, and bread and butter to 'make them go further'. To many still alive today, this remains the best way of serving them.

Savoury puddings

Sweet puddings ended a meal; savoury puddings started it, served as a separate first course and accompanied by rich gravy. Their purpose was to take the edge off the appetite, before tackling the main course. The proverb 'them as eats most puddin' can 'ave most meat', was as well-known here as in other parts of the county, since those who stuffed themselves with pudding would

---

[258] Travis, *Notes: (historical and biographical)*, p.256.

probably be too full to make substantial inroads into the roasted joints. The most popular of all savoury puddings made here was, obviously, the Yorkshire pudding.

The first recipe for a 'Yorkshire pudding' to appear in print formed part of Hannah Glasse's *Art of Cookery Made Plain and Easy* of 1747, but there is no real evidence for its attribution to Yorkshire. Her family came from Northumberland, and it has formed a major accompaniment to roast beef in the North East and Lancashire for at least 150 years, although its traditional place as a separate first course is distinctively Yorkshire. Today's puddings are light and crisp, having been baked in a hot oven, but are quite different from the original version, which was cooked in the radiant heat of a fire grate. As the joint rotated before the glowing coals, its juices dropped down into a metal dripping-pan, and it was here that the earliest Yorkshire puddings were made from a batter poured into a shallow tin. In 1822 Dr William Kitchener described how 'The true Yorkshire Pudding is about half an inch thick when done; but it is fashion in London to make them full twice that thickness'.[259] With its 6 tablespoons of flour, salt, 3 eggs and a pint of milk, browned on one side and then turned over to brown the other, it was essentially a rather greasy slab of stodgy solidity encased in delicious savoury crispness. It was still being made in the same way in the early 1900s.

Yorkshire pudding for meat cooked before the fire: Mrs Hall[260]

1½ oz/35 g flour
¼ tsp salt
1 egg, beaten
½ pt/300 ml milk
½ oz/12 g dripping

Beat the eggs in a basin, add the salt, then beat in the flour until smooth, and finally the milk, little by little. Set aside for 1–2 hours, stir well for 5-10 minutes, pour onto the warmed, not hot, dripping in a tin, and place beneath the roasting joint until baked firm, then cut into squares and serve hot.

Having tried this recipe, I can confirm that it could not be recognised as a Yorkshire pudding today.

---

[259] W. Kitchener, *The cook's oracle: containing receipts for plain cookery*, London, A. Constable & Co, 1822, p.445.
[260] Ashton et al, *The St Michael's recipe and quotation book*, p.13.

The later type, well-risen, light and crisp around the edges and softer within, only came into existence when iron ovens became available, which here was in the mid-nineteenth century. Every family claimed to have the perfect recipe, and no-one else's mother or grandmother could ever achieve such perfection, but in reality the basic recipe was quite simple and followed the same method.

Yorkshire pudding[261]

4 oz/100 g flour
½ tsp salt
2 eggs
½ pt/300 ml milk or milk and water
½ oz/12 g dripping

Put the flour and salt into a bowl, make a well in the centre, drop in the egg, and use a fork to beat in the milk little by little, drawing in the flour from the sides without forming lumps. Set aside for at least 30 minutes. Heat the oven to 400ºC/200ºF gas mark 6, (avoid using a fan oven as they tend to prevent the batter from rising), and put in a 12 x 9 in/30 x 23 cm dripping tin containing the lard. After 5-10 minutes, when the fat is smoking hot, pour in the batter and bake for about 30 minutes until risen and golden. Serve hot cut into squares.

This is a true Yorkshire pudding, always baked in a dripping tin to serve up to six people, and as made in most homes for every Sunday dinner up to around the 1950s. It then became fashionable to make small individual versions in bun tins. To be accurate, these should be called American puffs, or pop-overs, their earliest recipe probably coming from Mary Henderson's *Practical Cooking and Dinner Giving* published in the USA in 1877.

The basic recipes might vary in their primary contents, some using different proportions of eggs and flour, or using half milk and half water, but many families added further ingredients to give variety, or to flavour them for serving with different meats. These included:

3-4 oz/75-100 g minced cooked meat
3 oz/75 g minced raw onion
1 onion, boiled, chopped finely and mixed with 1 tsp dried sage or sage and thyme, to accompany mutton or pork.
8 sausages and a kidney cut into two, half-cooked in the dripping pan

---

[261] King Cross [Wesleyan] Circuit, *Recipes and quotations,* p.64.

before pouring in the batter enriched with 1 grated onion and ½ tsp vinegar.

3-4 oz/75–100 g grated apple, to be served as a last course

Although usually served with gravy, especially onion gravy, other local traditions included parsley sauce or a 'Yorkshire ploughman's' or 'mint sauce' salad. This comprised 3-4 spring onions, 6-7 large lettuce leaves and a handful of mint leaves all finely chopped together and mixed to taste with sugar and malt vinegar. Sufficient pudding might be made to provide a sweet at the end of the meal, the squares of pudding being served with golden syrup, raspberry vinegar and sugar, or a sweet white sauce.[262]

Next in importance to the Yorkshire pudding came the seasoned or savoury pudding. This was originally boiled in a cloth, probably alongside a joint of meat, when boiled meats were popular and many families had only a single kilp pot or cauldron in which to cook their meals.

Oatmeal pudding: Mrs F. Midgeley, Sowerby Bridge[263]

2 tbs oatmeal
3 tbs flour
3 tbs suet
1 onion, finely chopped
salt & pepper to taste

Mix the ingredients (using heaped tablespoonfuls) with just sufficient water to form a soft dough. Take a 15 ins/50 cm square of fine cotton or muslin, scald it, squeeze it dry, lay flat, sprinkle with flour and shake off the surplus. Place the mixture in the middle, gather the cloth around it, and tie with string. Plunge into a deep pan of boiling water, cover, and boil for 2 hours, adding boiling water as necessary. Turn the pudding out onto a hot dish and serve with gravy, either as a separate starter, or with the meat and vegetables. When ovens came in, this became a baked pudding.

Seasoning pudding: Mrs M. Rhodes, Halifax[264]

2 large onions, finely chopped

---

[262] Kaye, *Yorkshire cooking*, pp.164-169; Brears, *Traditional food in Yorkshire*, pp.191-192.

[263] Anon., *159 recipes from good kitchens*, p.29.

[264] Kaye, *Yorkshire cooking*, p.168

8 oz/225 g bread, crumbled
1 oz/25 g suet
1 heaped tsp mixed sage, thyme & marjoram
2 tsp oatmeal or rolled oats
½ tsp salt
⅛ tsp ground pepper
½ oz/12 g butter
1 egg, beaten
¾ pt/450 ml milk

Put the onions into a pan with 1 pt/600 ml cold water, bring to the boil, simmer for 5 minutes, then drain, retaining the liquid. Mix the dry ingredients, scald with the milk, add the onions and egg and beat thoroughly. Put into a greased 8 in/20 cm square tin, fork level, and bake at 180ºC/350ºF gas mark 4 for about an hour, until the top has browned.

To make the gravy, mix 2 tbs flour and 2 beef stock cubes and ½ tsp salt into the onion liquid, and bring to the boil while stirring. The fatless juices from a roast joint can also be stirred in.

Serve the pudding cut into large squares, accompanied by the gravy.

When cold, squares of this pudding were often wrapped in paper and slipped into a pocket ready to be eaten either at work or out of doors over the next few days. Another pudding which had started out as a boiled 'hunter's pudding' or 'spotted dick' to accompany meat on the eighteenth-century dining table, transformed itself into a baked pudding to be served as a first course. It was locally known as 'spare rib pudding', since it was made with the hot fat from roasting a spare rib of pork. Here this fat has been replaced with lard.

Spare rib pudding: Mrs E. Chambers, Greetland[265]

12 oz/350 g flour
1 heaped tsp baking powder
¼ tsp salt
4 oz/100 g currants
4 oz/100 g hot fat or melted lard

Mix the dry ingredients. Allow the fat/lard to cool until runny, but

---

[265] Ibid., p.169.

not set, then work into the flour along with just sufficient cold water to form a soft dough. Roll out and put into an 8 ins/20 cm square tin and use a sharp knife to deeply score its surface into small squares. Dot or brush the surface with hot fat, then bake at 200ºC/400ºF gas mark 6 for about 30 minutes until browned.

Another form of suet pudding took a simple dumpling mixture, formed it into balls, put them in the tin alongside the roasting beef for 20 minutes, then turned them over for a further 10 minutes before serving.

Figure 26. As this Edwardian postcard shows, large families used cheap Yorkshire pudding to satisfy hunger before serving the expensive meat.

CHAPTER 8

TEAS AND CAKES

Once tea had passed its name on to the social event at which it was served, as happened in the eighteenth century, it gradually came to mean different things to different people. To some, particularly the upper and middle classes and many in the southern counties, it remained an elegant, light snack mainly of dainty sandwiches and small cakes. To those in the north it became a substantial meal, something to look forward to, especially on family Sunday afternoons and large social gatherings. Housewives would always try to have some home-baked buns, biscuits and cakes to hand, just in case someone called, but this expected hospitality was never given the elevated title of 'tea'.[266]

Some teas were entirely charitable, a treat for the poorer members of society. For at least thirty years after 1859, Luddenden Foot Congregational Chapel's Old Folk's Treat saw around 150 local over-sixties sit down to roast beef, mutton, ham and tongue followed by confectionery and the gift of two oranges and 4 oz of tea, all paid for by subscribing donors.[267] Similarly a committee in Halifax issued 1,200 tickets to local churches and chapels for distribution to poor boys and girls, inviting them to a tea planned to take place in the Rifle Volunteers' Drill Hall on New Years Day, 1879. After 400 of the children had sung grace, they went on to consume:

> 276 x 2 lb loaves
> 90 lb beef
> 10 hams for sandwiches
> 1,400 oranges
> 1,400 x 5 oz buns
> 200 gallons of coffee[268]

These are just two examples of the charitable teas held locally in Victorian and Edwardian times, and represent only a tiny fraction of those provided here every year from voluntary subscriptions.

Other teas were designed to raise funds for a particular purpose. Some were

---

[266] Hamerton, *Olde Eland,* p.4.

[267] S. Ellwood, *At the foot of the Lud: a history of Luddenden Foot,* Hebden Bridge, Royd Press, 2010, p.47.

[268] Porritt, *It happened here: third series,* p.78.

Figure 27. *Every June Scar Top Charity's open-air service was held in the yard of Ponden Mill in the Sladen valley, crowds being seated in rows facing the stage erected for the speakers, musicians and choir. Meanwhile the fires were stoked to make tea that accompanied masses of sandwiches and cakes.*

quite grand affairs. In order to fund the re-seating of Christ Church, Todmorden, and maintain its Sunday School, a public tea party was held in Schofield and Booth's woodyard in February 1861. Here, in a large room decorated with evergreens and a mural, 500 people sat down at 5 p.m. to enjoy the fare prepared by Abraham Crossly, a nearby confectioner. This included various meats and a

> splendid assortment of pastry in every taste and shape and in a profusion that did great credit to the occasion … fairly eclipsing anything of this sort ever got up in Todmorden.

The proceedings closed with a performance of the oratorio *Israel in Egypt* by the Todmorden Harmonic Society, all of which raised a profit of £20.[269] In order to

---

[269] J. Travis, *Local historical notes and personal reminiscences,* Todmorden, Frederick Lee & Co,

reduce the £500 debt on its new premises, Stones Wesleyan Church in Ripponden attracted 500 to its Old Scholars' Re-union Tea in 1911.[270]

Helpful as these teas were, they were usually eclipsed by bazaars. These took more effort to organise but were usually the most profitable. Usually, a particular theme was chosen and committees formed to supervise each element. One might set up a savings fund so that individuals could subscribe small regular amounts to pay for an expensive household item to be purchased at the bazaar. Another might find suppliers of goods, donors of items, and creators of home-made artefacts for sale at this event, while others would arrange for performances to take place in the evenings, or the decoration of the room in which it was to be held, usually the Sunday School. Just as importantly, a large tea had to be provided as well as a refreshment stall. Everyone was busy for weeks beforehand, and there was an atmosphere of real excitement as the great day grew near, hopefully attracting hundreds to enjoy the fruits of their labour. Some bazaars raised further funds by gathering recipes and publishing them, examples including the *St. Michael's Recipe and Quotations Book* of 1905 from Mytholmroyd and *Recipes and Quotations* of 1913 from King Cross. Further fund-raising recipe books, such as St. George's Church, Sowerby Bridge's *Salute the Soldier Week: Souvenir Recipe Book* and the Red Cross and St. John Ambulance's *159 Recipes from Good Kitchens*, both of 1914, formed part of the local war effort. These are invaluable sources of what Calderdale families actually cooked and ate, for each recipe has the name and address of its contributor. Today it is difficult to appreciate the sheer quantity of hard cash that these communal efforts raised for communal use. In 1903 alone, the bazaars held in Halifax (excluding all the other jumbles, cake and apron sales) was £5,874, several millions at today's values. The average income was £90, varying from Illingworth Church's modest £30 to Pellon Church's massive £600.[271]

Some chapel teas were provided for their sect's major administrative meetings, their purpose being hospitable rather than profitable. These could prove extremely challenging for their lady organisers, as when Hebden Bridge's Hope Chapel hosted a meeting of the Yorkshire Baptist Association in 1911. Over just two days they served 575 lunches and 800 teas, preparing vast quantities of

> beef, mutton, white and brown loaves, dinner buns, salads of tomatoes,

---

1905, pp.88-90.

[270] Lonsdale Collection, *Newspaper cuttings*, vol.25, p.34.

[271] Ibid., vol.4, p.14.

THE

ST. MICHAEL'S

Recipe . .

and

Quotation

Book.

Mytholmroyd
October, 1908

Figure 28. Many churches and chapels published books or recipes and quotations contributed by members of their congregations as a means of raising much-needed funds. This is the elegant cover of a typical local example.

cucumbers, lettuce and parsley, [followed by] stewed prunes, figs and rhubarb, fruit tarts and custards, sultana cake, mixed tea cakes, mixed buns, eccles cakes, and turnovers, cracknels, coffee and cheese biscuits.[272]

In contrast, there were many lesser teas, those arranged informally with plainer, everyday home-made bread, cakes, buns, fatty-cakes and pastries. At some, even men were allowed, or almost allowed, to do the catering, having to insist that 'a fine of 1d will be levied on Ladies who assist or interfere' with their Sunday School's annual tea.[273] Just bringing along whatever one could spare and share, later known as 'faith teas', also took place as at Norwood Methodist Chapel in Todmorden. On Tuesday evenings during the summer months young folk gathered together for a meal of this kind before going for a walk, perhaps up Stoodley Pike, then returning to the chapel for cups of coffee or tea prepared by the caretaker.[274]

In many chapels, a good supply of cups, saucers and plates was built up to cater for their teas and meetings, these often being specially transfer-printed with the name and, sometimes, a picture of their place of worship. Not only did this give an additional touch of style and elegance to their tables, but it enabled any item that had gone astray to be easily recognised and returned to its proper place.

To those unfamiliar with the county, the scale and quality of a first-rate Yorkshire tea came as a complete revelation. The invitation was usually informal, but really sincere and welcoming, as a visitor to Haworth experienced early in the nineteenth century, when he was unexpectedly instructed

'Nah, Maister, yah mun stop an' hev sum te-ah, yah mun, eah, ya mun.' A bountiful table was soon spread … On sitting down to the table, a venerable woman officiated, and after filling the cups she addressed me: 'Nah, Maister, yah mun loaze th' table' (loose the table). The master said, 'Shah meeans yah mun sey 't greyce.' I took the hint, and uttered the blessing.'[275]

Similarly in 1859, when Stacy Marks was working in Halifax, decorating the magnificent interior of Colonel James Akroyd's new All Souls, Hailey Hill, he was invited to spend Sunday with a friend and his family. Already replete after

---

[272] A. Binns, *Valley of a hundred chapels,* Heptonstall, Grace Judson Press, 2013, p.65.

[273] Ibid., p.28.

[274] Calderdale Libraries, *Memory lane: recollections of Todmorden,* p.133.

[275] Gaskell, *The life of Charlotte Brontë,* p.565.

the mid-day dinner, only a short time elapsed

> before the table was spread again for an equally substantial tea … Huge hams, prodigious joints, eggs boiled or poached, with teacakes hot and buttered, washed down with copious draughts of tea, ensured present distension and future indigestion. After the entertainment of this kind it was difficult to waddle rather than walk like turkeys crammed for Christmas, to reach the station.[276]

Figure 29. *High teas in prosperous homes were quite impressive, as seen in these examples described by Charlotte Bronte (above) in 1849 and Stacy Marks in 1859 (below).*

---

[276] Crump, 'Halifax Visitors Book, Vol.1', p.121.

Had he read Charlotte Brontë's *Jane Eyre,* he would have realised that

> Yorkshire people at that time took their tea round the table. It was essential to have a multitude of plates of bread and butter, varied in sorts and plentiful in quantity; it was thought proper, too, that on the centre plate should stand a glass dish of marmalade; among the viands was expected to be found a small assortment of cheesecakes and tarts; if there was also a plate of thin slices of pink ham garnished with green parsley, so much the better.[277]

In most households this quality and range of foods made for Sunday afternoons and family celebrations was rare, being governed by the state of the local economy. When times were hard and money scarce, even a buttercake, just 'cake', meaning a piece of wheat bread or slice of bread, spread with butter, represented a luxurious treat.[278] As conditions improved, so did the teas, especially when new and cheaper ingredients became affordable due to technical innovations and the expansion of the British Empire from the middle of the nineteenth century. If possible something substantial, such as sliced boiled ham, would appear either in a mixed salad or in sandwiches, but its place could be taken by tinned lobster, Canadian salmon or sardines, often mixed with breadcrumbs, salt and pepper to make them go further.[279] Tinned fruits, such as pineapple or pears, were also popular, being eaten with sliced bread and butter for the same reason. As much variety as possible was offered, sometimes pork pies, potted meat, fish paste, jams and packet jellies joining these specially purchased foods. Just as important, or probably more so, were the home-made cakes and pastries.

Most housewives took a great pride in their home baking since it was considered to be a really important feminine skill. Most of their confectionery was baked after the bread on Thursdays, some being based on yeast-raised dough.[280] Especially from the middle of the nineteenth century, it became much easier to make a great variety of cakes and pastries as ingredients such as cornflour, ground rice, different kinds of sugars, golden syrup, currants, raisins, sultanas, candied peel, glacé cherries, and all manner of spices became both available and affordable in local shops. Even more importantly, new chemical raising agents came onto the market, bicarbonate of soda, cream of

---

[277] Brontë, *Wuthering Heights,* chapter 7.

[278] Wright, *English dialect dictionary,* under 'Cake'; Lonsdale Collection, *Newspaper cuttings,* vol.25, p.120; Travis, *Notes: (historical and biographical),* p.42.

[279] *Todmorden & Hebden Bridge Historical Almanack,* 1876, p.42.

[280] Calderdale Libraries, *Memory lane: recollections of Elland,* p.51.

tartar and a range of baking powders. Now good cakes could be easily made without the use of time-consuming yeast or expensive eggs, a great benefit for women who had to run homes with few labour-saving devices and usually spent every weekday in the mill. The following recipes are those that they baked not only for their own families, but as contributions to their chapel teas.

Pasties and Pastries

Just as oven-bottom cakes originated from bakestone cookery, so did some of the area's most characteristic confectionery, pasties or plate-pies made of a thin layer of filling sandwiched between two rounds of pastry. When cooked on a bakestone they could be baked on one side before being turned over with spittles to bake on the other. Once ovens had come into use they were simply slid onto an oven-sheet, or, for deeper fillings, put into a heat-proof plate made either of pottery or of tinplate. They remained very popular up to the 1970s-80s but are harder to find now in local shops. The simplest had a layer of jam enclosed in sweet, short pastry, and were known by various names, including short sandwich, raspberry shortcake, or:

Shortcake with jam: Mrs S. Smith, Sowerby Bridge[281]

8 oz/225 g flour
¼ tsp bicarbonate of soda
4 oz/100 g butter or margarine
4 oz/100 g sugar
1 egg, beaten
2-3 tbs raspberry jam

Sift the flour and bicarbonate, rub in the butter, mix in the sugar and finally the egg, and work gently to make a soft dough. Roll out into two 9 in/23 cm rounds, spread the jam to within ½ in/12 mm of the edge of one, dampen the edge, cover with the other round, seal the edges, pressing with a fork all round and prick the top. Bake at 180ºC/350ºF gas mark 4 for about 15 minutes. They were often brushed with milk or beaten egg and sprinkled with sugar just before going into the oven.

Deeper plate-pies were made with a plainer pastry:

---

[281] Anon., *159 recipes from good kitchens*, pp.13-14.

Figure 30. This selection of local cakes includes (1) jam filled shortcake or short sandwich, (2) bilberry pie, (3) egg custard, (4) curd cheesecake, (5) Vicarage cake, (6) gingerbread or moggy, (7) mint pasty and (8) scones.

Shortcrust pastry

8 oz/225 g flour
pinch of salt
4 oz/100 g butter, lard or dripping

Rub the fat into the flour and salt until they resemble fine breadcrumbs. Sprinkle in 2-3 tablespoons cold water and stir with a round-bladed knife until it has formed into lumps. Knead these very lightly to form a smooth pastry, cover, and leave to rest in a cool place for about 30 minutes before rolling out for use.

The local moorlands, although treeless, provided delicious wild fruits that were freely available to all who put in the time needed to gather them, for they were tiny and usually well hidden within their foliage. They were, and remain, unpredictable, some years producing bumper crops, and others virtually none. As the Rev. John Watson described in 1775, the cranberries *Vaccinium oxyoccus* as found on Warley, Sowerby and Rishworth moors were 'in high estimation for tarts', while he thought that the local cloudberries *Rubus charnaemorus* 'would make an agreeable tart'. Most popular and widespread of all, bilberries *Vaccinium myrtillus,* were 'used as food by the poor people in the months of July and August.'[282] This disparaging remark gives the impression that they were only fit for the paupers, but nothing could be further from the truth, their rich flavour and colour placing them among the finest of fruits. Even in a good year it can take hours to collect sufficient for a large pie, but it is well worth the effort and the purple-stained fingers. In use, they were usually combined with apples, since their pulp was ideal for absorbing the berries' juices.

Bilberry pie: Haworth 1867[283]

1 batch of pastry, as above
4 oz/100 g bilberries
1 medium cooking apple
2 oz/50 g sugar
beaten egg white and
sugar for glazing

Wipe the apple, make a cut around its middle, stand in an ovenproof dish with 4 tbs water and bake at 200ºC/400ºF gas mark 6 for about 40 minutes until tender and scoop out the pulp. [Alternatively peel, core and chop the apple, microwave until tender and beat with a fork]. Mix the hot pulp with the berries and sugar. Roll the pastry out into two large rounds. Use one to line a greased deep pie plate, spread the filling across it, dampen the edges, cover with the other piece having cut a hole in its centre, seal the edges, brush with the egg white and sprinkle with sugar. Bake at 200ºC/400ºF gas mark 6 for about 10 minutes, then reduce to 180ºC/350ºF gas mark 4 for a further 10 minutes.

Before leaving bilberries, as they are known throughout most of Yorkshire, it is revealing to note that their name originates from *böllebaer*, this word being introduced here by the Danish invaders of the ninth century. Before this time their Old English name was *winberige*, which explains why places where they grow at the head of the valley have names such as Whinberry Clough on Heptonstall Moor.[284]

Other fruits popular for plate pies included apples, blackberries and rhubarb.

---

[282] Watson, *The history and antiquities of the parish of Halifax,* pp.736, 741.

[283] F. White (ed.), *Good things in England: a practical cookery book for everyday use,* Originally published 1932, London, Futura, 1974, p.231; Shackleton, 'Reminiscences of shopping' in Bailey et al, *Pennine perspectives,* p.305.

[284] Grid ref SD 924303.

The rhubarb was not the delicious thin-stemmed bright pink forced rhubarb of the 'Rhubarb Triangle', south of Leeds, but the ordinary thick stemmed garden variety, from which a few plants could provide a 'fruit' when others were out of season. Despite its sour acidity, it was delicious when combined with plenty of sugar, when its raw stems were dipped into it, when stewed to accompany ground rice moulds, or when made into a plate pie.[285]

Rhubarb pie

1 batch of pastry as above
8 oz/225 g rhubarb
3 oz/75 g sugar

Remove the poisonous leaves from the rhubarb, wash the stems and chop into small lengths. Cook as in the previous recipe, but continue baking for a further 20 minutes.

Instead of retaining the original rounded shape of the bakestone and girdle, later pasties took on the square shape of the baking-sheet, this being much easier to cut into squares when divided into individual portions. Typical recipes include:

Currant or mint pasty: Mrs J. Reat, Illingworth[286]

1½ batches of pastry, as above
8 oz/225 g currants
1½ oz/35 g soft brown sugar
2 tsp finely chopped fresh mint leaves
a few drops of lemon juice or rum
1½ oz/35 g butter or margarine
milk and sugar for glazing

Roll the pastry out into a 14 in/35 cm square. Spread the mixed currants, sugar and mint over one half, add the lemon juice or rum, and dot with the butter or margarine. Dampen the edges, fold the empty half over to form a lid, seal the edges, prick with a fork, brush with milk and sprinkle with sugar. Bake at 200°C/400°F gas mark 6 for 20-25 minutes.

---

[285] Shackleton, 'Reminiscences of shopping' in Bailey et al, *Pennine perspectives,* p.307.
[286] Kaye, *Yorkshire cooking,* p.199.

How d'you pasty: Mrs A. Terry, Skircoat Green[287]

1½ batches of pastry, as above
12 oz/350 g currants
2 oz/50 g candied peel
2 tbs brown sugar
1 tbs golden syrup

Wash the currants, shake off the surplus water in a sieve and mix with the peel, sugar and syrup over a gentle heat for a few minutes, then leave to cool and bake as in the recipe above for 30 minutes.

The advent of ovens enabled deeper pastries to be baked, one of the most popular being 'flawns' or egg custards, both large and individual. As the following recipe shows, their crusts were thick and, not being blind-baked beforehand, rather soggy. These features mattered little when cheap pastry was essential to make a meal substantial and satisfying for people used to hard physical labour.

Baked egg custard: Mrs G. Greaves, Mytholmroyd[288]

2 eggs, beaten
4 tbs caster sugar
pinch of salt [pinch of nutmeg]
1 pt/600 ml milk

Pastry
1 lb/450 g flour
1 tsp baking powder
¼ tsp salt
8 oz/225 g lard

Sift the baking powder and salt into the flour, rub in the lard and mix with 3-4 tbs cold water to make the pastry. Roll this out and use to line a greased 8 in/20 cm diameter pie dish. Beat the eggs, sugar and salt into the milk for 5 minutes, stir over a gentle heat until starting to thicken, but without boiling, pour into the pastry case, sprinkle on the nutmeg, and bake at 150ºC/300ºF gas mark 2 for about an hour, until the custard has set but not curdled. Serve cold, directly from the dish.

---

[287] Ibid.

[288] Ashton et al, *The St Michael's recipe and quotation book,* p.29.

Yorkshire is known for its cheesecakes, also known as curd tarts. Their main ingredient, curds, were made from various combinations of fresh milk, buttermilk, Epsom salts and rennet that produced something like a cottage cheese. They were popular in the Dales and other dairying areas, but not in the South Pennines, since there was such a great demand for fresh milk and butter.[289] As a result, none of the local cheesecakes contained curds. Beestings cheesecakes were sometimes made from the rich milk produced by a cow just after calving, the result being a thick custard, but others were based on apples, almonds, potatoes or rice.

Apple cheesecakes[290]

4 oz/100 g peeled, cored and grated apple
4 oz/100 g sugar
4 oz/100g. melted butter
grated zest of ½ lemon
1 egg, beaten

Mix together the grated apple, sugar and butter and zest, finally beating in the egg. Put into deep individual tart tins lined with shortcrust pastry (see p.123) and bake at 180ºC/350ºF gas mark 4 for about 30 minutes.

Almond cheesecakes[291]

6½oz/165 g ground almonds
6½oz/165 g caster sugar
2 egg yolks, beaten
1 drop almond essence
raspberry jam

Mix the almonds with the sugar and beat in the yolks and essence. Put a little raspberry jam into the bottom of each cheesecake before adding the mixture. Bake as the recipe above.

Potato cheesecakes[292]

6 oz/150 g mashed potato

---

[289] Brears, *Traditional food in Yorkshire,* p.207.
[290] West family, *Manuscript,* pp.14, 29, 30.
[291] Ibid., p.30.
[292] Ibid., p.14.

1½ oz/35 g melted butter
3 oz/75 g currants
½ oz/12 g candied peel or grated rind of ½ lemon
4 oz/100 g sugar
1 egg, beaten

Beat the butter into the potatoes, then the dry ingredients, and finally the egg. Bake as the apple cheesecake above.

Rice cheesecakes[293]

3 oz/73 g each of melted butter, sugar and currants
2 oz/50 g rice flour
1½ oz/35 g flour
½ tsp bicarbonate of soda
1 drop lemon essence [or grated rind of ½ lemon]
2 eggs, beaten

Mix the dry ingredients, then stir in the melted butter, the essence and the eggs. Bake as the apple cheesecake above.

Scones

Just like pasties, scones appear to have developed from crude suet cakes baked on bakestones and girdles, the addition of raising agents, butter and eggs, along with oven-baking, making them much lighter and richer. They were usually served cold, split across the middle, thickly buttered and sometimes spread with jam too.

Sultana scones: Miss D. Grimshaw, Todmorden[294]

8 oz/225 g flour
½ tsp salt
½ tsp bicarbonate of soda
½ tsp cream of tartar
2 oz/50 g margarine [or butter]
1 oz/25 g sultanas
1 egg, beaten
¼ pt/150 ml milk

Sift the flour, salt, bicarbonate of soda and cream of tartar together,

---

[293] West family, *Manuscript recipe book*, p.29.

[294] Grimshaw, *Manuscript recipe book*.

rub in the margarine or butter and add the sultanas. Mix in the egg with sufficient milk to make a soft dough, turn out onto a floured board, roll out about ¾ in/2 cm thick and cut into rounds. Bake at 200ºC/400ºF gas mark 6 for about 10 minutes until well-risen and browned.

Wheaten scones: Miss D. Grimshaw, Todmorden[295]

4 oz/100 g wholemeal flour
4 oz/100 g plain flour
½ tsp bicarbonate of soda
½ tsp cream of tartar
1 oz/25 g margarine [or butter]
7 tbs milk

Mix the flours, bicarbonate of soda and cream of tartar, rub in the margarine or butter, and work in just sufficient milk to make a soft dough. Bake as in the recipe above.

Cakes

Up to the mid-nineteenth century, the absence of ovens made it impossible for most working families to bake their own cakes, but fortunately the spread of ovens coincided with the growing availability of wheat flour, raising agents and the increased ability to afford ingredients such as sugar, eggs and spices. These enabled housewives to make a number of cakes that had previously been restricted to middle-class households and professional bakeries. They included plain sponges, flavoured sponges and fruit cakes.[296] Feather cakes, 'light as a feather' featured in a local folk song that questioned the domestic skills of an intended bride. Sung to the tune of 'Billy Boy' it asked her boyfriend:

> Can she cook and can she bake?
>   Billy Boy, Billy Boy.
> Can she cook and can she bake?
>   Charlie Willy
> She can cook and she can bake,
>   Aye, and make a feather cake,
> But she's young and she can't leave her mammy.[297]

---

[295] Ibid.

[296] King Cross [Wesleyan] Circuit, *Recipes and quotations,* p.39.

[297] Brears, *Traditional food in Yorkshire,* p.212.

Feather cake: King Cross[298]

8 oz/225 g flour
8 oz/225 g sugar
3 tsp baking powder
4 oz/100 g butter
3 eggs, beaten

Mix the dry ingredients, rub in the butter, stir in the eggs, pour into a 12 x 8 in/30 x 20 cm greased and lined dripping tin and bake at 180°C/350°F gas mark 4 for 30 minutes.

Norland cake: Mrs A.E. Whiteley, Sowerby Bridge[299]

4 oz/100 g butter
4 oz/100 g sugar
2 eggs, beaten
6 oz/150 g flour
2 tsp cream of tartar
1 tsp bicarbonate of soda
¼ pt/150 ml milk

Cream the butter with the sugar and beat in the egg little by little. Sift the flour with the cream of tartar and beat into the mixture, then beat in the bicarbonate of soda dissolved in the milk. Put into a greased and lined 8 in/20 cm square tin and bake at 150°C/300°F gas mark 2 for 1 hour. Serve cut into either slices or squares.

Seed loaf: Mrs J. Mitchell, Mytholmroyd[300]

8 oz/225 g flour
3 oz/75 g butter
6 oz/150 g sugar
2 tsp baking powder
3 tsp caraway seeds
2 eggs, beaten
6 tbs milk

---

[298] King Cross [Wesleyan] Circuit, *Recipes and quotations*, p.39; Ashton et al, *The St Michael's recipe and quotation book*, p.30.

[299] Anon., *159 recipes from good kitchens*, p.40.

[300] Ashton et al, *The St Michael's recipe and quotation book*, p.27.

Rub the butter in to the flour, mix in the dry ingredients, then the eggs and milk. Put into a greased and lined loaf tin and bake at 150°C/300°F gas mark 2 for 50 minutes.

The homes of the clergy, whether Church of England, Roman Catholic or Nonconformist, were always busy social hubs, with a constant stream of callers who all expected the basic hospitality of a cup of tea and a slice of cake. Wives and housekeepers, therefore, needed to have easily-made and good quality cakes always ready in their pantries.

[Vicarage] cake: Mrs Metcalf, Mytholmroyd[301]

8 oz/225 g flour
1 tsp bicarbonate of soda
½ tsp allspice
½ tsp mixed spice
4 oz/100 g butter or dripping
4 oz/100 g demerara sugar
8 oz/225 g Valencia raisins
½ pt/300 ml milk

Sift the bicarbonate of soda and spices with the flour, rub in the fat, mix in the sugar and raisins and then the milk to produce a soft mixture. Put into a greased and lined loaf tin and bake at 150°C/300°F gas mark 2 for 2 hours.

In the period when the Bible was studied in Sunday schools, in churches, in chapels and in private, it is not surprising that someone managed to combine various ingredients listed in its chapters and verses into a cake recipe. Considered to be particularly appropriate for all manner of religious meetings, it is found in numerous church bazaar cookery books. The instructions usually quote King Solomon's advice for making a good boy in Proverbs chapter XXII verse 14 'Thou shalt beat him with a rod'.

Scripture or bible cake: King Cross, Halifax[302]

4 oz/100 g butter	*Judges v 25*
4 oz/100 g sugar	*Jeremiah vi 20*

---

[301] Ashton et al, *The St Michael's recipe and quotation book*, p.8.

[302] King Cross [Wesleyan] Circuit, *Recipes and quotations*, p.50; Ashton et al, *The St Michael's recipe and quotation book*, p.26.

3 eggs, beaten	*Jeremiah xvii 11*
8 oz/225 g flour	*I Kings iv 22*
½ tsp mixed spice	*II Chronicles ix 9*
pinch of salt	*Leviticus ii 13*
1 tbs honey	*I Samuel xiv 25*
4 oz/100 g raisins	*I Samuel xxx 12*
4 oz/100 g figs, chopped	*Nakum iii 12*
4 oz/100 g almonds,	*Numbers xvii 8*
bleached & chopped	
½ tsp baking powder	*Amos iv 19*
2 tbs milk	*Judges iv 19*

Cream the butter with the sugar then beat in the eggs, little by little, and mix in the flour, mixed spice, salt and honey, followed by the raisins, figs and almonds, and finally the baking powder dissolved in the milk. Put into a greased and lined 8 in/20 cm diameter cake tin and bake at 180ºC/350ºF gas mark 4 for about 1 hour.

Currant loaf: West Family[303]

3 oz/75 g butter
3 oz/75 g sugar
2 eggs, beaten
1 tsp bicarbonate of soda
¼ tsp cream of tartar
8 oz/225 g flour
4 fl. oz/100 ml milk
6 oz/150 g currants
1 oz/25 g chopped candied peel

Cream the butter with the sugar, then beat in the eggs little by little. Sift the bicarbonate of soda and cream of tartar with the flour and beat into the creamed mixture little by little, adding just sufficient milk to form a dropping mixture. Mix in the currants and peel, turn into a greased and lined loaf tin and bake at 170ºC/325ºF gas mark 3 for about 1½ hours.

In the late nineteenth century commercial bakers began to sell fruited malt loaves sweetened, flavoured and enriched with sticky brown malt extract. Home made versions used cheaper black treacle to produce similar results.

---

[303] West family, *Manuscript recipe book*, p.27.

Sticky bread: Mrs Joe Siddall, Sowerby Bridge[304]

6 oz/150 g wholemeal flour
2 oz/50 g plain flour
3 oz/75 g sugar
2 oz/50 g sultanas
2 tsp baking powder
1 tsp bicarbonate of soda
¼ pt/150 ml milk

Mix the dry ingredients together, except the bicarbonate of soda, which should be dissolved in the milk before stirring into the mixture to produce a dropping consistency. Put into a greased and lined loaf tin and bake at 150ºC/300ºF gas mark 2 for about 50 minutes. Keep for a few days to soften before eating.

Traditional oatmeal-based parkins had long been popular for Plot Night on 5 November, but now much lighter flour sponge gingerbreads became popular, these often being known as 'moggy'. There are numerous recipes, some retaining oatmeal, some including eggs, some with black treacle and some with golden syrup, but all were baked in a shallow rectangular dripping pan and served cut in thin slices.

Gingerbread: Miss R. Greenfield, Dean Hey[305]

12 oz/340 g flour
1 heaped tsp ginger
1 tsp bicarbonate of soda
½ tsp cream of tartar
6 oz/150 g sugar
1½ oz/35 g melted lard or butter
8 oz/225 g black treacle or golden syrup
½ pt/300 ml tepid milk

Sift the flour with the bicarbonate of soda and cream of tartar, and mix in the sugar. Make a well in the centre, pour in the melted lard or butter with the warmed treacle or syrup and the milk and stir together until smooth. Put into a greased and lined 7 x 9 in/18 x 23 cm dripping tin and bake at 150ºC/300ºF gas mark 2 for about 1

---

[304] Anon., *159 recipes from good kitchens*, p.9.

[305] Ashton et al, *The St Michael's recipe and quotation book*, p.22.

hour. If liked 2-3 tsp of caraway seeds may be mixed in before baking.

As described earlier, the use of oatmeal as the area's main bread-corn declined during the Victorian period, but home bakers soon developed new recipes for retaining it on the tea-table.

Oatmeal biscuits: Mrs A. Wilcock, Hall Gate[306]

6 oz/150 g fine or medium oatmeal
5 oz/125 g flour
3 oz/75 g sugar
1 tsp baking powder
1 egg, beaten
4 oz/100 g lard

Mix the dry ingredients, then work in the egg and melted lard to form a stiff pastry. Roll out thin on a floured board, cut into rounds and bake at 150°C/350°F gas mark 4 for about 20 minutes.

Oatmeal buns: West Family[307]

6 oz/150 g fine or medium oatmeal
5 oz/125 g flour
4 oz/100 g sugar
¼ tsp salt
1½ tsp baking powder
1 egg, beaten
6 tbs milk

Mix the dry ingredients, then work in the egg with just sufficient milk to form a dropping consistency. Drop golf-ball sized lumps from a fork onto a greased baking sheet and bake at 150°C/350°F gas mark 4 for 35 minutes.

With the bakery completed, the housewife could confidently provide the contents of the tea table that could satisfy her family, friends and visitors. This was certainly the experience of the Rev. Patrick Brontë, who clearly enjoyed being entertained in the homes of his parishioners, the 'Happy Cottagers', where:

---

[306] Ibid., p.24

[307] West family, *Manuscript recipe book*, p.49.

The table-cloth, though coarse,
Was of a snowy white;
The vessels, spoons and knives
Were clean and dazzling bright;
So down we sat – devoid of care,
Nor envied Kings – their dainty fare.[308]

Composed in 1811, in the hungry years of the Napoleonic wars, many really would have envied the lavish dishes being set before their Regent, the Prince of Wales, but fortunately these were well beyond their comprehension.

Figure 31. *The Rev. Patrick Brontë was impressed by the pristine tablecloths and polished tablewares set before him when being entertained in the homes of local cottagers.*

[308] J.H. Turner, *Haworth past and present: a history of Haworth, Stanbury & Oxenhope*, Brighouse, J.S. Jowett, 1879, p.171.

Figure 32. The mistal (cow-house) at Walt Royd, Wheatley, showing the shorthorn cows in their individual 'booses'.

CHAPTER 9

FROM THE DAIRY

Today there are relatively few dairy herds in the South Pennines compared to earlier centuries. This is partly due to economic changes, and partly to the banning of cattle from the uplands that fed the reservoirs providing water to the adjacent cities, towns and villages. This absence is deceptive, since dairying has always formed an important part of local farming and industrial life. As the Rev. Watson explained in 1775,

> everyone who can, takes as much [land] as will yield a sufficient quantity of milk and butter for the support of his family; on this account it proves difficult for many of the poor to get these things.[309]

For this reason, most clothiers' houses on the hillsides had a cow-house called a mistal (Old English for a dung-place for cattle) in their barn or outbuilding. Here the cows were tethered in 'booses' by rope or chain seals passed around their necks from autumn through to the spring. They were fed here on hay which had been harvested the previous summer and packed down hard in the haymow above.[310] This was now cut out in blocks and shaken loose to drop down into the 'hecks' or racks before each animal. With the arrival of warmer weather and a new growth of vegetation, they were turned out either into closes to pasture, or the fringes of the moors to graze.

From the early nineteenth century most were Dairy Shorthorns with grizzled red and brown coats and patches of white, this breed being good milkers that could be fattened up for the beef trade at the end of their working lives. According to Betty Sunderland of Far New Fly near Nab Hill, a good cow should be

> … but short in her face, fine in her horn;
> She'll quickly get fat, without cake or corn;
> She's clean in her jaws, she's full in her chine;
> Heavy in flank, and wide in her loin,
> Broad in her ribs, long in her rump.
> Straight, and flat back, with never a hump;
> She's wide in her hips, calm in her eyes,
> Broad in her shoulders, thick in her thighs;
> Light in her neck, small in her tail;

---

[309] Watson, *The history and antiquities of the parish of Halifax*, p.8.
[310] Crump, *The little hill farm*, pp.36-37.

Broad in her breast, good in her pail;
Fine in her bone, silky of skin,
Greasy without, all soundness within.[311]

Milk

The importance of milk production on the hill farms from the late seventeenth century saw some farmers investing considerable resources and labour into making new enclosures from the moors. Some, such as in Haworth, had detached field barns with mistals for housing and milking their enlarged herds. Those now standing as ruins in the Withins area of Stanbury Moor date from c.1620-1679, but remained in use through to the mid-nineteenth century.[312] The reason for providing far more milk than was needed for home consumption was due to the demands of the domestic textile workers. They always ate their daily meals of porridge with milk, and if they couldn't keep a cow for themselves, they had to find it elsewhere. Their usual practice was to collect it from the farms soon after morning milking. William Hanson who was born in Soyland in 1804 had the childhood memory of his mother who 'rose early to attend to the milk and prepare it for those who came for it'.[313] Charlotte Brontë was familiar with this practice, describing it in her 'Shirley' of 1849:

> the court and kitchen [were] crowded with excited milk-fetchers – men, women and children, whom Mrs Gill, the housekeeper, appeared vainly persuading to take their milk-cans and depart. It is, or was, by-the-by, the custom in the north of England for the cottagers in the country squire's estate to receive their supplies of milk and butter from the dairy of the Manor House.[314]

The same scene took place most mornings in small farms too, some Stanbury folk walking down to Dolly Moor on the opposite side of Sladen valley to collect their milk from Mrs Sunderland about the same period.[315]

As the domestic industry declined in the early to mid-nineteenth century, the new textile mills drew in thousands of workers who, living in small terrace houses, had no land, but still required their daily milk. This resulted in a milk famine around the time of the Napoleonic wars, when George Haigh of Copley Gate was told by the Luddites that they would shoot him unless he agreed to

---

[311] Turner, *A spring-time saunter,* p.75.

[312] Wood & Brears, *The real Wuthering Heights,* p.15, plates 1-3, 7, 11

[313] Crump, *The little hill farm,* p.14.

[314] C. Brontë, *Shirley,* 1849. Reprinted London, Everyman's Library, 2008, pp.360-361.

[315] Craven, *A Brontë moorland village,* p.88.

sell his milk to his neighbours. It was this shortage that promoted the use of tea as a substitute for milk.[316] To meet this growing demand, a number of large households invested in new large purpose-built dairies. In order to keep them ideally cool and fresh, many were built underground and so remain largely hidden today. One at Forks House on Stanbury Moor took the form of a cellar extending northwards from the back of the house, the stones of its vaulted roof being protected by a ground-level stone-flagged roof.[317] More sophisticated examples involved excavating a new basement storey beneath the housebodies or halls of major period houses, a considerable feat of domestic engineering. This took place at Great House, Colden, where stone shelves were installed to carry large lead cream-settling pans, and a channel left in the floor for a constant stream of spring water.

The work of a dairy revolved around morning milking at around 6 a.m. and evening milking at 5 p.m., these taking place indoors in winter, and outdoors in summer, as on Milking Hill.[318] Using coopered wooden milk kits, usually replaced by metal ones around 1900, the milk was carried into the dairy. Here, probably being cooled in a trough of running water, it was strained through a sile. This was a wooden bowl with a hole in its base across which a piece of clean muslin was tied, or later one of metal fitted with a piece of fine brass gauze sometimes covered by a cotton wool filter cloth. This removed all dirt, scraps of vegetation and bovine dandruff, leaving the milk to pass through into a cream-settling pan.

Some of these were wide, shallow lead-glazed bowls made at one of the local potteries, while those who could afford them preferred large rectangular ones of sheet lead with sloping sides and a plug-hole sealed with a long conical brass plug.[319] After a day, or possibly two, the cream had risen to the surface from where it was carefully skimmed off using a 'shank', a saucer-like turned wooden bowl that took its name from an Old English word meaning 'to pour out'.[320] Those using lead dishes simply eased up the plug, allowed the milk to drain off, and gently scrape off the remaining cream. These practices generally ceased from around 1900, when the first of the local farmers invested in one of

---

[316] T.W. Hanson, *The story of old Halifax,* Halifax, 1920, p.235

[317] Grid ref. SD 984358.

[318] Grid ref. SD 984358.

[319] Calderdale Libraries, *Memory lane: recollections of Sowerby Bridge,* p.8.

[320] Watson, *The history and antiquities of the parish of Halifax,* p.546; Wright, *English dialect dictionary,* under 'Shank'.

the new centrifugal milk separators. Though expensive, these hand-turned machines extracted far more cream than any of the older methods, and soon covered their costs.[321]

Figure 33. Setting off to deliver the milk from Kitson Royd Farm, Cornholme.

Once the cream had been removed, the remaining skimmed milk was kept cool in jugs ready to be collected, as long as that arrangement worked. However, it soon broke down as larger quantities were demanded by factory workers. At this stage milk began to be delivered either to small shops or as door-to-door sales directly from the farm. Small family farms in the Upper Calder valley now used special saddle-shaped tinplate milk churns that fitted on a donkey's packsaddle, a tap on each side running the milk off into measures.[322] Customers could now leave their jugs out on their doorsteps or windowsills, often with a saucer on top to keep out birds, insects and smuts of soot, and have them filled when the milkman called. Others used tall cylindrical churns that could be carried round the streets with a horse and trap, the predecessor of the later milk-floats and their crates of bottled milk.

Butter
A little of the cream may have been used in hot drinks, poured over desserts or

---

[321] Crump, *The little hill farm*, p.32.

[322] *Milltown Memories*, 2004, 7, p.51.

used as a cooking ingredient, but most was converted into butter. To do this it was stored for a few days in glazed earthenware cream pots before being agitated in a butter churn, causing the fat globules to gather together. The earliest churns were of the vertical cylindrical plunge-type, in which a pierced piston-like plunger, called a dasher, was worked up and down by hand. The older ones were cooper-made in oak with iron bands, but by the mid-nineteenth century local potteries were producing them in black or brown lead-glazed earthenware, while at Eccleshill Pottery in north-west Bradford they were of brown salt-glaze, with bands of impressed decoration. One of these was collected from Ripponden Wood Farm by W.B. Crump in 1913.[323]

Later churns were sometimes made of light, tough tinplate, easy to use, clean and easy to handle, but subject to rust if they got scratched.[324] Where larger quantities were to be churned, barrel churns were used, the cream being poured through a hatch into a horizontally-mounted barrel with a turning handle to one side.[325] In 1880 end-over-end churns having the barrel rotating on pegs projecting from their sides were invented by William Wade & Sons of Leeds, these becoming quite popular. A typical 20 gallon model would produce about 65 lb of butter at a single churning.

Sometimes, particularly if the temperature was unsuitable, the butter would not separate, even after several hours of labour. This was usually attributed to witchcraft and could only be solved by consulting one of the local wise men. At a farm near Pecket Well they churned for two days before going to see a 'witch doctor' in Cragg Vale. He gave them a written charm to be taken home and placed over the verse in the family bible reading 'Thou shalt not suffer a witch to live', after which the churn and its contents had to be put into the nearest stream. Not surprisingly, this worked![326] When the same problem arose in Todmorden, another 'witch doctor' was called in who first tried various methods of exorcising 'the old bitch' who was deemed responsible. As this met with no success, his next attempt involved heating an iron chain red-hot in a fire and then wrapping it around the bottom of the churn. This also failed completely and the 'doctor' could suggest nothing else. Eventually the family

---

[323] Crump, *The little hill farm,* p.32. P. Brears, *The old Devon farmhouse,* Tiverton, Devon Books, 1998, p.105 no.1432.

[324] Cliffe Castle Museum, Keighley, no.159.55.

[325] Wood, S., *Haworth, Oxenhope & Stanbury from old photographs,* Stroud, Amberley, 2011, p.51.

[326] Lonsdale Collection, *Newspaper cuttings,* vol.5, p.2.

added fresh cream brought from a relative living two miles away, and success was finally achieved. One way of averting such witchcraft was to nail up a rusty horseshoe in the mistal.[327]

Local farmers experienced a quite different problem during the First World War when the Food Committee for Todmorden and Sowerby Bridge ruled that all milk had to be available to the public. Some had continued to make butter, which was now considered to be an unacceptable luxury, and when threatened with prosecution decided to strike, halting milk deliveries into the villages and towns. As a result, local people carried all manner of containers up to the farms to collect their milk just as their parents and grandparents had done, but fortunately everything quickly returned to normal.[328] In many homes butter and cream were still considered to be rare luxuries. One family remembered skimming the cream from the top of the milk and pouring it into an old treacle tin on the mantelpiece so that everyone who came by could give it a good shake until small balls of butter finally formed.[329]

Churning was just the first step of butter making. If left as it came out of the churn, it would rapidly turn rancid as its intermixed buttermilk turned sour. To prevent this, the butter was taken out of the churn using wooden scoops. It was then put into a large, freshly scalded and cold-rinsed sycamore bowl that was held crooked in one arm, while the free hand pressed and beat it to expel the buttermilk.[330] Once the bowl had been rinsed again and dried, the butter was replaced and kneaded with the salt that would both improve its keeping qualities and enhance its flavour. Finally the butter was turned out onto a scalded and rinsed butter board, divided into lumps of standard weights and either beaten into rectangular blocks using grooved 'scotch hands' or turned out of cylindrical moulds ready for sale. At Upper Hanroyd in Midgley, the butter was stamped with a butter pat bearing a sheaf of corn design, other farms having different stamps by which customers could recognise where their butter came from.[331] As for the buttermilk, this might be drunk or used for making cakes and sponges, but most was fed to livestock, especially the pigs.

---

[327] Travis, *Notes: (historical and biographical)*, pp.17-18.

[328] Thomas, *Hardship and hope*, pp.89, 95.

[329] Calderdale Libraries, *Memory lane: recollections of Todmorden*, p.14.

[330] Wood, *Haworth, Oxenhope & Stanbury from old photographs*, p.51. Crump, *The little hill farm*, p.29; Cliffe Castle Museum, Keighley, no.877.

[331] Hartley and Ingilby, *Life and tradition in West Yorkshire*, p.104; Calderdale Museums, 1952/8, 1952/15.

Figure 34. *Mrs Greenwood moulding butter in her dairy at Outwood, Crimsworth Dean.*

Cheese

Since there was such a great local demand for skimmed milk and butter, only small cheeses were made here, just sufficient for home consumption. For these the milk was warmed to blood heat and curdled with 'keslops', a home-made rennet made from the salted stomach and contents of a young calf, rich in the necessary enzymes. This turned the milk into a delicate almost jelly-like curd which was sliced into small cubes and hung in a piece of muslin to drain. Rather than the normal cylindrical cooper-made cheese vats and large cheese presses used elsewhere, here lead-glazed earthenware versions were produced by the local potteries. They took the form of tall jars pierced by numerous holes and having a very thick, heavy plunger or 'follower' to slide down inside.[332] Having been mixed with a little salt, the curds were next packed into the muslin-lined vat, the follower placed on top, and then left for a few days to drain. Now compacted into a 2-3 lb/900 g-1.3 kg cheese, it was stored in a cool place and turned upside down every day until required for use.

---

[332] There are examples in Calderdale and Cliffe Castle Museums no.740.

143

To make a 2 lb cheese

This recipe recreates the method probably used to make cheese in a Halifax Pottery cheese press.

12 pt/6.9 l whole milk
7 tbs junket rennet
1 oz/25 g salt

Equipment: a large pan, a thermometer, a 30 in/75 cm and two 20 in/12.5 cm squares of muslin, a sieve, string, a cylindrical plastic storage jar 5 in/12.5 cm in height and diameter with its sides and base drilled with a series of small holes, and a disc to fit within it and a weight.

Gently heat the milk in the pan to 37ºC, remove from the heat, quickly stir in the rennet, cover, and set aside for 1 hour. Using a long knife, cut the curd into ½ in/1 cm squares and leave for a further 30 minutes. Having lined a large bowl with the large square of muslin, use a sieve to scoop the curd from the pan into the muslin, gather the corners together and hang up over a bowl to drain for 12 hours.

Put the drained bag into a bowl, open the top and use the hands to break up the curds and mix in the salt. Line the plastic jar with a smaller piece of muslin, pack in the curd, place the disc on top, add 3 lb/1.35 kg weight on top and leave in a cool place to drain over the next three days, changing the muslin and inverting the cheese once every day. Remove the cheese from the mould, and replace the muslin with circular pieces overlapping each end and a strip wrapped around the sides. Store in a cool, well-ventilated place for a few weeks, inverting it every day, and then use as required.

The whey was usually fed to the pigs, but today it may form a smooth cooling drink, perhaps flavoured with fresh fruit juice and a little sugar.

For those who wanted to include cheese in their diet, the nearest source was North Lancashire, that county's delicious cheese being carried over the border by cheesemongers and cheese factors from the early nineteenth century.[333] It was also stocked on market stalls and in grocers' shops, just as it is today. In later years, particularly with the spread of Co-operative stores, other cheeses became available, especially Cheshire, to provide 'bait' or 'jock' to take to work, to be eaten with raw onions for suppers, and to accompany onions in pasties.

---

[333] *The Commercial Directory for 1818-19-20*, Manchester, James Pigot, 1818, p.147.

When toasted as a rarebit, it formed a quick snack, or could be baked as a savoury custard:

Figure 35. To be exempt from window tax, dairy windows bore the word 'DAIRY' (1 Top Withins). Pails full of milk were carried in using a yoke (2 from Keighley), their contents being strained through a 'sile' supported on a 'brig' over a milk-pan (3). The cream was then skimmed off using a fleeting dish (4), leaving the skim-milk to be distributed in a delivery churn, a donkey 'saddle' churn or a milk can (5-7 from Todmorden). Having been stored in a cream-pot (8) the cream was churned in a barrel-churn (9 from Farther Isle Farm, Stanbury c.1890) or a plunge churn (10 from Keighley, 11 Halifax pottery, 12 Eccleshill stoneware, from Ripponden Wood Farm) until it turned into butter. The small quantity of cheese made locally was pressed either in Halifax pottery vats (13) or in wooden vats under a screw press (14 from Cowhouse Farm, Cullingworth).

Savoury toasts: R.H., Mytholmroyd[334]

crustless bread ½ in/1.3 cm thick and 2½ in/6.4 cm square
4 tbs grated cheese
4 tbs minced boiled ham
a little mustard
butter for frying and spreading

Thickly butter the squares of bread, add a thin layer of mustard, then a thick layer of the mixed cheese, ham, and cayenne. Shallow fry in a little butter, melt the cheese under the grill (originally a Dutch oven in front of the open fire) and serve piping hot.

A nice supper dish: Miss L.A. Sharp, Halifax[335]

2 thick slices of bread, buttered
4 oz/100 g grated cheese
2 eggs, beaten
1 pt/600 ml milk
pepper & salt to taste

Butter a fireproof dish, then the bread, and spread with half the cheese. Beat the remaining ingredients together, pour over the bread and bake at 180ºC/350ºF gas mark 4, for 30 minutes, until browned on the top.

Bread & cheese pudding: Mrs M. Fowler, Stainland[336]

2oz/50 g each, grated cheese & fresh breadcrumbs
⅛ tsp mustard powder
pinch cayenne pepper
1 egg, beaten
1 oz/25 g butter

Mix the dry ingredients, then the egg, and finally the butter warmed until just liquid. Put into a pie dish and bake at 180ºC/350ºF gas mark 4 for about 30 minutes.

---

[334] Ashton et al, *The St Michael's recipe and quotation book,* p.10.

[335] King Cross [Wesleyan] Circuit, *Recipes and quotations,* p.27.

[336] Kaye, *Yorkshire cooking,* p.186.

Cheese & onion pie: Nurse Wall, Hebden Bridge[337]

2 large or 3 smaller onions
3 oz/75 g grated cheese
2 tbs milk
1 tsp salt
pinch ground black pepper
1 oz/25 g butter
Shortcrust pastry made with 12 oz/350 g flour and 6 oz/175 g lard.

Boil the onions for 15-20 minutes until tender, drain, remove the outer brown skin and finely chop the rest. When cold, mix in all but the butter. Use half the pastry to line a shallow greased pie dish or plate, put in the onion mixture, dot with the butter, cover with the remaining pastry, seal the edges, prick the top with a fork, and bake at 190°C/375°F gas mark 5 for about 25-50 minutes. Serve either hot or cold.

Figure 36. Cheese and onion pie was popular for both family and communal meals.

---

[337] St John's Church, *Good recipes: a souvenir*, Hebden Bridge, 1933, p.11.

Figure 37. This former well at Hebden Bridge had carved stone 'Old Man's Faces' to protect its water as it emerged from beneath the ground.

CHAPTER 10

DRINKS

One of the great advantages of living on Pennine hillsides was the ready availability of plentiful supplies of clean, soft, fresh-tasting drinking water. Much of the 40-60 in of rain that fell on 225 days of each year was captured in the peaty moorlands, from which it gradually descended over the impervious gritstone beds of countless narrow 'sykes' to eventually join the rivers flowing along the bottoms of the valleys. As the Rev. John Watson described in 1775, the Halifax parish 'abounds with common springs, as most hilly countries do'.[338] These often rise just below the tops, that at Top Withins being 1,376 ft (420 m) above sea level, for example, enabling villages and numerous farms to be established along their channels as they splashed down the hillsides. Most were open to the air, while many others, those flowing through pastures, have lengths enclosed in stone-lined culverts and grassed over to keep them free from pollution. This was particularly important when successive properties lay one below another down their course, a geographical situation that often led to disagreements among neighbours. Water was not only essential for drinking, but also for cooking, brewing, washing, dairying, wool-textile production and watering cattle over-wintering in the barns.

The rights to take water have long been established by legal agreements, as William Bentley's will carefully specified when dividing his land on Stanbury Moor between his three sons in 1591.[339] A few years earlier, in 1586, Ambrose Greenwood and William Briggs had disputed how the water of the syke of their village of Old Town should be controlled, Greenwood winning the case.[340] Over three centuries later, to make sure that everyone knew who owned Old Town's major source of water, the following lines were carved on stone tablets above their long troughs:

> THIS IS THE SPOUT & SITE OF
> THE OWLER-SYKE & ANCIENT WATERCOURSE OVER WHICH
> BRIGWELLHEAD WATER HAS
> FLOWED CONTINUOUSLY FROM 1600 A.D. UNTIL 1900
> A.D. WHEN IT WAS TURNED INTO

---

[338] Watson, *The history and antiquities of the parish of Halifax*, p.17.

[339] Wood & Brears, *The real Wuthering Heights*, p.10.

[340] Ogden, J.H., 'Burlees and Old Town', *Transactions of the Halifax Antiquarian Society*, 1904, 73-92 at p.89.

OLD TOWN RESERVOIR BY Wm., Hy.
& JOHN COUSIN MITCHELL.

THIS IS THE NO. 1. DIVISION STONE
WHICH UNTIL A.D. 1900 DIVIDED
BRIGEWELLHEAD WATER, ONE
PART FLOWING TO BOSTONHILL &
THE REMAINDER TO OLD TOWN HALL
ESTATES. THIS DIVISION STONE WAS
PLACED IN ANCIENT WATERCOURSE AT
THE JOINT EXPENCE OF JOHN COUSIN
OF OLD TOWN HALL & Wm. COUSIN
OF BOSTON HILL A.D. 1838.

THIS IS THE SITE WHERE THE
ANCIENT WATERCOURSE
CROSSED THE OLD TOWN ROAD
ALL THE WATER FLOWING
DOWN THE CHANNEL ON TO
OLD TOWN HALL ESTATE.

The expense involved in erecting permanent immovable memorials of this kind clearly demonstrates the importance attached to water rights in the area.

For practical purposes, the water was usually fed into stone troughs hollowed out of massive rectangular blocks of gritstone, these being found both close to houses and set into roadside walls, an overflow at the rim running off the surplus into a drain below. Despite having no deep shafts and containing running rather than static water, they were usually called 'wells', whether springs or conduited from streams. Most towns and villages had their own communal well. Since before 1398 the Old Well Head spring had served Halifax half a mile to the north-east, where Well Street ran just north of the parish church.[341] Similarly the spring at Well Head Lane supplied Sowerby half a mile to the north-north-east of the village and Todmorden's wells lay just north of the railway viaduct and south of the canal bridge, as commemorated in Well Lane and Well Street. In Haworth there were two public wells, the Head Well on Well Street off West Street, north of the church, and the Brigg Well towards the bottom of Main Street. All those dependent on such wells, usually women, scooped up their water into cans, of which there were two kinds. The larger metal cans were almost cylindrical, tapering towards their rims, and about 18

---

[341] Roth, *The Yorkshire coiners and notes on old and prehistoric Halifax*, p.139.

Figure 38. Before the development of municipal water supplies, most local villages had to rely on their local spring or 'well'. Queuing at the well, as seen here at Heptonstall, provided a welcome opportunity for exchanging gossip.

in/45 cm tall, with a semi-circular handle across the top for carrying, and a second at the side for tipping. The smaller hand-cans or water-pots, most probably of either tinplate or the locally made lead-glazed earthenware were carried on top of the head, supported on a pad.[342] Those who preferred not to queue at the wells, and had surplus funds, could use the services of professional watercarriers such as 'Molly Water' of Elland.[343]

If coming directly from springs, these wells should have provided water of a reasonable quality, but all might become contaminated with all manner of impurities. This was particularly the case where well-shafts were sunk into the ground, either where springs were rare, as on the coal measures to the east of Halifax, and along the flat valley bottoms, or where private wells were sunk in the backyards and gardens of the increasingly crowded villages and towns. By the mid-nineteenth century the combination of overflowing privy-middens, over-used churchyard cemeteries and the complete lack of sewers was causing the subsoil and its ground water to be dangerously poisonous. As Dick o'th Clough complained from Haworth:

> Th' beer is noan what it war, … I mind th' time when th' Bull watter ran right

[342] Craven, *A Brontë moorland village,* p.115.

[343] Hamerton, *Olde Eland,* p.125.

through th' kirkyard – thick an' strong it war, afore iver it touched th' malt. I tell ye, th' beer had *body* in't i' them days.[344]

The water from the Head Well was now so foul that even the cattle refused to drink it.[345] Meanwhile those who relied on the Brookfoot Well just west of Brighouse found its water both scarce and filthy, since passing gypsies and tramps washed both themselves and their shoes in it, and it was also used for drowning mice.[346] Open wells could be dangerous in other ways too, those going to Heptonstall's well on 14 January 1874, discovering that it contained the drowned remains of James Holt, a local farmer.[347] Sealing the top of a well with flagstones and installing a pump certainly reduced the risk of surface contamination and accidents, but did nothing to cure the problem of organic poisons seeping in from below.

There were a number of attempts to improve the quality of local water supplies. In Stanbury a pipe was laid from Enfield Side at the opposite side of the Sladen valley into a cistern built on top of a well-house in the village, this simple inverted siphon's clear spring water negating the use of old roadside and field wells.[348] In Halifax, the celebrated engineer John Smeaton had prepared a new scheme for carrying in water from Well Head back in 1761. It provided conduits near the top of Cheapside and at the top and bottom of Woolshops.[349] Remains of water-pipes made out of bored tree-trunks jointed at each end have been dug up in the town, as have early lead pipes that would have served individual houses.[350]

The increasing number of earth closets and privy-middens in the rapidly expanding towns in the opening decades of the nineteenth century soon fouled much of the groundwater that supplied both these public wells, and those in numerous private back-yards. As in other parts of the country, the great cholera epidemic of the 1830s brought matters to a head, making the provision of sewage disposal systems and the supply of clean water a priority. Even so, the

---

[344] H. Sutcliffe, *By moor and fell: landscapes and lang-settle lore from West Yorkshire*, London, T.F. Unwin, 1899, p.24.

[345] Baumber, *A history of Haworth from the earliest times*, p.139.

[346] Brighouse & District Local History Society, *What was happening in Brighouse* p.14.

[347] *Todmorden & Hebden Bridge Historical Almanack*, 1876, p.65.

[348] Craven, *A Brontë moorland village*, p.115.

[349] Roth, *The Yorkshire coiners and notes on old and prehistoric Halifax*, p.112.

[350] Calderdale Museums, AH 148.57, 1902 from Wards End.

necessary funds, local authority powers and parliamentary consents, took many more years to assemble. A number of small-scale reservoirs were started in the 1850s, but the larger ones that form such a prominent feature of the main upland valleys were mainly constructed from around 1870 to the 1920s to serve the towns of Halifax, Bradford and Keighley. As a result, most communities had access to a supply of 'town' water by 1900, only those in the more remote parts of the hills remaining reliant on local springs. It is remembered that Mary Alice Grimshaw of Todmorden had three taps in the kitchen – hot, 'town' (cold) and spring (cold).

As described in Chapter 9, skimmed milk was an essential part of the everyday diet of most of the farming and factory-working families here. It had the advantages of being nutritious and requiring neither heat nor utensils for its preparation. From the early eighteenth century fashionable China tea had been drunk by the wealthier clothiers, but, since it was expensive and required the use of a kettle and a hot fire, it was little used by most local people until the opening years of the nineteenth century, when there was a milk famine.[351] In the 1830s its use was becoming widespread, but when Peter Suter, druggist and tea dealer of Crown Street, Halifax, advertised his green tea at 12s (80p) and black tea at from 4s 6d to 13s 4d (22.5 - 66p) a pound, he was aiming at the wealthier classes, for these prices were well beyond the means of most families. By the 1850s black tea had dropped to 3s 8d - 4s (19 - 20p) a pound, falling to 1s (5p) in the 1870s as new tea plantations opened in India and Ceylon.[352] As a result, it became the most popular of all drinks, taken at breakfasts and teas in the home, and at every communal tea organised by local churches, chapels and other groups. It was usually served with milk, perhaps cream, and sugar and, as an extra treat, with a dash of rum. Those who could not afford black tea, cream and sugar mashed the leaves of mint or pennyroyal and stirred in black treacle for sweetening, the result tasting very similar to tea, also being just as warming and satisfying at a fraction of the prices.[353]

The simplest way of making tea was to pour boiling water onto the leaves in either a pint pot or else a tea-can carried to work, but by the 1860s many were using teapots made in the local potteries. The traditional pint-size mess pots remained the most popular drinking vessels in many households, but these

---

[351] Brears, *Traditional food in Yorkshire*, pp.241-245; Hanson, *The story of old Halifax*, p.235.

[352] Turner, *The Rev. Oliver Heywood, 1630-1702*, vol.4, p.124; *Halifax Courier*, 22 December 1855.

[353] Travis, *Notes: (historical and biographical)*, pp.28, 237.

were gradually replaced with cheap and colourful cups and saucers from Staffordshire and other pottery factories. From 1891 to 1907 Nicholas Taylor of Denholme Pottery made finely-thrown brown-glazed copies of these wares, selling them as 'Denholme China'. These were very popular around Calderdale and Haworth, families such as the Stanleys of Oakworth buying sets comprising a teapot, cream jug, sugar basin, butter dish, cups, saucers and tea plates.[354] The saucers were not used as mere drip-trays, but served as drinking vessels, tea from the cup being poured into one to cool quickly before being lifted to the lips, this representing good, not bad manners here.[355] As today, many considered cups and saucers to be a refinement best kept for polite use, preferring a pottery mug for everyday use. If ordered from a local pottery they could have your name or favourite motto inscribed across their sides.

Figure 39. Local potteries made a variety of attractive yet affordable teawares throughout the nineteenth and early twentieth centuries. This teapot, probably made at the Cliviger pottery, was used by the Taylor family of Queensbury, while the tea caddy was made at Howcans, just north of Halifax.

In addition to tea, both coffee and cocoa became popular hot drinks in the later nineteenth century, their use, along with tea, being championed by the teetotal / temperance movement which sought to suppress the consumption of alcohol.

---

[354] Cliffe Castle Museum, 456, December 1913.

[355] Pickles, *Between you and me*, p.45.

This cause was promoted by the nonconformist churches, mill and factory owners and organisations such as the Band of Hope. Dobson's of Elland aided their efforts by making conversation lozenges inscribed 'drink causes nine-tenths of the crime in this country' and 'the hardest work may be performed without intoxicating drink'.[356] Drunkenness was seen as a major social evil, one that was easily developed where those who wanted a drink, meal or warm social environment had no alternative but to use a public house. One answer was to provide what were essentially alcohol-free pubs. A number were set up by the Halifax Cocoa House Company, its Winding Road Railway Branch opening at 5.30 a.m. for up to 300 workers on their way to the mills for 6 a.m., and operating through to 10 p.m. A pot of tea, or cocoa, or a bun, cost just a ha'penny (0.2p) each, fruit pasties 3d (1.2p), and meat, three vegetables and a pudding 6d (2.5p). Customers at Christmas were given spice cake and cigars for free.[357] At the other end of the valley, in Todmorden, John Fielden of Dobroyd Castle and the leading local mill owner set up the superior "Fielden" Coffee Tavern and Temperance Hotel in Pavement in 1880/81 at the huge cost of £4000. Here, from 5 a.m. to 10 p.m. tea, coffee and cocoa were 1d (0.4p) a cup, breakfasts and teas 6d (2.5p), and dinners 3d - 1s (1.2 - 5p) each. Both were forced to close in 1913, just before the outbreak of the First World War.[358]

In the home, many made fresh non-alcoholic cold drinks because they were both cheap and refreshing. These included:

Lemonade: Mrs M. Marsden, Parkinson Lane, Halifax[359]

juice & pared zest of 6 lemons
12 oz/350 g sugar

Boil the sugar in 2 pt/1.2 l water, stir in the zest and leave for 2-3 hours. Add the strained juice and 4 pt/2.4 l cold water, strain through a fine muslin [or a coffee filter paper] and serve chilled.

Orangeade: Mrs M. Fowler, Stainland[360]

juice & pared zest of 2 oranges

---

356 Personal communication, Mr T. Chadwick.

357 Porritt, *It happened here: third series*, p.77.

358 B. Rudman, *Todmorden old pub trail*, Littleborough, George Kelsall, 1989, p.26; Travis, *Notes: (historical and biographical)*, p.353.

359 Kaye, *Yorkshire cooking*, p.224.

360 Ibid., p.225.

1 oz/25 g sugar

> Put the ingredients into a jug, pour in 1 pt/200 ml boiling water, leave to cool, and strain as before.

Alternatively, cordials were made when fruits were in season, so that they could be used throughout the year, their store-cupboard recipes being given in the next chapter.

Teetotalism, however strongly supported from church and chapel pulpits, temperance societies and employers, never provided serious competition to ale and beer as the favourite drinks of the majority of the population. They had made and drunk them for countless centuries because they were safer, more nourishing and more palatable than most available alternatives. Children were expected to drink beer, Methodists often fortifying their Sunday School congregations with it at Whit Walks up to around the 1840s.[361] Many local families continued to brew their own beer up into the 1920s and 30s, one Sowerby Bridge inhabitant remembering how 'we used to make beer for our own use in the cellar at home, I can smell the hops now.'[362] Considering that this was such a widespread practice it is surprising that little evidence of home brewing remains today. Local museums hold little more than 'an old brewing spoon' and a number of brewing pots and drink pots, while the methods were so well-known that no-one appears to have needed to write them down. The raw materials were readily available, water being plentiful, while around 1800 'badgers' (itinerant traders) such as Dearden who attended Todmorden market were selling malt in suitably small quantities, and farmers such as Cornelius Ashworth were collecting 2½-hundredweight 'pockets' of hops from the canal wharf at Salterhebble for delivery to local customers.[363] Some families actually grew their own hops; they were to be seen in the garden of a demolished cottage on the hillside above Shibden Hall in the 1960s. In later years supplies were probably obtained mainly from grocer's shops.

One of the most useful sources of information on small-scale home brewing comes from the 1836 inventory of Ovenden Workhouse since, although this was a public institution, it operated its domestic affairs in a similar manner to

---

[361] M. Heaton, *Recollections and history of Oxenhope,* Oxenhope, 2006, pp.106-107; S. Davids, *Oxenhope in times past,* Chorley, Countryside Publications, 1986, p.18.

[362] Calderdale Libraries, *Memory lane: recollections of Sowerby Bridge,* p.7.

[363] Dugdale, *Todmorden market,* p.40; Davies et al, *The Diaries of Cornelius Ashworth 1782-1816,* pp.179, 186, 231, 244.

Figure 40. *Most of the drinking vessels used in Calderdale and Haworth were made in the local potteries, these typical examples including a meas pot (1), named mugs (2 & 3 made by Nicholas Taylor at Denholme around 1905), a puzzle jug made at Howcans in 1883 (4), a knurr and spell pot of 1857 (5) and a Howcans frog mug of the 1880s (6).*

those of its neighbouring small farms. Here the chamber over the kitchen held 3 strikes of malt, while the back kitchen-cum-brewhouse contained:

1 set-pot [boiling copper] and grate	17s
2 brewing tubs	13s
1 sieve and briggs [a strainer with a frame to hold it over a tub]	2s
1 pail	2s

and the cellar below had six barrels valued at 21s (105p) and a tunnel [a funnel for filling them] at 6d (2.5p).[364] Most homes would use the identical items to brew their beer but on a smaller scale, perhaps having a communal set of tubs which each might use in turn. Alternatively, the tubs were often replaced by large brewing jars, and the barrels by 'drink pots' made in the Halifax potteries. The latter have been called 'cider jars' locally for the last half century or so. This is romantic stupidity, since this was not a cider-making area, and the cider would have dissolved the lead from the glaze, poisoning the drinkers into insanity.

Local dialect words include 'gailker' for the fermenting vessel, 'stingo' for strong 'ale', 'tiplash' for medium-strength beer, and 'grout' for small beer. These three grades were all made from the same batch of malt, almost like mashing three pots of tea from the same teabag, the terms 'brewing' or 'mashing' a pot of tea coming directly from their use in beermaking.[365] The following recipe follows the local method of home brewing using about half the quantities, since each drink pot holds about 2½-3 gallons (20-24 pt).

To brew 5 gallons of beer in three strengths

Equipment
1 20 pt/11 l boiling or stock pot as the copper
1 30 pt/15 l polythene tub with a corked hole near its base as the mash tub.
1 coarse-meshed nylon bag to line the mash tun to replace the original wicker 'betong' or strainer.
3 20 pt/ 15 l polythene tubs with corked holes near their bases as wort tub and 3 gailkers.
1 large, thick blanket or duvet.
1 large sieve.
3 large bottles as drink pots.

Ingredients
6 lb/1.7 kg. ground pale malt
2 oz/50 g hops
6 tsp dried real ale yeast

1. Boil 16 pt/9.5 l of water in the copper and leave to cool to 68°C/155°F.

---

364 West Yorkshire Archives, Calderdale, *Daybook*, HAS:123(209).

365 Watson, *The history and antiquities of the parish of Halifax*, p.538; Travis, *Notes: (historical and biographical)*, p.142.

Figure 41. For home brewing water boiled in a set pot (left) was ladled in a pottery lading-can onto malt in a brewing pot (centre), from which the sweet 'wort' was strained into a brewing tub. After being re-boiled with hops, it was fermented with yeast, the froth being skimmed off into a barm-pot (on the table) for future brews, before being poured into a drink pot (right) to clear ready for drinking.

2. Pour the water into the lined mash tub, stir in the malt thoroughly, cover and wrap in the blanket or duvet, leave for 2 hours, then drain into the wort tub.

3. Repeat stages 1 and 2 with a second batch of water.

4. Meanwhile return the wort from stage 2 to the boiler with one third of the hops, boil gently, covered, for 1 hour, making sure that it does not boil over, then pour through the strainer into one of the two gailkers, and leave to cool.

5. Repeat stages 1 and 2 with a third batch of water, discard the spent malt, and wash out the mash tub.

6. Meanwhile repeat stage 4 with the second batch, straining it into the second gailker.

7. Repeat stage 4 with the third batch, stirring it into the mash tub.

8. This has produced three gailkers of wort, each of a different strength. As each cools to 16°C/60°F stir in 2 tsp of the yeast and leave in a warm place to ferment. Skim off the initial foam and the deposit around the edge, stir, leave for about five days, and then

159

put in a cool place for a few days to settle.

9. Pour or syphon the clear beers into separate bottles. There will be around 10 pt/6 l strong ale or stingo, 14 pt/8.4 l beer or tiplash and also 15 pt/9 l of small beer or grout, which should be drunk as soon as possible as it sours in a few days.

All the local public houses brewed their own beers using the same method, but with appropriately larger and more specialised equipment. The brewhouse of the Old White Bear, Norwood Green, was removed into the original brewhouse at Shibden Hall in 1953, together with its equipment. An extremely rare survival, it includes a pump to draw water from an underground cistern along an elevated gutter into the cast-iron 'copper', a long cooling trough with a pump to return the malted 'wort' back to the boiler, a huge 'gailker' or fermenting vessel, a stillage holding a number of barrels, and a number of smaller utensils.

After brewing, the weak 'grout' was not worth selling, and so local publicans gave it away to their poor neighbours and cottagers. They then added a little treacle or sugar along with more yeast, put it into bottles and allowed it to ferment from the neck overnight. It was then drunk on its own, or with old milk and eaten with porridge.[366]

Herb beers and ginger beer were also home-brewed using the following ingredients:

Dandelion beer[367]

2 oz/50 g dandelion root
1 oz/25 g root ginger
1 lemon, sliced thinly
1 lb/450 g sugar
1 oz/25 g cream of tartar

Hop beer

1 oz/25 g hops
8 oz/225 g brown sugar

---

[366] Travis, *Notes: (historical and biographical)*, p.142.

[367] Kaye, *Yorkshire cooking*, p.225.

160

Figure 42. The brewhouse of the Old White Bear, Norwood Green, now re-erected at Shibden Hall Museum. Its equipment includes an oar (1) for stirring the mash, a tempse or horsehair sieve (2) to strain the wort, and a brewers' jet (3) used to ladle the wort into a tundish or funnel (4) when filling barrels. The tub (5) was placed beneath the barrels to collect the overflow of frothy yeast.

Ginger beer[368]

1 oz/25 g bruised root ginger
1 lemon, thinly sliced

---

[368] Ibid., p.226.

1 lb/450 g sugar
1 tsp cream of tartar

Treacle beer

1 lb/450 g golden syrup
8 oz/225 g black treacle
½ oz/12 g ground ginger (optional)
pared zest of 1 lemon (optional)

For all of these, boil the ingredients in 8 pt/5 l water for 15 minutes, strain into a clean vessel, allow to cool to 16ºC/60ºF and stir in 2 tsp dried yeast. This is to replace the traditional method of floating a piece of toast spread with yeast on top of the liquid. Leave in a warm place for 48 hours to ferment, then syphon off the clear liquid into sterilised bottles and cork lightly before storing in a cool place, such as a cellar. Home-brewed beers were notoriously unpredictable, causing glass bottles to unexpectedly explode like grenades. Today it is safer to use plastic bottles with tops that can be screwed down tightly.

Home brewing was a laborious, time-consuming operation that required both equipment and real practical skill, but it was cheaper than buying commercially brewed beer. As incomes improved and nonconformists and others adopted teetotalism, it slowly declined, those who still enjoyed drinking in the home starting to collect supplies in their own jugs from the out-sales of their local pub. The public houses remained as popular as ever, however, with their combination of warmth, good company, social activities and a range of ales, beers, wines and spirits. To some, they provided a welcome retreat from their cold, dull, damp, dim and overcrowded homes. Many developed their own character and clientele appropriate to the needs of their communities. In Todmorden in 1802, for example:

> Should thirsty you be, there's the sign of the Hart,
> Or a bottle you want, they there play their part;
> For the landlord's so mild, the men who are able,
> May demolish his chairs, or break him a table.
> But the Royal's the place for to sit at your ease,
> For Howorth's chief object his guests is to please.[369]

---

[369] Dugdale, *Todmorden market*, pp.40-41.

162

Those who liked to make their own beer even more warming and intoxicating heated it up and stirred in a noggin (here 5 tbs) of gin to each pint to transform it into 'dogs-nose'.[370] It is a stimulating liquid, but one rather difficult to drink, since the rapidly-evaporating alcohol shoots up the nostrils with every sip. Spirits were readily available from public houses and other retailers, but their prices were much higher than their production costs due to the duty imposed by the Inland Revenue. For those prepared to take the risk, it was much cheaper and more profitable to set up an illegal still. The former 'Golden Fleece' in Sowerby used to make its own whisky, for example.[371] Another still was set up at Woodcock Farm on Nab Hill in the 1850s. Here, on the high watershed of the Calder and Worth valleys, Sarah Lister had found an ideally secluded location on the track linking Oxenhope to Luddenden Dean and Halifax, and where thirsty quarrymen were opening up the Woodcock and Fly delphs. When discovered in December 1856, she had 20 gallons/88 l of 'wash' in an advanced state of fermentation and a still set in stonework. John Brigg, a local magistrate, fined her the enormous sum of £30, which she was quite unable to pay, and so she had to spend three and a half months in gaol.[372] Further details emerge from a raid on a house on Highwell Road, Halifax shortly before Christmas, 1860. Here, in an upstairs room, was 10 lb/4.5 kg of black treacle to start the fermenting stage, low wine (the product of the first distillation), 4½ gallons (21.5 l) being distilled, and a quantity of whisky 15 per cent over proof.[373] These are examples of stills that were discovered, but the remote hilltop farmsteads were ideally sited for illicit whisky stills that may have remained undetected. Some stills were set up for legitimate use by firms such as Gibson Dixon of Woolshops, Halifax, but there must have been a constant temptation to use them for illegal purposes.

Making wines in the home tended to be more of a hobby for the few, rather than a popular everyday task. Those who practised this craft often did so with real skill and enthusiasm. There are memories of the huge back kitchen of a large house in Todmorden in the 1960s, where half the stone-flagged floor was covered with demijohns containing fine wines of all manner of colours and flavours, and being pressed to try many of them by their maker. The recipes for damson, cowslip, coltsfoot, oak leaf, and elderberry wines, along with

---

[370] Wright, *English dialect dictionary,* under 'Dog (37)'.

[371] H.P Kendall, 'Quickstavers in Sowerby', *Transactions of the Halifax Antiquarian Society,* 1914, 173-196 at p. 195.

[372] *Leeds Mercury* 20 December 1856; Personal communication Mr E. Kelly.

[373] Porritt, *It happened here: third series,* p.132.

Figure 43. Stills, such as this legitimate example from Gibson Dixon's shop in Woolshops, Halifax, could also have been used to make illicit spirits.

elderflower champagne, are identical to those found in recipe books elsewhere, but the following local wines are worth trying; the first four relying on natural yeasts.

Blackberry wine[374]

1 lb/450 g blackberries
sugar

Soak the fruit in 2 pt/1.2 l cold water for three days, stirring 2-3 times a day. Strain and squeeze out the clear liquid through a fine sieve or piece of muslin, measure, and add 1 lb/450 g sugar to each 2 pt/1.2 l Stand for three more days, stirring as before, then pour into sterilized bottles and cork lightly before storing in a cool place.

Elderberry wine[375]

elderberries
sugar
stick cinnamon, root ginger, cloves

Boil equal volumes of berries and water for 20 minutes. Strain, measure, and to each 4 pt/2.4 l of liquid add 2 lb/900 g sugar and ½ oz/12 g each of the spices. Boil, strain, leave until cold, then bottle.

Elderflower champagne[376]

2 large heads elderflower
1 lemon, sliced
1½ lb/675 g sugar
2 tbs white wine vinegar

Steep the ingredients in 8 pt/5 l cold water for 24 hours, then skim, bottle and keep for 2 weeks before drinking.

Red currant wine: Mrs Culpan, Mytholmroyd[377]

red currants
sugar

---

[374] Kaye, *Yorkshire cooking,* pp.225-226.

[375] Ibid., p.226.

[376] Ibid.

[377] Ashton et al, *The St Michael's recipe and quotation book,* p.37.

Soak the currants in an equal volume of cold water for fourteen days, stirring well every day. Strain off the clear liquid, measure and stir in 1 lb/450 g sugar to each 2 pt/1.2 l, stir until dissolved, then bottle.

Elderberry wine: Mrs W. Carter, Mytholmroyd[378]

elderberries
sugar, cloves, ground ginger, Valencia or Muscatel raisins,
yeast

Scald the elderberries in 1½ times their volume of boiling water, cover and stand for 24 hours. Strain the liquid and measure into a large boiling vessel. Add to each 2 pt/1.2 l, 12 oz/350 g sugar, 1 clove, 1 tsp ginger and 4 oz/100 g raisins, simmer for 1 hour, and pour into a sterilised vessel. Leave until cooled to 16ºC/60ºF, stir in ¼ tsp of yeast to each 2 pt/1.2 l, cover, and leave for 2 weeks to ferment. Cork lightly, leave in a cool place for 3 months, then strain and bottle.

---

[378] Ibid., p.38.

CHAPTER 11

THE STORE CUPBOARD

Few houses today have to rely on home-preserving, since supermarkets offer foods either imported fresh from distant parts of the world, or preserved by refrigeration, deep freezing, drying or canning, all at affordable prices. Up to the middle of the twentieth century things were quite different, for there was much more reliance on home-grown and seasonal foods that had to be preserved for use throughout the year. Green beans, for example, had to be sliced, salted and packed down in jars, while soft fruits were bottled in hermetically sealed glass jars, and eggs submerged in isinglass or lime solutions. The most popular methods of preparation were those by which the final product tasted better than the raw ingredient, either by pickling with vinegar or preserving in sugar.

Plain food, however economical and nourishing, eventually becomes unpalatable and boring unless accompanied by something to add piquancy. This was the role of the pickles and savoury sauces that could be either home-made or purchased from a grocer. Pickled onions, piccalilli and chutneys were all popular, using recipes identical to those found in most cookery books, but one was a particular favourite here, being regularly served with hot-pots.

Pickled red cabbage[379]

1½ lb/1.2 kg. red cabbage
2 tbs salt
1 tbs each whole allspice & cloves
6 peppercorns
2 cinnamon sticks
2 pt/1.2 l. malt vinegar
1 tbs sugar (optional)

Finely shred the cabbage, layer with the salt in a deep bowl, cover, and leave overnight. Meanwhile bring the vinegar and remaining ingredients to the boil in a stainless steel or enamel covered pan, remove from the heat, pour into a jar or jug, and leave overnight. Next day drain the cabbage, rinse off the surplus salt, drain again, and pack into sterilised jars with vinegar-proof lids. Strain in the

---

[379] Kaye, *Yorkshire cooking*, p.228.

vinegar through a piece of muslin, and seal down for use. The cabbage tends to lose its crispness after 2-3 weeks.

Another pickle, pickled eggs, was often enjoyed in public houses, where jars stood on the bar ready for sale to those who wanted something sharp-flavoured to accompany their pints. Commercial versions tended to use a rather acidic white vinegar, while home-made ones preferred the everyday brown malt kind.

Pickled eggs

6 eggs
1 tbs each whole allspice & peppercorns
¼ oz/12 g bruised root ginger
1 pt/600 ml malt vinegar

Boil the eggs for 10 minutes, put into cold water, remove the shells, and pack into jars with vinegar-proof lids. Tie the spices in a piece of muslin, simmer the vinegar for 5 minutes in a covered pan, pour over the eggs, and seal down. They are best kept for 4 weeks before eating.

From at least the early nineteenth century cheap blends of black treacle mixed with twice their volume of malt vinegar and a pinch of salt had been used to dress shredded lettuces and spring onions for 'Yorkshire ploughman's salad'. From this, firms such as Goodall and Backhouse of Leeds developed their Yorkshire Relish as the world's most popular bottle sauce, selling six million bottles a year, while Henderson's Relish, 'The Spicy Yorkshire Sauce' flourished around Sheffield.[380] A dash of these made cold meats much more appetising, and led many housewives to make their own versions to suit their particular tastes.

A Yorkshire relish: Mrs J. Harrison, Halifax

6 pickling chillies
1 tbs cloves
2 tbs peppercorns
2 tbs mustard seeds
4 oz/100 g salt
8 oz/225 g sugar

---

[380] Brears, *Traditional food in Yorkshire,* pp.173, 192.

4 oz/100 g black treacle (for 'burnt sugar')
2 pt/1.2 l green gooseberries (optional)
2 pt/1.2 l malt vinegar

Boil for 20 minutes, cover, simmer for 30 minutes, then sieve and bottle.

Relish: Mrs Walton, Southowram[381]

4 oz/100 g boiled tomato pulp (may used tinned)
2 oz/50 g salt
4 tsp mustard powder
1 oz/25 g flour
5 oz/125 g sugar
1 pt/600 ml malt vinegar

Rub the tomato through a sieve. Mix the flour and mustard with a little of the vinegar. Bring the remaining vinegar to the boil, stir in the flour and mustard mixture together with the tomato pulp and remaining ingredients and boil for 5 minutes before bottling. If a more spiced flavour is wanted, a few tablespoons of Henderson's Relish or other brown sauce may be stirred in.

Home made sauce: Mrs T. Horsfall, Sowerby Bridge[382]

3 beef stock cubes
½ oz/12 g pickling spice
2 tbs mustard powder
3 oz/175 g sugar
1 oz/25 g flour
1 pt/600 ml malt vinegar

Mix the flour into a quarter of the vinegar in a 1½ pt/900 ml basin and set aside. Boil the remaining ingredients together for 5-10 minutes, strain out the spices, and beat the liquid into the flour mixture. Return to the pan and stir as it simmers for 3 minutes, then pour into bottles and seal down for use.

The other sharp bottle sauce, a particular favourite with mutton and lamb, was:

---

[381] Ashton et al, *The St Michael's recipe and quotation book,* p.39.
[382] Anon., *159 recipes from good kitchens*, p.28.

Mint sauce for winter: Miss Parker, Hebden Bridge[383]

8 oz/225 g finely-chopped mint leaves
1 pt/600 ml malt vinegar
1 lb/450 g sugar

Put the mint into a bowl or pan, scald with the boiling vinegar, stir in the sugar until dissolved, cover, leave until cold, then bottle for use.

As these recipes show, sugar was available to most families from the mid-late nineteenth century, but before that time it was far too expensive for everyday use except by the well-to-do. The equally precious alternative was honey.

Honey

The only natural source of sweetening in this area was honey, the huge areas of heather moorland being ideal for producing supplies of the finest flavour, so long as the bees were protected against the harsh climate. This was done by building open-fronted boxes of brick or stone into sheltered hillsides to hold the hives, a good example being seen just below Ponden Hall, Stanbury. The hives themselves were of the traditional tall domed shape, made of straw ropes bound together with strands probably made from the long stems of blackberry plants. In 1775 the Rev. Watson defined 'A Hive to take bees in after they have swarmed' as a 'poich'. This very localised dialect word was also spelled as 'peitch' or 'puche' and originated from their resemblance to 'pikes', the mounds into which hay was raked before being led into the barn, or round haystacks. Each one would produce 6-7 lb/2.7-3.1 kg. of honey after leaving enough for the bees to feed on over the winter months.[384] Although it is hard to imagine today, the polluted air blown in from industrial Lancashire, further contaminated by the numerous belching chimneys of Calderdale's crowded houses and mills, killed off not only the trees on Halifax's Beacon Hill, but also many of the valley's bees.

Local honey was used mainly as a delicious, luxurious spread, being sealed down in jars for safe keeping. Once the combs had been drained of their rich contents, they were placed in a large pancheon and scalded with boiling water to separate their remaining sweetness from the wax. The liquid was then left to

---

[383] Kaye, *Yorkshire cooking,* p.228.

[384] Watson, *The history and antiquities of the parish of Halifax,* p.544; Travis, *Notes: (historical and biographical),* p.146; Wright, *English dialect dictionary,* under 'Bee (6)'.

ferment, before being bottled as honey-drink or honey mead, which, when old, was intoxicating.[385]

Jams and Jellies

Once sugar had become affordable, it enabled working families to make the jams and jellies that had previously been beyond their means. Some were made from fruits that could be gathered from the local countryside.

Crab apple jelly[386]

crab apples, sugar, butter

Cover the apples in water, stew to a pulp, drain the liquid through a fine sieve and measure into a pan. Add 1 lb/450 g sugar for each 1 pt/600 ml, stir until boiling, add ½ oz/12 g butter for each pint/600 ml, and boil quickly for 10 minutes. Try a sample for setting on a cold saucer, then pour into sterilised jars and seal down.

Blackberry jelly: J. Crowther, Mytholmroyd[387]

blackberries, sugar

Pick the berries when dry, barely cover with water, boil until soft, pour into a piece of muslin and hang up to drain without squeezing. To each pint/600 ml add 1 lb/450 g sugar, boil for about 40 minutes until a sample will set on a cold saucer, pour into sterilised jars and seal down.

Blackberry & apple jam

1½ lb/675 g blackberries
1½ lb/675 g apples
3 lb/1.4 kg sugar

Peel, core and chop the apples, put into a pan with the blackberries, barely cover with water, simmer gently until all is soft, then boil rapidly until the setting point is reached, pour into sterilised jars and seal down.

---

[385] Wright, *English dialect dictionary,* under 'Honey (3)'.

[386] Kaye, *Yorkshire cooking,* p.234.

[387] Ashton et al, *The St Michael's recipe and quotation book,* p.34.

Damson jam: Mrs M. Crossley, Hebden Bridge[388]

2 lb/900 g damsons
2 lb/900 g sugar
½ pt/300 ml malt vinegar

Rub the damsons clean, prick well with a darning needle or skewer. Boil the sugar, vinegar and 3 tbs water for 10 minutes, add the damsons, bring to the boil, boil for 8 minutes, without skimming, then put into sterilised jars and seal down. As this had far too many stones for convenience, most preferred to remove them.

Bullace or damson cheese

bullaces or damsons, sugar

Bake the fruit at 140ºC/275ºF gas mark 1 for about 1 hour until very soft, remove, rub the pulp through a sieve, measure, and add 8 oz/225 g sugar to each pound/450 g and boil until it sets. Put into sterilised jars and seal down.

Other jams were made from garden fruits such as blackcurrants, raspberries, strawberries, gooseberries and rhubarb.

Rhubarb marmalade: Mrs C. Bottomley, Mount Tabor[389]

1 lb/450 g rhubarb
12 oz/350 g sugar
pared zest of 1 lemon
⅛ tsp almond essence (instead of bitter almonds)

Cut the rhubarb into 2 in/5 cm lengths, put into a pan, stir in the remaining ingredients and leave for a few hours, or overnight, to extract the juice. Boil for about 45 minutes to 1 hour until thick, then put into sterilised jars and seal down.

Another local favourite was lemon cheese to be used either as a spread or a filling for individual tarts. Today it can accompany ice cream.

---

[388] Ibid., p.32.
[389] Kaye, *Yorkshire cooking*, p.234.

Lemon cheese: Mrs H. Baldwin, Cragg[390]

juice of 2 large lemons
12 oz/350 g sugar
2 oz/50 g butter
3 eggs, beaten

Put all the ingredients into a large jar, stand in a pan of boiling water over a gentle heat and stir well until mixture thickens, but does not boil and curdle. Pour into sterilised jars and seal down.

Marmalades were also home-made from Seville oranges, sweet oranges and/or lemons, using their standard recipes. Fruits and sugar were also used to make a number of home cures.

Home Cures

Before the National Health Service was set up in 1947 medical services usually involved expensive doctors' bills, unless they were one of the benefits of a friendly society or were provided by the workhouse infirmary or other charitable institution. As a result, most families still relied on the home-made folk medicines developed from generations of personal experience. Even if a person was not ill, there was a strong belief that they needed a tonic every spring, when their blood had to be cleaned by 'cleaning out the system' with concoctions of green herbs or natural laxatives. Among these, syrup of figs was a rich, sweet favourite, certainly more palatable than one Todmorden alternative:

> Granny used to make me go to the slaughter-house for a pint of blood. She
> mixed it with milk and made us drink it as a "health tonic". She was a right
> old Bugger![391]

The following recipes are more typical:

Blood purifier

1 lemon, sliced
2 tbs blackcurrant jam
10 red sage leaves
sugar to taste

Scald the ingredients with 2 pt/1.2 l boiling water.

---

[390] Ashton et al, *The St Michael's recipe and quotation book,* p.31.
[391] Calderdale Libraries, *Memory lane: recollections of Todmorden,* p.1.

For impurity of the blood

1 oz/25 g each horehound, burdock root, hops & gentian root
5 oz/125 g root ginger
2 oz/50 g Spanish juice [liquorice dissolved in water]
1 tbs yeast

Boil the ingredients in 40 pt/23 l water for an hour, strain, add yeast when tepid, ferment 24 hours, then bottle.

Spring mixture: Miss C. Harwood, Norton Tower[392]

3 oz/75 g Epsom Salts
1 oz/25 g cream of tartar
½ oz/12 g flowers of brimstone
½ oz/12 g ground ginger
12 oz/350 g brown sugar
grated zest & juice of a lemon

Simmer all the ingredients with 4 pt/2.4 l water for 10 minutes and bottle when cold. A wineglass was to be taken every night and morning, but this recipe ***should not*** be used today.

The other main concern was to relieve the symptoms of the colds which made wintertime a misery for many. Some believed that inhaling the smoke of freshly burnt camphor would provide a cure, for it would certainly give the impression of being powerfully effective.[393] Most families preferred remedies that blended fruits rich in vitamin C with sugar and alcohol that tasted far better and were much more soothing. Today they make good drinks in their own right, being just as enjoyable when still in perfect health.

Elderberry syrup: Sowerby Bridge, 1897[394]

ripe elderberries, black treacle or golden syrup, brandy

Wash, crush and strain the berries into a measuring jug. Put the juice into a pan with 1 pt/600 ml treacle or golden syrup to each pint, simmer for 20 minutes, skim off any scum, then leave to cool overnight. Next morning mix in 1 pt/600 ml brandy and keep in a corked bottle ready for use, especially for 'a tight cold'.

---

[392] Kaye, *Yorkshire cooking*, p.240.

[393] Anon., *159 recipes from good kitchens*, p.36.

[394] Calderdale Libraries, *Memory lane: recollections of Sowerby Bridge*, p.15.

Elderberry syrup: Miss Culpan, Mytholmroyd[395]

elderberries, demerara sugar, root ginger, cloves

Remove the berries from their stalks using a fork, put into an earthenware jar and bake at 150ºC/300ºF gas mark 2 for about 30 minutes, until their juices have been released. Strain through a sieve and to each pint/600 ml juice add 1 lb/450 g demerara sugar, 1 clove and ⅛ oz/12 g bruised root ginger. Simmer for 30 minutes, skim and strain through fine muslin into sterilised bottles. This was reputedly 'Excellent for bronchitis'.

Blackberry cordial: Mrs H. Helliwell, Halifax[396]

1 lb/450 g blackberries
2 ins./5 cm stick cinnamon
1 tsp cloves
12 oz/ 350 g sugar
1 tsp blade mace
4-6 tbs brandy

Simmer the blackberries in ¼ pt/150 ml water until soft, break them up with a wooden spoon and strain into a large jar with the remaining ingredients. Cover closely and shake or stir every day for a week. Finally strain through a piece of fine muslin and bottle for use. It makes a pleasant short drink, especially in wintertime, and today makes an excellent sauce to accompany ice cream, or to flavour gin.

Raspberry vinegar: Mrs Tom Farrer, Halifax[397]

raspberries, vinegar, sugar

Fill a glass or stoneware jar with raspberries, cover them with vinegar and leave for ten days before straining off the clear liquid through a piece of muslin. To each pint add 1½lb sugar, simmer for 10 minutes until it has dissolved, skim off any scum, then cool and bottle for use. A teaspoonful was taken to ease chest complaints and sore throats, others dissolved it in a cup of hot water, while some poured a little on their Yorkshire puddings.

---

[395] Ashton et al, *The St Michael's recipe and quotation book,* p.39.

[396] Kaye, *Yorkshire cooking,* p.223.

[397] Ashton et al, *The St Michael's recipe and quotation book,* p.35.

Figure 44. Most of the events that marked the passage of each year were celebrated with traditional foods, starting with spice cake and cheese to welcome first-footers just after midnight on January 1.

CHAPTER 12

JANUARY TO DECEMBER

The progress of each year was marked by a succession of customs, most being celebrated with their own particular foods. Some were based on centuries-old Christian festivals, while others originated either from agricultural and trading activities, or the recreational opportunities provided by the long, warm days of summer. None were exclusive to Calderdale and Haworth, but were essentially representative versions of more widespread regional or national practices, Even so, the details of each custom, including any rhymes, songs and recipes associated with it, often reveal strong local characteristics. They commenced in the first moments of each new year with New Year's Day.

New Year's Day
The stroke of midnight, marking the start of the New Year, saw the arrival of a First Footer, ideally dark haired and carrying a small shovel bearing a piece of coal, a little salt, and a piece of bread along with best wishes for 'A happy New Year'. The usual reward was a piece of spice-cake and cheese, for people believed that 'the more different samples of this delightful Christmas fare you could obtain, the more happy years you will have before you'.[398]

Some chapels celebrated this day with a communal tea-party. At Old Town 350 people sat down to 'snow-white tablecloths, gas brackets entwined with multi-coloured tissue paper, strips of holly and paper roses looped from the ceiling, seasonable mottoes decorating the walls, the laughter of children and the musical jingle of spoons and crockery' as everyone tucked in.[399]

Pancake Day: Shrove Tuesday
In order to use up eggs before fasting in Lent, they were made into pancakes around mid-day. This was one of the rare annual holidays enjoyed by young people who were released from both school and work on the sounding of the pancake bell at their parish church.[400] In Halifax they chanted:

> When pancake bell begins to toll,
> Mother begins with thible and bowl..
> When pancake bell begins to ring,

---

[398] Lonsdale Collection, *Newspaper cuttings*, vol.17, p.138.

[399] Binns, *Valley of a hundred chapels*, p.28.

[400] Hamerton, *Olde Eland*, p.31.

> Mother begins a' tumblin them in.[401]

or;

> When pancake bell begins to ring,
> All Halifax lads begin to sing.[402]

The thible, pronounced with a long 'i', was a flat-sided, porridge-stirring stick.

Pancakes: West Family[403]

4 oz/100 g flour
pinch of salt
1 egg
½ pt/300 ml milk
fat or oil for frying

Sift the flour and salt into a bowl, make a well in the centre, drop in the egg and beat in with the milk added little by little, drawing the dry flour in from the sides to form a smooth batter. Heat a little fat or oil in a frying pan, pour in just sufficient batter to cover the base, cook for 1-2 minutes until set, then toss or turn over and cook the reverse side until golden. The batter improves if left for about half an hour before use.

The pancakes were usually spread with either treacle/golden syrup or sugar with orange or lemon juice before being rolled up and served. In Todmorden anyone leaving even a trace of pancake on their plate was severely warned that unless they finished every scrap "You'll be put into a wheelbarrow and tipped on the muck-midden!"[404]

Good Friday

The legally enforced 'fish days' of the medieval and Tudor periods, when the eating of meat on Holy days was forbidden, had not been enforced for centuries, but was still practical in some families on Good Friday, the commemoration of Christ's death. Meals of salt cod, or the 'somewhat more

---

[401] Calderdale Museums 1949.15. This information came with the donation of a thible.

[402] W.J. Haliday, and A.S. Umpleby, *The white rose garland of Yorkshire dialect verse and local and folk-lore rhymes,* London, J.M. Dent, 1949. p.15; Calderdale Libraries, *Memory lane: recollections of Todmorden,* p.68.

[403] West family, *Manuscript recipe book,* p.14.

[404] Calderdale Libraries, *Memory lane: recollections of Todmorden,* p.68.

Figure 45. *Pancakes were made in most homes on Shrove Tuesday. They were usually served with sugar and orange or lemon juice, or treacle or golden syrup.*

tolerable' salt herring were dutifully eaten, rather than enjoyed.[405] However, there were compensating treats such as 'Friday Cakes', now better known as Hot Cross Buns, to be bought from the local bakers and confectioners.[406] Today's buns are more richly fruited and spiced than their predecessors, and have a white flour-and-water cross, over their tops. Victorian buns were plainer and had the cross impressed with a tin cutter.

Hot Cross Buns: West Family[407]

1¼ lb/550 g strong white flour
1 tsp dried yeast
1 oz/25 g sugar
½ tsp salt
1 oz/25 g lard
1 oz/25 g currants
½ oz/12 g candied lemon peel
1 egg, beaten
¼ pt/150 ml tepid milk

Sift together the flour, yeast, sugar and salt, rub in the lard, and mix in the currants and peel. Beat the egg into the milk, pour into the dry ingredients, mix to form a soft dough, turn out onto a floured board and knead for 10 minutes. Cover and leave in a warm place until doubled in size, then knead for a further 2-3 minutes, divide into twelve and mould as round buns, cutting a shallow cross on top of each. Arrange on a greased baking sheet, cover, and return to the warm until doubled in size. Bake at 190ºC/375ºF gas mark 5 for 15-20 minutes until golden brown. They may be glazed as they come out of the oven with a mixture of equal quantities of sugar and milk melted together.

Good Friday was better known as Pace Egg Day in Calderdale. Eggs have been used as symbols of re-birth and resurrection for centuries, especially Christ's resurrection on Easter Sunday. Pace Eggs, which took their name from Paschal, meaning Easter, were traditionally begged by children on this day, ready for being decorated for games on Easter Monday. To do this, groups of boys performed their Pace Egg Play before those who might have eggs to give, the

---

[405] Hamerton, *Olde Eland,* p.93.

[406] Ibid.

[407] West family, *Manuscript recipe book,* p.44.

best-known local version being enacted at Midgley up to the First World War. Largely due to the effort of H.W. Harwood and F.H. Marsden, it was revived in 1932 and is still performed today on Good Fridays.

Figure 46. *The Pace Egg Play performed every Good Friday in the village of Midgley was originally a way for boys to ask adults to 'give us your Pace Egg for Easter Monday'. Here, as seen in 1913, the doctor (third from the left) is about to revive the slain Slasher; 'Here, Jack, take a little out of my bottle, And let it run down thy throttle.'*

It starts with the Fool ringing a bell as he walks round and asks the crowd to remember that it is 'Pace-Egging time'. The main characters, St George of England, the Black Prince of Paradine, the King of Egypt, Hector and Slasher then appear in sequence. Duels are re-enacted, and St George triumphs over all. After the Doctor has revived Slasher, Little Devil Doubt appears and demands donations:

> It's money I want, it's money I crave,
>
> If you don't give me money I'll sweep you all to the grave.[408]

The texts were printed in small woodcut-illustrated chap books, printed by

---

[408] H.W. Harwood and F.H. Marsden (eds.), *The Pace-Egg: the Midgley version. With an introductory study.* Originally published 1935. Reprinted Halifax: David Bland, 1977, p.9.

Walker's of Otley, and others in Leeds, Bradford and Manchester, throughout the middle and late nineteenth century. To refresh themselves, the pace-eggers drank 'spo', 'popollolly', or 'Spanish juice'. This was a stick of brittle liquorice broken up, put into a bottle with sugar and warm water, and left in a cupboard for as long as possible with regular shakings until it turned 'nice and black'.[409]

The eggs given as presents by family, friends and neighbours were dyed in various ways, a much easier process in the past when eggs were white rather than the modern induced brown. Some might have the brown outer skins of onions tied around them with yarn or a piece of soft cloth before being boiled for 15 minutes to produce a richly marbled red-brown finish that might be enhanced by polishing with a little bacon fat. Since many dyes were not as fixed as they are today, pieces of coloured cloth bound round the egg would transfer their bright hues in a similar manner. Being a major textile area, industrial dyes from local dyehouses were also used.

Easter Sunday

As the day of the Resurrection, most families attended services at their church or chapel, with a Sunday afternoon tea as usual, but with one special item, a simnel cake. Originating as cakes made by adult children when visiting their mothers on Mothering or 'Mid-lent' Sundays, they had become associated with Easter by the mid-nineteenth century. At first, they were simple lightly fruited cakes:

Simnel cake: Morley Family, Halifax[410]

4 oz/100 g butter
4 oz/100 g sugar
2 eggs, beaten
6 oz/175 g flour
1 tsp baking powder
6 oz/175 g currants
2 oz/50 g candied peel
1 oz/25 g chopped almonds

Cream the butter and sugar, beat in the eggs little by little, sift in the flour and baking powder, beat again, and mix in the remaining ingredients. Put into a greased and lined 7 in/18 cm round cake tin and bake at 180ºC/350ºF gas mark 4 for 1½ hours.

---

[409] *Leeds Mercury*, Supplement, 11 April 1896.

[410] King Cross [Wesleyan] Circuit, *Recipes and quotations,* p.42.

Figure 47. *Local simnel cakes were authentically plain fruit cakes, made without the thick layers of almond paste introduced by confectioners around the 1890s.*

However, by 1900 commercial confectioners, especially those around Bury, began to make much richer versions with a layer of almond paste through their middles and further almond paste decoration on top.

Simnel cake: Mrs A. Ainley, Mytholmroyd[411]

8 oz/225 g ground almonds
4 oz/100 g icing sugar
4 eggs
8 oz/225 g butter
6 oz/150 g caster sugar
4 oz/100 g sultanas
4 oz/100 g chopped raisins
1 oz/25 g mixed candied peel
1 oz/25 g nibbed almonds
1 tsp baking powder
8 oz/225 g flour

Mix the ground almonds and icing sugar, then work in one of the eggs to form the almond paste (don't use commercially produced almond paste, since it contains far too much sugar), and roll into a 7 in/18 cm disc. Cream the butter with the caster sugar. Separate the remaining eggs, beating the yolks into the butter and sugar, and then the stiff-beaten whites, followed by the dried fruits and almonds. Finally sift the baking powder with the flour, and fold into the mixture. Put half the mixture into a greased and lined 8 in/20 cm round tin, put the almond paste on top and pat it level before adding the rest of the mixture. Bake at 150°C/300°F gas mark 2 for 2-2½ hours.

Like all fruit cakes, it should be made a few weeks before required in order to soften and mature. The original recipe scattered tiny caraway sweets over the surface half-way through baking, but today a border of small Easter eggs of almond paste may be added after the cake has cooled.

Easter Monday
This was the day for playing with the pace-eggs, either 'jauping' them together like conkers, the losers forfeiting their shattered eggs, or rolling them down steep grassy slopes until they broke.

---

[411] Ashton et al, *The St Michael's recipe and quotation book*, p.20.

May Day: 1 May

Maypoles were set up in Halifax from before 1680, the last one, in Warley, blowing down in 1899, but no particular food or drinks were linked to their dances.[412] Instead, the onset of spring was celebrated on Spa Sunday.

Spa Sunday: First Sunday in May

It was popularly believed that people's blood needed to be cleaned and refreshed every spring to compensate for the long months of stodgy wintertime diet. Some did this with home-made herbal brews or doses of brimstone (sulphur) and treacle 'to clear the system'. It was just as popular to drink the waters of one of the valley's sulphur springs or 'spas'. These included one in Spa Wood, Cragg Vale, a mile up the road from Mytholmroyd, one in Spa Wood, on the west side of Luddenden Brook, a mile north of Luddenden village, and others at Simm Carr, a mile north-west of Stump Cross in Shibden Dale, and at Upper Edge, Elland.

The earliest mention of Luddenden Spa was in 1801-2, when three boys were already there at 3 a.m. when they were surprised by the arrival of a group of the local volunteer soldiery.[413] In the later nineteenth century, young people gathered here from 5 a.m., continuing to visit throughout the day to drink, fill their bottles, and hear impromptu sermons given by John Preston, a local well-intentioned character who supported himself by doing odd jobs around Luddenden Dean. He was succeeded by the Rev. John Poynton of Mixenden, and later by the Salvation Army.[414] Meanwhile Mr Major Wilde was at Cragg Vale spa,

> When as lads in our clogs and our smocks we did go,
> When the bright mantle of May did appear;
> With bottles and Spanish [liquorice], over Heathershelf Scout …
> Then we've raced down the wood to the mineral spring,
> Filled our bottles and then felt as proud as a king.
> Then we've played in the fields and the brooks,
> And there heard the music that charms us today.
> Played by Nature, as only Nature can play.[415]

The Sim Carr spa was appropriated by the Halifax Temperance Society to

---

[412] E. Webster, 'Some Dean Clough archives', *Transactions of the Halifax Antiquarian Society,* 1988, 41-56 at pp.47-49.

[413] *Halifax Courier*, 21 November 1857.

[414] Turner, *A spring-time saunter*, pp.10-12.

[415] Mellor, *Biographies, sketches, & rhymes by the Calder Valley Poets*, p.101.

promote the virtues of pure cold water, being followed by the Labour Party promoting its socialist policies.[416] Youngsters were still gathering at these spas just before the First World War, but then this custom began to die out, although the springs continue to flow as they have done for centuries.

Whit Sunday

Whit Sunday, the seventh after Easter, commemorated the descent of the Holy Spirit at Pentecost, and was also chosen by most churches and chapels as the day on which to celebrate their Sunday school anniversaries. After the usual morning service and mid-day dinner, all those involved would gather at their place of worship. The children would wear their new clothes with pride, usually showing them off to their families and neighbours who would be expected to put a penny into their pockets, if new clothes and pennies could be afforded.[417] Processions were then marshalled, some being simple affairs led by the teachers and youngsters carrying patriotic flags, some with a borrowed horse-drawn farm wagon bearing the little ones, the church officials and perhaps a harmonium, while others might have a brass band.[418] Having marched around their area, singing long-practised hymns learnt from specially printed sheets, stopping particularly in front of the houses of significant members of the community and the housebound, they usually ended up in a field for refreshments and sports.

Back in 1815 the Luddenden Methodists paid 11s 7d (59p) for bread, cheese and beer for the children, while at Hawksbridge Chapel, Oxenhope, 'Susan Boocock brews half a stroke [9 lb] of malt for the singers to drink with their bread and cheese after the anniversary', since the nonconformists only turned teetotal in the 1840s.[419] As Charlotte Brontë described in her *Shirley* of 1849:

> [At four] long lines of benches were arranged in close-shorn fields round the school: there the children were seated, and huge baskets, covered up with white cloths, and great smoking tin vessels were brought out. Ere the distribution of good things commenced, a brief grace was pronounced … and sung by the children, their young voices sounded melodious, even touching, in the open. Large currant buns, and hot, well-sweetened tea, were then administered in the proper air of liberality: the rule for each child's allowance

---

[416] Crump, *The little hill farm*, p.77.

[417] Lonsdale Collection, *Newspaper cuttings*, vol.31, p.25; Hamerton, *Olde Eland*, p.93; Blinman, *Sowerby Bridge: our memories, our history*, p.17; *Siddal: our memories, our history*, p.28.

[418] Calderdale Libraries, *Memory lane: recollections of Brighouse, Rastrick & Hipperholme*, p.81.

[419] Binns, *Valley of a hundred chapels*, p.46.

being that it was to be about twice as much as it could possibly eat, thus leaving a reserve to be carried home for such as age, sickness, or other impediment, prevented from coming to the feast. Buns and beer circulated, meanwhile amongst the musicians and church-singers; afterwards the benches were removed and they were left to unbend their spirits in licensed play.[420]

Figure 48. *Churches and chapels celebrated Whit Sunday by processing through their area and singing hymns before enjoying their walk cakes as at Heptonstall (left) and Oxenhope Sawood Wesleyans at Old Town (right).*

In some chapels this scene was still being re-enacted almost unchanged over a century later, while in others more distant journeys were being made as new transport facilities became available. At Halifax's Square Chapel in 1914, fifty of the youngest scholars were carried off to a field at Bailiff Bridge in Thomas Greenwood & Co.'s new Austin motor wagon after it had been specially adapted with rows of wooden seats. The rest caught a train to Lightcliffe before walking the rest of the way for an afternoon of sports and refreshments including buns, oranges and huge Thermos flasks of hot coffee.[421]

---

[420] Brontë, *Shirley*, pp.310-311.

[421] Lonsdale Collection, *Newspaper cuttings*, vol.31, p.99.

Buns remained staple fare at the Whit Walks for many years. At some chapels they were eaten plain, at others the teachers brought their own butter, until as conditions improved over the years, all the buns could be served thickly buttered.[422]

As Martha Heaton remembered from the 1890s, Oxenhope's Sunday School scholars assembled at their respective chapels for a hymn and prayer before walking to the home of one or other of the major local families. Here, in the gardens, they sang hymns and heard speeches, sometimes being entertained with light refreshments, or else gifts of oranges handed out by their host's children. Afterwards they returned to their chapels for their 'walk cake tea'. The records of Oxenhope's Horkinstone Baptists detail the arrangements made for the Whit Walk of their new Sabbath School back in 1838:

> James Hartley of Haworth to make 140 cakes for the children at 2d each as good as he can afford.
> That 2 stone of flour, 6 oz of currants to be made into bread for the teachers. John Whitaker is to be engaged to see the making of it.
> Mr M. Saunders to provide tea & sugar for 140 scholars & 50 teachers and some few others, say to friends.
> John Hey to wait upon some female to provide tea things etc.[423]

Similarly, in May 1853, Hawksbridge Baptists ordered 'that 11 stones of flour be baked into cakes, 24 cakes to the stone, and 5 lb currants 24 to each stone.'[424] In other words, into 264 cakes, each weighing 1 lb 5 oz/575 g. In later years the dough was being enriched with eggs, milk and candied peel, and given a glossy glaze. Those seen in photographs of around 1900 and the 1930s appear as large flattish teacakes that were nibbled from one side, rather than being sliced and buttered. One was provided to each person attending the walk, those who were entered on the Sunday School's register being entitled to a second one, as authorised by a named bun ticket. As a result, those with large families had full bread-pots after the walk, ready to be enjoyed with a pot of milk at suppertime.

Walk cakes: Hawksbridge Baptists, Oxenhope, 1853[425]

For two cakes take:

---

[422] Calderdale Libraries, *Memory lane: recollections of Sowerby Bridge*, p.78; Calderdale Libraries, *Memory lane: recollections of Todmorden*, p.126; Binns, *Valley of a hundred chapels*, p.46.

[423] Heaton, *Recollections and history of Oxenhope*, p.106-107.

[424] Davids, *Oxenhope in times past*, p.18.

[425] Ibid.

Figure 49. *This group of Hawksbridge Baptists are enjoying their walk cakes at a Whitsuntide in the 1930s. Around the close of the nineteenth century those on the register of the Hawksbridge Sunday School were issued with named bun tickets that authorised them to receive a second bun.*

1 lb3 oz/525 g strong white flour
½ tsp salt
1 tsp dried yeast
2 oz/50 g lard
6 oz/150 g currants

Mix the salt and yeast into the flour and make a well in the centre. Melt the lard in ¾ pt/450 ml hot water and leave until tepid. Mix sufficient into the flour to form a soft dough, turn out onto a floured board, knead for 5 minutes, place in a bowl, cover, and set aside in a warm place until doubled in size. Knead in the currants, and form into two flat 7 in/18 cm rounds on greased baking sheets, cover lightly and return to the warm until risen, then bake at 200ºC/400ºF gas mark 6 for 20-25 minutes until a pale brown. Remove from the oven and brush with a glaze of

2 tbs sugar dissolved in 2 tbs milk

189

Return to the oven for a few minutes to dry, then leave on a wire tray to cool.

1890s Walk cakes[426]

Follow the recipe above, but
- add 3 oz/75 g sugar to the flour
- replace the lard and water with butter and milk
- add a beaten egg to the tepid liquid
- add 3 oz/75 g candied peel with the currants.

At the tea, the men and boys used mugs provided by the chapel, while the girls and ladies brought their own mugs sometimes inscribed with their names and reserved as 'walk pots' for this special day. The hot tea was then distributed by the superintendents and male teachers using borrowed milking cans. Later, in the evening, all kinds of games and races were enjoyed in a farmer's field, perhaps with dancing too if a band had been hired.[427]

The following recipe produces even richer buns.

Whitsuntide buns: Joseph Dobson's of Elland, 1884[428]

1 lb/450 g flour
1 tsp salt
3 oz/75 g lard
3 oz/75 g butter
2 tsp dried yeast
5 oz/150 g sugar
1 egg, beaten
about ¼ pt/150 ml milk
13 oz/375 g currants
3½ oz/100 g chopped candied peel
[For the glaze: 1 tbs sugar dissolved in 2 tbs milk]

Sift the salt into the flour, rub in the fats, mix in the yeast and sugar, then the egg with just sufficient milk to produce a soft dough. Turn out onto a floured board and knead for 5 minutes, then knead in the currants and peel, divide into 10 oz/275 g or 4 oz/100 g pieces.

---

[426] West family, *Manuscript recipe book*, [loose paper].

[427] Hartley & Ingilby, *Life and tradition in West Yorkshire*, p.95.

[428] Personal communication, Mr T. Chadwick.

Mould each one into a round bun and arrange on greased baking sheets, allowing room for them to expand, lightly cover and leave in a warm place for at least an hour to rise. Bake at 180ºC/350ºF gas mark 4 for about 20 minutes, brush with the glaze as soon as they come out of the oven and leave to cool. Serve cut across and thickly buttered.

N.B. This appear to be the richest dough of any traditional English fruit bun and, being the recipe of a professional baker, can be difficult to use successfully in the home. For this reason, the yeast may be replaced with 1½ tsp baking powder, cutting out the need for the dough to rise.

In later years the traditional buns were supplemented in some chapels with potted meat sandwiches and special treats such as an orange or even a bar of chocolate in the twentieth century. These were often packed into individual paper bags so that they could be quickly handed out in the field where the sports were being held. If there was a shortage of crockery, or if it was unsuitable for use outdoors, each child would be expected to bring their own mug for the tea or coffee, parents often wrapping coloured thread around the handle as a means of identification.

Some chapels held their anniversaries on different days, omitting the walks and the field sports, but replacing them with a service with hymns and a popular preacher followed by a lavish tea provided by the ladies. This led to great rivalry as visitors from other congregations carefully and critically compared the chapel's fare with the one they provided for their own anniversaries. Those who assembled at Lighthazles New Connexion Chapel, north-west of Ripponden, on the first Sunday in June in its early days found nothing but rhubarb pies and pasties, earning it the derisory name of 'Th' Rhubarb Charity', 'charity' being a West Riding name for an anniversary. One year a gang of lads tied a mocking bunch of rhubarb to the chapel chimney![429] More conventionally, Siddal Strict Baptist's Zion Chapel anniversary every Good Friday saw over 100 seated in their schoolroom, the long tables covered in white cloths, a tea urn and cups and saucers at each end, ready for a beef salad followed by jelly, custard, and cakes, all home-made.[430]

---

[429] Lonsdale Collection, *Newspaper cuttings*, vol.27, p.37.

[430] *Siddal: our memories, our history*, Halifax, Workers Educational Association, 1989, p.24.

Some alive today can still remember the last of the anniversaries and charities, when only a few score of mainly elderly ladies and their young grandchildren came together for a service and communal meal. In their heyday, however, these were great days of enthusiastic rejoicing. At the famous Scar Top Charity near the head of the Worth, close on 2,000 were still attending in 1905 to hear the harmonium, violins, cornets, piccolo, trombones and double bass accompany the huge choir to make the valley ring with hymns. Then came the sermon, hot and impassioned, delivered by a popular lay preacher who farmed in Luddenden Dean. A final anthem and a collection followed before all dispersed.[431] As at Blake Dean, at the head of Hardcastle Crags, and at many other chapels, the anniversary had been one of the major events that marked the passage of each successive year.

Rushbearing and Feasts (March – September)
Up to around the eighteenth century the soft *Juncus* field rushes, common to the wetter meadows and moors of the area, were gathered each year to provide an aromatic, absorbent, insulating floor covering of the local churches. This practical chore was then turned into a communal celebration with the rushes built up into tall convex-sided pyramids mounted on two-wheeled carts drawn by long teams of men. Usually setting off from a convenient inn, they would then tour their neighbourhood, accompanied by a fiddler, or later a brass band. Most of these rushbearings died out during the hard days of the 1840s, very few being held in later decades. After some seventy years, the Sowerby Bridge rushcart was revived in 1977, and still takes place on the first weekend in September.[432]

Feasts and fairs had a quite different origin as church festivals held on the day of the patron saint. For example, Halifax Feast is held on the feast of the birth of St John the Baptist, 24 June. After the Reformation they continued as semi-commercial annual events at which employers and potential employees gathered for hirings and itinerant traders attended to sell livestock, household goods and foods not generally available locally. In Todmorden, for example, the yearly Pot Fair, held in November, sold all manner of household goods, everything from chairs, tables, clothes horses, chaff and straw mattresses, to pottery.[433] At Haworth Tide, the lanes were filled with pens of sheep, trotting

---

[431] Turner, *A spring-time saunter*, pp.196-199.

[432] G. Stringfellow, *The Sowerby Bridge rush bearing*, Halifax, Metropolitan Borough of Calderdale, 1980.

[433] Travis, *Notes: (historical and biographical)*, p.35.

horses, geese, and crates of pullets brought from Ireland.[434]   By the early nineteenth century every town and village had its own event of this kind, some calling them feasts, others calling them rushbearings, even if there wasn't a single rush in sight. They were the only secular day's holiday in the entire year, providing an opportunity for family and friends from the surrounding area to meet up hospitably. For this reason, they were spaced out throughout the lighter and warmer months, so that each could be visited in turn.

A typical rushbearing or feast around the 1860s would include footraces, clog dancing competitions, drinking, and, as a result, fighting. Stalls set up along the roadsides sold locally grown damsons, pears, apples and nuts, and most probably professionally baked gingerbreads moulded as figures, horses, watches or ornamental slabs.[435]   Those made by Joseph Dobson (1829-1885) of Elland included crowns, fiddles, anchors, swans, Prince of Wales feathers and a lion.

Moulded gingerbread: Haworth, 1860s-70s[436]

1 lb/450 g flour
3 heaped tsp ground ginger
¼ tsp ground aniseed
½ tsp each ground clove, cinnamon, allspice
8 oz/225 g black treacle
2 oz/50 g muscovado sugar
2 oz/50 g butter

Sift together the flour and spices, make a well in the centre. Melt the remaining ingredients without boiling, pour into the flour, mix, and knead until smooth. Cover with a cloth to keep warm, break off pieces, roll out about ¼ in/7 mm thick, dust with a little mixed flour and ginger on both sides and press into the mould. Trim off the surplus with a knife, invert and tap one end of the mould to turn the gingerbread out onto a greased or non-stick baking tray. If the mould tends to stick it may be brushed with a little of the melted butter.

Bake at 130ºC/250ºF gas mark 1 for about 45 minutes, then remove

---

[434] Hartley & Ingilby, *Life and tradition in West Yorkshire,* p.146.

[435] Savage, *Sam Banks: his life and times,* p.15.

[436] Brears, *Traditional food in Yorkshire*, p.305.

Figure 50. *Sweets or 'fairings' were among the rare treats to be enjoyed at the annual village fair or feast, most being made by local confectioners. Gingerbreads were made by Joseph Dobson of Elland using these carved moulds. He also stamped out these conversation lozenges so that youngsters could exchange surreptitious messages.*

onto a wire cooling tray. The gingerbreads will be too hard to eat when fresh but will soften if left in a kitchen or cellar for a day or more, and then stored in airtight containers.

Dobson also made sweets in the form of small, flat round lozenges stamped with popular mottoes. Those of the mid-1850s celebrated the Crimean War with 'LORD RAGLAN', 'BATTLE OF BALACLAVA' and other battles. Later in the century more suggestive ones were made for the younger fairgoers, with lines such as 'MEET ME BY MOONLIGHT', 'MAY I KISS YOU', 'YES AND WELCOME', 'CAN YOU KEEP A SECRET', 'NAME THE DAY', or 'WELL I NEVER'.[437]

In addition to buying these professionally produced treats, many families saved money by making their own, especially brandy snaps which, despite their name, never contained any brandy.

Brandy snaps: Miss S. Spencer, Hollock Lee[438]

2 oz/50 g each butter, brown sugar, treacle and flour
1 tsp ground ginger

Cream the butter and sugar, beat in the treacle, then the flour sifted with the ginger. Form the mixture into walnut-sized balls, place 6 in/15 cm apart on a greased baking sheet and bake at 180°C/350°F gas mark 4 for about 7-10 minutes until spread and bubbling. Remove from the oven, allow to cool 1-2 minutes, free from the sheet with a knife and roll around a ½ in/1.5 cm diameter rod, such as the handle of a wooden spoon, and leave to cool until brittle. Slide off and store immediately in an airtight tin.

Some of the foods associated with feasts were used to provide highly amusing competitions. The classic local version was the 'meyl-eating match'. For this, each competitor was given the same amount of dry oatmeal, but nothing to drink, the first to prove he had finished by whistling being declared the winner.[439]

In Halifax itself the Midsummer Fair was held in various locations: Cadney's Croft and New Market in 1832, Horton Street in 1838, then Northgate, the Market, Lister Lane, the Piece Hall, and from the 1890s, the Victoria Cattle Market. Over the years it transformed from a mainly hiring and retailing fair into a pleasure fair, where many people gathered simply to enjoy an hour or two's entertainment. Around 1900 there were shooting galleries, coconut shies, 'Aunt Sallies' featuring heads of the hated Boer leaders, distorting mirrors, prize bullocks, fat women, midgets and huge steam-powered roundabouts, all along with the usual range of sweets and fruits.[440]

---

[437] Personal communication, Mr T. Chadwick.

[438] Ashton et al, *The St Michael's recipe and quotation book*, p.23.

[439] Savage, *Sam Banks: his life and times*, p.16.

[440] *Halifax Courier*, 27 June 1905; Lonsdale Collection, *Newspaper cuttings*, vol.4, p.68; vol.11,

Thump Sundays

The Sundays immediately following the annual fair were known as Thump Sundays, 'because all those entering an ale-house and refuse to pay for liquor for the jollification of the company are soundly thumped.' Thumps were celebrated in Halifax, Illingworth, Brighouse, Denholme and Queensbury, where 'the natives who live elsewhere make a rule to visit their old home, and the re-assembling of scattered families causes much social happiness …' 'every house has its family party' usually centred on a substantial meal.[441]

Trips

Today, when cars, buses, trains and planes form part of everyday life, it is hard to imagine a time when, for most people, travel meant walking, and long walks could only be made by taking time off work. The first opportunities for long-distance travel came with the arrival of the railways. The Manchester-Leeds line through the Calder Valley in 1841 was later extended to Burnley, Preston and Blackpool, while the line up the Aire Valley through to Keighley in 1848, eventually gave access to Morecambe and Windermere too. Churches, chapels, societies and factory-owners now started to organise large-scale excursions that enabled huge numbers of people to leave their valleys to see different landscapes and the sea for the first time.

This was very exciting, but, since no-one knew if food was going to be available in these unexplored regions, most took their own provisions for the day. One elderly farmer, on being told by youngsters that London was a bad place for food, arrived at the station struggling under the weight of a huge carpetbag. As he explained it contained a home-cooked:

> shoulder lump an' a couple o' ducks, an' aw've hawf a cheese, an' a rowl or
> two o' butter, an' some apple pasties, an' a bottle o' wine. We're nooan baan
> to pine [starve]; we're baan to enjoy 'uzzens![442]

Similarly, when Mr.Lund of Keighley's Turkey Mill sponsored a works outing to Windermere, Joe o' Raygill brought three 'curnberry' (redcurrant) pasties, while a group from Exley Head carried

> their rhubub pasties an' treacle parkins. Harry o' Bridget's had a treacle
> parkin t' size of a pancake in his hat crahn, an' Joe o' owd Grace's had a gert

p.136.

[441] Wright, *English dialect dictionary,* under 'Thump (5)'; *Halifax Courier*, 3 July 1897; W.B. Trigg, 'Excursion to Ovenden', *Transactions of the Halifax Antiquarian Society*, 1925, 81-104 at p.99.

[442] Lonsdale Collection, *Newspaper cuttings*, vol.26, p.24.

bacon collop in his pocket t' size of an oven tin. Somebody remarks, "Tha'll grease thi owd chops wi' that, Joe."[443]

On arrival, the women needed cups of tea. Apparently having carried their mill tea-cans with them, they approached some of the numerous houses that displayed 'Hot water sold here' in their windows. The price, tuppence a piece, was shocking, twice as much as they paid for a whole week's supply back at the mill, but it had to be paid. It was well worth the expense, however, as they set off from Bowness Pier to cruise to Newby Bridge, Wray Castle or Ambleside, before returning to the train, exclaiming 'i's 'ommost like bein' i' Heaven.'[444] Home-made pasties proved to be so popular, especially in the bilberry time in summer, that Oats Royd Mills' annual excursion to Blackpool became popularly known as 'the pasty trip'.[445]

Some found it more convenient to buy their trip food from their local baker and confectioner, from whom this was a welcome source of extra trade. These shops already produced the popular pasties and parkins, but other items were particularly popular with trippers, these including:

Pork pie: West Family[446]

Filling
2 lb/900 g minced pork
1 tsp salt
½ tsp pepper
½ tsp sage

Pastry
1 lb/450 g flour
5 oz/125 g lard
½ tsp salt

Mix the pork, salt, pepper and sage together with cold water and set side. Bring the lard and salt to the boil, pour into the flour, quickly work together to form a dough and knead when just cool

---

443 Bill o' th' Hoylus End, *Revised edition of poems*, pp.78, 79, 82.

444 Ibid., pp.79, 80.

445 J. Billingsley, 'Families, friends and neighbours: folklore and cultural tradition in Midgley' in I. Bailey, D. Cant, A. Petford, & N. Smith, *Pennine perspectives: aspects of the history of Midgley*, Midgley, Midgley Books, 2007, p.136.

446 West family, *Manuscript recipe book*, p.11.

enough to handle to form a stiff pastry. Use two thirds of the pastry to line either an 8 in/20 cm greased shallow round cake tin, or six 3½ in/9 cm diameter individual pie tins, cover and set aside for 20 minutes, keeping the remaining pastry covered to prevent it drying out. Spoon the pork into the pies, roll out the remaining pastry to form lids, carefully sealing the edges and cutting a small round hole in the centres. [The pies may be glazed with beaten egg at this point.] For a large pie, bake at 200ºC/400ºF gas mark 6 for 30 minutes, then reduce to 160ºC/310ºF gas mark 3 for a further 2 hours, or a further 30-40 minutes for the small ones.

Picnic pie: West Family[447]

Filling
8 oz/225 g minced raw beef or pork
4 oz,/100 g minced ham
4 oz/100 g breadcrumbs
½ tsp salt
⅛ tsp pepper

Pastry
12 oz/325 g flour
1 tsp baking powder
½ tsp salt
5 oz/125 g lard

Mix the meat, breadcrumbs and seasoning with ¼ pt/150 ml cold water and set aside. Sift the flour, baking powder and salt together, rub in the lard, and mix in 6 fl oz/200 ml hot water to form the pastry. Knead smooth and use two-thirds to line the lower two-thirds of a greased and lined loaf tin, working the pastry evenly up the sides with the fingers. Fill with the meat, use the remaining pastry to form a lid, seal the edges, brush with beaten egg, and bake at 200ºC/400ºF gas mark 6 for 30 minutes, then reduce to 160ºC/310ºF gas mark 3 for a further 1½ hours.

Excursion buns a penny each: West Family [448]

1 lb/450 g strong white flour

---

[447] Ibid., p.10.
[448] Ibid., p.33.

1½ oz/35 g sugar
pinch of salt
1 tsp dried yeast
1 egg, separated
2 oz/50 g melted butter
½ tsp lemon essence
½ pt/300 ml tepid water
roughly crushed sugar crystals for sprinkling

Mix the dry ingredients, make a well in the centre, pour in the water, beaten yolk and butter, mix to form a soft dough, turn out onto a floured board, and knead for 5 minutes. Place in a bowl, cover lightly and leave to rise in a warm place, for about an hour. Divide the dough into 8 pieces, form each into a ball and place on a greased baking sheet, well spaced apart. Lightly cover and return to the warm until doubled in size, then bake at 190ºC/375ºF gas mark 5 for 15-20 minutes. The buns may be brushed with beaten egg and sprinkled with crushed sugar candy as they come out of the oven.

Towards the end of the nineteenth century the day trips were being extended into Wakes Weeks, when the mills closed down for important maintenance work, and almost the entire population went on holiday, often to the same resort, as 'Tom Halifax' discovered:

I 'waked' and wandered where she stands,
That Queen of tripping places,
And met on Blackpool's breezy sands
Men of all lands and crazes -
Yes! Tykes from Barkis-land were there,
From Stain-land, El-land too,
From Greet-land there were some I'll swear,
And Soy-land not a few.[449]

Staying in a boarding-house was relatively expensive, involving the costs of the room, the food to be provided for the landlady to cook and charges for 'cruet'. There were also the attractions to be paid for, the piers, funfairs, donkeys, theatres, rock, and so on. To pay for these Halifax pawnbrokers took all manner of items just before the holidays began, even 'the pans, dishes, cutlery, hardware etc.' that would not be needed for that week.[450] For many, dining with

[449] J. Lister, *Poems by Tom Halifax*, Halifax, [n.d.], vol.1, p.65.
[450] Lonsdale Collection, *Newspaper cuttings*, vol.36, p.24.

strangers at a large communal table with shared tureens was a new and rather challenging experience, as everyone tried to adopt formal manners quite different from those usual at home. Young Wilfred Pickles dreaded it, particularly

> that awful silence at meals with everyone asking in whispers for the salt to be passed and scared lest their stomachs should rumble … I felt quite guilty when I crunched my roast potato, for the noise in my mouth seemed to shatter the silence.[451]

Pub Food

All those who called into a public house, while away from home, expected to be able to buy food to accompany their drinks, the quality and range of the fare varying considerably from one house to another. It might be as simple as a bit of oatcake and cheese, or the staple of 'beef brawn'/'pressed beef' and oatcake, better known towards the Lancashire border as 'stew an' 'ard'. At the Black Horse, Thornton, a meos-pot of broth and a pint of ale cost only 3½d, while at the Old Mason's Arms, Gauxholme, joints of beef were roasted over the taproom fire and served with oatcakes.[452]   Anyone calling at the Eagle Inn in Stanbury, and asking for food around 1920 was shown into the back parlour and silently served with 'two eggs, delicious bread and butter, cakes and pastry, tea and cream', all for a shilling.[453]

The larger pubs would offer to cook more substantial dishes for casual callers, relying on any ingredients illustrated by an incident at an inn near Midgley around 1870. Here five young men had already eaten over a pound of steak and a penny breadcake each when a local butcher came in and, impressed by their appetites, offered to pay 6d each for more food. A further 12 lb of steak and an 18½ lb joint of beef were cooked, served and eaten along with fish, loaves of bread and several quarts of ale – an average of over 5 lb of beef per man![454]

In some pubs, where there was a regular demand for meals, an 'ordinary' or dinner-of-the-day was usually available. That at Todmorden's York Hotel around 1900 was typical: oxtail soup, a main course of roast beef, mutton,

---

[451] Pickles, *Between you and me,* p.14.

[452] W. Cudworth, *Round about Bradford,* Bradford, Thomas Brear, 1876, p.166; Rudman, *Todmorden old pub trail,* p.17.

[453] Southwart, *Brontë moors & villages,* p.155.

[454] Turner, *A spring-time saunter,* p.37.

turkey or duck with potatoes and vegetables, then apple or gooseberry pie, cheese, and a dessert.[455]

In addition to these routine meals, most public houses competed for the provision of bespoke catering for special events, particularly wedding 'breakfasts' and funeral teas. The larger ones also provided formal dinners for all manner of civic events and social celebrations. The following typical menu was served at the Queen Hotel in 1879 to celebrate the opening of Todmorden's new market hall. The range and quality of its dishes shows the enormous contrast that existed between the foods eaten by the prosperous well-to-do and those of the ordinary working population.

Soups	Macaroni
	Clear Hare
Fish	Turbot & Lobster Sauce
Entrées	Boiled Mutton & Tongue, Boiled Turkey & Ham, Boiled Fowl
Roasts	Crop of Beef, Pork, Veal, Goose, Turkey & Sausage, Grouse, Chicken
Sweets	Tartlets, Custards, Jellies, Blancmanges, Cream &c.
Dessert	[probably fresh fruits, dried fruits and nuts]
Wines	Port, Sherry, Claret
	Champagnes of Moet & Chandon, Roerderer, Mumm & Co.
	Hock, Moselle, Burgundy
	Lemonade, Seltzer, Soda & Potash Waters.[456]

Hen-Pecked Husbands' Clubs

Despite their name, these clubs that were being set up in small towns around the 1870s were essentially popular social societies more intent on fun and good fellowship than for providing a refuge for brow-beaten menfolk. However, as 'Tom Halifax' stated;

Its members must be married,
No bachelors allow'd,
No bachelors might mingle
Among the "hen-pecked" crowd,
But poor hard-harass'd hubbies
Who fly from women's claws -
For them the "Henpeck'd Club" is
A place where sufferings pause.[457]

---

[455] Rudman, *Todmorden old pub trail,* p.57.

[456] Dugdale, *Todmorden market,* pp.27-28.

[457] Lister, *Poems by Tom Halifax*, vol.1, p.65.

One club that met on the old packhorse bridge at Hebden Bridge used to remove chosen husbands from their homes by force, mount them on a hand-truck and jolt them down the roughest roads back to the bridge, where the local inns presumably served their needs. No wonder it was described as a 'notorious fraternity'![458]

Meetings just before the First World War were much better organised and respectable, taking place on Easter Mondays, when fifty or sixty men would travel to the pre-arranged location from all parts of this area, and even from distant Sheffield and Lancashire. In 1910 they gathered at Luddenden Foot and walked the four miles to Cragg Vale to picnic at Turvin. Loaves of bread, tins of tongue and joints of beef were then made up into sandwiches, some people slicing and others buttering. Tinned pineapple provided the dessert, after which the club's Mayor presided over a meeting, and hymns were sung before all returned down towards the station. Next year they chose Boothtown United Methodist Church as their base, commencing with 'well-filled plates of roast beef or boiled ham and confections of many kinds' before going to visit Shibden Hall and park as guests of John Lister. Having returned by way of Shibden Valley and Pule Hill they enjoyed a tea, spent the evening with stories and songs, and finally dispersed at 9 p.m. Such joyous, innocent meetings failed to survive the Great War, probably because it caused the deaths of too many of the former members.[459]

Haymaking
The local hay harvest started in mid-June, some waiting until Halifax Feast on St. John's Day, 24 June, before starting to scythe. As this work required extra help, some farms hired Irish mowers from around the 1840s, usually paying them an agreed wage plus their food and lodgings.[460] Some local farmers provided a good breakfast beforehand and an hour-long dinner, with a half-hour 'drinking time' each morning and afternoon.[461] It was thirsty work, with some farms buying up to five barrels of beer to help keep everyone going throughout the day, along with supplies of oatcake and treacle parkin. The carting of the last load, called 'churn-getting', was usually celebrated with further beer and refreshments.[462]

---

[458] *Todmorden & Hebden Bridge Historical Almanack,* 1876, 5 June.

[459] Lonsdale Collection, *Newspaper cuttings,* vol.21, p.43; vol.25, pp.55, 61.

[460] Crump, *The little hill farm,* pp.54-56.

[461] Travis, *Notes: (historical and biographical),* p.47.

[462] N. Arnold, *Edwardian Cornholme,* Cornholme, Workers Educational Association, 1981,

Harvest

Since most of the farms in the Upper Calder Valley stopped growing corn towards the end of the nineteenth century, there are few memories of the traditional Harvest Homes that celebrated the cutting of the final sheaf. At Shays, Cornhome, an old trestle table and forms were set up in a disused cottage ready for a meal of two or three hens stewed with vegetables, accompanied by a barrel of beer left over from the hay harvest. Music then followed, two men having fiddles and another a concertina.[463]

Pig Fair Monday

Since pigs formed an important part of the domestic economy of the cottagers and tenant farmers in Brighouse and the surrounding townships, a pig fair was established in the Black Swan field on the first Monday after 12 October 1850, and over subsequent years. This soon developed into a very popular event attracting thousands of visitors, to whom local confectioners began to sell parkin pigs in 1866. By 1873 H.B. Turner of Bethel Street was producing 7,000 of them, but by 1889 he was baking 12,000, G. Hoare of Briggate 11,000 and D. Hartley also of Briggate a further 4,000, a total of 27,000 parkin pigs for this one-day fair. In addition, both H. Smythe, a Bethel Street pork butcher and Turner now introduced 'sausage pigs' making 2,000 of these between them.[464] The pigs would have been made from recipes such as:

Gingerbread snaps: Mrs Oates, Mytholmroyd[465]

8 oz/225 g flour
2 tsp ground ginger
4 oz/100 g sugar
3 oz/75 g butter
4 oz/100 g treacle or golden syrup
1 tsp bicarbonate of soda

Sift the flour and ginger together. Heat the sugar, butter and treacle or syrup *very* gently together until the sugar has dissolved, then mix into the flour along with the bicarbonate of soda dissolved in 2 tsp water to form a dough. Roll out on a floured board, cut into pig shapes, place on a greased baking tin and bake at 180°C/350°F gas mark 4 for about 12 minutes

p.16; Greenwood, *Life on a Pennine farm*, p.36.

[463] Arnold, *Edwardian Cornholme*, p.17.

[464] Brighouse & District Local History Society, *What was happening in Brighouse* p.23.

[465] Ashton et al, *The St Michael's recipe and quotation book*, p.19.

Figure 51. Founded in 1850, Brighouse's Pig Fair Monday drew in enormous crowds for whom the local bakers made parkin pigs. In 1889 27,000 of these were sold on this single day, each stamped out using a tinplate cutter.

Plot Night 5 November

For centuries special 'tharf' or unleavened cakes made from oatmeal had been baked to celebrate All Hallows on 1 November and All Souls the following day. As these feasts declined in popularity, their cakes became associated with Plot Night on 5 November, transferring themselves into 'parkins'.

As early as 1728 parkins were being made throughout the year, one Sarah Priestley of Halifax being accused of stealing oatmeal for making one, her mistress having sent her to Elland for the treacle.[466] Before the introduction of baking soda, parkins were made with a simple mixture of oatmeal, treacle and lard, resulting in a solid cake of brick-like hardness that took weeks of storage in a damp room to become soft enough to eat. Even when soda came into use, they still had to be kept for at least a week or more before use.

Parkin: West Family[467]

8 oz/225 g medium oatmeal
8 oz/225 g flour

---

[466] Brears, *Traditional food in Yorkshire*, pp.163, 171.
[467] West family, *Manuscript recipe book*, p.23.

1 tsp bicarbonate of soda
4 oz/100 g lard
8 oz/225 g black treacle

Mix the dry ingredients, make a well in the centre, pour in the lard and treacle melted with 4 tbs water, mix together and put into a greased and lined 7½ ins./18 cm. square tin. Bake at 150ºC/ 300ºF gas mark 2 for 45 minutes. Store for at least a week until soft enough to eat.

This is a basic parkin recipe, but there were numerous others, some without treacle, some without oatmeal, some using sugar and golden syrup, some adding eggs and ginger. Most took the form of a flat cake, while others resembled round ginger biscuits. The following recipe gives a much lighter cake made without the oatmeal that most people expect to find in parkins.

Sponge parkin (1900): Mrs Marsden, Halifax[468]

1 lb/450 g flour
8 oz/225 g sugar
2 tsp ground ginger
½ tsp ground nutmeg
1 tsp bicarbonate of soda
pinch of salt
4 oz/100 g lard
8 oz/225 g treacle or golden syrup
½ pt/300 ml milk

Mix the dry ingredients, stir in the lard melted in the treacle, then the milk, and bake as the previous recipe.

As John Hartley described in 1867, having lit their bonfire in the early evening

> they all sit raand th' fire wi' ther parkin an' milk, or else rooasted puttatis, an' they tell tales [among the] Squibs and crackers! Star leets an' cattering wheels.[469]

Toffee Joins 5 November

Plot night was also the time for 'toffee-joins' at which youngsters would gather at a friend's house, each contributing part of the ingredients needed for boiling

---

[468] Kaye, *Yorkshire cooking,* p.213.

[469] Hartley, *Clock Almanack,* 1867, November.

a large batch of toffee. These were usually very lively affairs as one of the great sports was to try and smear one another's faces with the black treacle.[470] For one join in the early 1860s, the girls made the following budget for purchases from a grocery shop:

3 girls donating	6d	1s 6d
6 boys donating	9d	2s 3d
		3s 9d
2 lb butter	2s 6d	
2 lb sugar	1s 0d	
1 lb treacle	3d	
		3s 9d

Unfortunately, their accountancy was far better than their cooking skills. After arguments as to which ingredient was to be boiled first, interference from one of the lads, boiling it for two hours, and even leaving it overnight, it still refused to thicken and set. As a result, it had to be 'teamed with a weshing-bowl … sou thay hed ta eit er raither sup t'toffee we' spooins![471]

Those with more experience used more reliable recipes. By the Edwardian period some were replacing the traditional black treacle with golden syrup to give a milder flavour.

Treacle toffee[472]

1 lb/450 g demerara sugar
4 oz/100 g butter
4 oz/100 g black treacle
1 tbs vinegar
1 tbs water
1 tbs milk

Gently boil all (except the vinegar) together, starting slowly until the sugar has completely dissolved, then more rapidly for 15-20 minutes until at 149ºC/300ºF, a drop becoming brittle when put

---

[470] Billingsley, 'Families, friends and neighbours' p.138; Harwood, H.W., 'As things were: a social study of Upper Calder Valley', *Transactions of the Halifax Antiquarian Society*, 1968, 15-26 at p.20.

[471] Slyman, T' *story o' th' pudding macking un eiting*, p.15.

[472] Brears, *Traditional food in Yorkshire*, p.278.

into cold water. Stir in the vinegar and pour into a shallow greased tin, marking it into squares with a butter smeared knife when half set. Wrap in clingfilm and store in airtight containers to prevent the pieces from sticking together.

Toffee: Mr L.B. Harvey, Brearley[473]

1 lb/450 g brown sugar
8 oz/225 g butter
1 tbs golden syrup
¼ pt/150 ml milk

Follow the instructions above.

The tricks played at toffee joins often went beyond mere face-daubing. When the toffee had nearly finished its boiling at a house in Stanbury, a group of youths once climbed on to the roof and let a rope down the chimney, so that one of their friends inside could hook the pan onto it. What screams followed from the girls as their prized toffee shot up the chimney, never to be seen again.[474] It could also be very unwise to accept the sweets made by one Todmorden individual, since they were just short lengths of fatty tallow dusted in cocoa. One man was rendered completely speechless after trying one – they had stuck his false teeth solidly together!

Preparing for Christmas

As Christmas marked the greatest family gathering of the entire year, it was essential for every household to assemble all the good things they would need over the festive period. This involved buying in both raw and ready-made foods especially for those most important of meals, Christmas dinner and Christmas tea. Bakers were particularly busy, since many wives preferred to buy their Christmas cakes rather than risk spoiling expensive ingredients in their own ovens. To promote his wares, Mr H.J. Turner of Bethel Street, Brighouse, decided to advertise his Monster Currant Loaves, one to be cut up on 23 December 1871 weighing 220 lb and containing a hundred silver coins. His 1875 'Monster' was even larger, a massive 330 lb embedded with 330 silver threepenny bits, all available at 6d the pound.[475] Local bakers appear to have produced two kinds of Christmas cake, one raised with yeast and another with baking powder.

---

[473] Ashton et al, *The St Michael's recipe and quotation book*, p.32.

[474] Craven, *A Brontë moorland village*, p.123.

[475] Brighouse & District Local History Society, *What was happening in Brighouse* p.48.

Christmas bread: West Family[476]

1 lb/450 g strong white flour
½ tsp salt
½ tsp ground nutmeg
½ tsp ground mace
6 oz/150 g caster sugar
3 oz/75 g butter
3 oz/75 g lard
1 tsp dried yeast
1 egg, beaten
½ pt/300 ml tepid milk
8 oz/225 g currants
4 oz/100 g raisins
2 oz/50 g candied peel

Sift the flour with the salt and spices, mix in the sugar, rub in the fats, mix in the yeast, egg and milk to form a light dough, knead 10 minutes on a floured board, cover, and leave in a warm place for 1 hour to rise. Knead in the dried fruits and peel, form into two loaves, put into greased loaf tins, cover, and return to the warm until doubled in size. Bake at 190ºC/375ºF gas mark 5 for about 30-35 minutes. They may be brushed with a glaze of equal volumes of milk and sugar melted together as they come out of the oven.

Christmas cake [plain]: M.H., Haworth[477]

1 lb/450 g flour
½ nutmeg, grated
2 oz/ 50 g baking powder [today, 2 tsp]
2 oz/ 50 g butter
2 oz/50 g lard
8 oz/225 g caster sugar
2 eggs, beaten
8 oz/225 g currants
4 oz/100 g raisins
2 oz/50 g candied lemon peel
2 drops lemon essence
a little milk

---

[476] West family, *Manuscript recipe book*, p.19.

[477] Hawksbridge Baptist Church, *A useful recipe book.*

Figure 52. Victorian Christmas bread, Christmas cake, mincemeat, mince pies and Christmas puddings ignited with brandy were much plainer than those of the present day.

Sift the flour with the nutmeg and baking powder. Cream the butter and lard with the sugar, beat in the eggs, a little at a time, then the flour, little by little, and finally the remaining ingredients with a little milk to form a dropping consistency. Put into a greased and lined 7 in/18 cm square or 8 in/20 cm diameter round tin and bake at 150ºC/300ºF gas mark 2 for 2–2½ hours, covering with a piece of greaseproof paper after the first hour.

Christmas cake [rich]: Mrs Mary Wright, West Shaw[478]

Ingredients: as above, plus 4 oz/100 g currants, 2 oz/50 g each of butter, lard, and ground almonds, and 2 more eggs. Leave out the lemon essence.

Follow the instructions above.

The reason why some families made cakes of different qualities was because they might need a very rich one for special occasions and important visitors, a

---

[478] Oxenhope Church, *Recipe book*. See also Anon., *159 recipes from good kitchens*, p.5.

plainer one for ordinary use, and a basic 'plum spice bread' to be eaten with cheese and beer for 'the kitchen company', as back-door servants and visitors were known.[479] Even the richest of the recipes, given above, has only about a third of the dried fruits of the modern Christmas cake. It was only when wages increased and the cost of ingredients fell as a result of cheap imports from around the Empire, that home bakers competed with their neighbours to see how much fruit, butter, fruits and eggs they could add to the mixture. As a result many people find that today's Christmas cakes are far too heavy and indigestible for comfort.

The same effect overtook the Christmas pudding. Originating as a large suet dumpling containing only a small amount of dried fruit and for eating as an accompaniment to meat, it became ever richer during the late nineteenth and early twentieth centuries. It too has now become so rich, sweet and heavy that it has often become more of burdensome duty than a pleasure when served at the end of the Christmas dinner. For this reason, it is worth trying the following recipes. The authentic way of pre-cooking them months in advance was to tie the mixture in a large square of cotton or linen that had been scalded, shaken to remove most of the water, and then had its upper side sprinkled with flour. Having shaken off the surplus, the mixture was placed on it, the cloth gathered up and tied at the top with string, after which it was plunged into water boiling in a pan over the fire, or in the set-pot usually used for doing the laundry. This is still a practical way of producing the traditional flattened ball-shaped pudding. However, it is easier to use the popular late Victorian method of packing the mixture into a greased pottery basin, covering it with a piece of pleated greaseproof paper and a cloth tied over the rim, or the modern equivalent of a piece of kitchen foil, pressed tightly around the top, before cooking in a steamer.

Christmas pudding [plain]: K. Fogden[480]

5 oz/125 g each of fresh breadcrumbs, suet, sugar, currants and raisins, and chopped candied peel
¼ tsp each bicarbonate of soda and grated nutmeg
1 tsp golden syrup
grated zest of a lemon
2 eggs, beaten
a little milk

---

[479] Hamerton, *Olde Eland*, p.89.

[480] Anon., *159 recipes from good kitchens*, p.5.

Mix the dry ingredients, then stir in the syrup, eggs, and sufficient milk to form a stiff mixture. Pack into a greased basin or mould, cover with greaseproof paper and a piece of cooking foil pressed closely round the rim, and steam for 4 hours. It may be stored in a dry place for a week or two before steaming for 4 hours just before serving.

Christmas pudding [rich]: Miss Hutchinson, Ewood Hall[481]

4 oz/100 g flour
4 oz/100 g fresh breadcrumbs
8 oz/225 g suet
8 oz/225 g each chopped raisins, sultanas and currants
2 oz/50 g candied peel
6 oz/150 g sugar
1 oz/25 g ground almonds
¼ tsp grated nutmeg
4 eggs, beaten
⅛ pt/75 ml brandy
a little milk

Mix the dry ingredients, then the eggs, brandy, and just sufficient milk to make a medium mixture. Pack firmly into greased basins, cover as above, and steam for 12 hours.

At the table, a little brandy would be poured over the pudding and set alight after which it was served, except in poor or teetotal families, with either:

Brandy butter: Miss Hutchinson, Ewood Hall[482]

4 oz/100 g butter
3 oz/75 g icing sugar
brandy

Cream the butter with the sugar, beat in the brandy a little at a time, spread as a flat slab, chill, and cut into fancy shapes to serve with the pudding.

or

---

481 Ashton et al, *The St Michael's recipe and quotation book,* p.17.
482 Ibid.

Brandy sauce

2 tbs cornflour
5 tsp sugar
½ pt/300 ml milk
1-2 tbs brandy

Blend the cornflour and sugar with 2 tbs of the milk, scald with the remaining milk, bring to the boil while stirring, until it thickens, continue for 2 minutes more, then stir in the brandy and serve.

Today most people imagine that everyone used to have mince pies at Christmas, but this was not so. Though affordable by the well-to-do, their expensive ingredients put them well beyond the reach of most working families up to the end of the Victorian period, when prices fell. It was only then that they began to appear in ordinary family recipe books.

Mincemeat [plain]: Mrs Greenwood[483]

1 lb/450 g peeled, cored and finely-chopped apple
5 oz/125 g each chopped currants, raisins and suet
2 oz/50 g candied peel
10 oz/275 g sugar
2-3 tbs brandy

Mix all together, seal down in sterilised jars and keep in a cool place for a few weeks before use.

Mincemeat [rich]: Mrs Whittingham, Shelf[484]

4 oz/100 g each currants, raisins, sugar, peeled, cored and finely-chopped apple
1 oz/25 g each chopped candied lemon peel and suet
¼ nutmeg, grated

Mix all together, add a little water, seal down in sterilised jars and store in a cool place.

These mincemeats can be used to make shortcrust individual or plate pies to be baked at 200ºC/400ºF gas mark 6 for about 20 minutes. Even when the baking

---

[483] Ibid., p.34.

[484] Kaye, *Yorkshire cooking*, p.232.

had been completed, there was still much to do, especially shopping. As Bill o' th' Hoylus End expected, any Yorkshireman's Christmas should include:

> … ten or twelve pounds o' gooid meit,
> A small cheese and a barrel o' beer,
> Aw'll welcome King Christmas to neet,
> For he nobbut comes once in a year.
>
> Them bairns they care nowt abaht drink,
> Like us 'at's advancing into years;
> So Sally, lass, what does ta think,
> If ta buys them some apples an' pears?[485]

The best time to shop was the late evening of Christmas Eve, when butchers and greengrocers had to progressively reduce their prices in order to clear their stock before it went off over the coming holiday.

Christmas Day 25 December

With the house to prepare and the food and drink to make ready for probably this most important family gathering, Christmas morning was always a busy time, especially when these practicalities had to be fitted in between church and chapel services. The children would probably find apples, pears or oranges in their stockings when they got out of bed, but after breakfast would have to set off to their Sunday School. At Portsmouth, near Todmorden, in the 1850s-60s some 400 children would be seen leaving their homes before 9 a.m., each carrying a penny to put into old Abraham Greenwood's hat as he stood at the top of the schoolroom steps. Once seated upstairs, they sprang up at the sight of five or six men carrying in great trays loaded with pieces of spice bread and currant bread. After these had been rapidly distributed and munched, a second group carried in cans of hot coffee, for which each child had brought their own mug.[486] Later in the day, and just as they would do on Boxing Day and New Year's Day, the children would set off in small groups to sing carols from one house to another. Their main carol was *Here we come a-Wassailing* which included the lines:

> Bring us out a table, and spread it with a cloth,
> Bring us out a mouldy cheese, likewise a Christmas loaf

However, their gifts were much more likely to be a penny or two.[487]

Back at home, mothers and sisters would be busily employed preparing for the

---

[485] Bill o' th' Hoylus End, *Revised edition of poems*, p.57.

[486] Savage, *Sam Banks: his life and times*, pp.14-15.

[487] Billingsley, 'Families, friends and neighbours', p.138; Hamerton, *Olde Eland*, p.90.

main meal of the entire year, Christmas dinner. Beef was the usual joint, being served hot with potatoes, vegetables and Yorkshire pudding, and large enough to provide cold meat over the following days.[488] Unlike today, when most families have poultry as their main meat, relatively few could afford to buy chicken, ducks, geese and turkeys, though those who kept them might kill off one of their own. As with the Cratchit family in Dickens' *A Christmas Carol*, the gift of that most prestigious of birds, the goose, would represent almost unbelievable good fortune. Just being invited to share the taste of one was an exceptionally grand experience, one that moved Bill o' th' Hoylus End to his poetry. As he was returning home from the army on Christmas Eve, 1863, he met Harry Smith, a local manufacturer, who invited him to dine on roasted goose and a giblet pie. The latter does not sound particularly appetising, but in reality was truly delicious.

Yorkshire goose giblet pie[489]

raw neck, liver & heart of a goose
1 onion, sliced
6 peppercorns
1 bouquet garni
1 lb/450 g steak, thinly sliced
1 tsp salt
¼ tsp pepper

Pastry
12 oz/350 g flour
1 tsp salt
6 oz/150 g lard

Cut the neck into four lengths and the liver and heart into two, place in a stewpan with the onion, peppercorns and bouquet, barely cover with water, cover, and simmer for 1½ hours. Meanwhile sift the flour and salt together, rub in the lard and work in about 5-6 tbs cold water to make the pastry. When the giblets have cooled, cut their meat into small pieces and layer them with the steak in a pie dish, seasoning with at the salt and pepper, and top with the strained giblet stock. Use the pastry to form a lid with

[488] *Siddal: our memories, our history,* Halifax, Workers Educational Association, 1989, p.20.

[489] P. Haslehurst, *The family friend and young woman's companion,* Sheffield, [1814], p.59; T. Garrett, *The encyclopedia of practical cookery,* London, L. Upcott Gill, 1894, pp.696-7.

a hole in the centre and bake at 190ºC/375ºF gas mark 5 for 1½ hours. It may be served either hot or cold.

As Bill later remembered:

> I've been i' lots o' feeds, mi lads,
> An' had some rare tucks-aght;
> Blood-puddin days wi' killin' pigs,
> Minch pies an' thumpin' tarts;
> But I wired in, an' reight an' all,
> An' supp'd whe I wor dry,
> Fer I wer dinin' wi' a gentleman
> O' goose an' giblet pie.
>
> I often think o' t' feed, mi lads,
> When t' gentleman I meet;
> Bud nauther on us speicks a word
> Abaht that glorious neet;
> In fact, I hardly can misel,
> I feel that fearful shy;
> Fer I ate a deal o' t rosted gooise,
> An' warm'd his giblet pie.[490]

Bill appears to have seen but never tasted that most impressive of all Christmas foods, the Yorkshire goose pie. Only made in the grandest of households or for the most lavish entertainments, it was based on boned-out poultry stuffed one inside the other, all packed round with masses of game and a rich forcemeat. Place on a sideboard, it would be dug out and served cold throughout the twelve days of Christmas. He was not exaggerating when he told of:

> pies made so big that it take a toathree [small crowd of] foak to lift um on t' table; sum war 9 or 10 feet i' circumference 'appen weyd as far as 20 stone.[491]

Such gargantuan gastronomic delights were totally beyond the expectations of most families, particularly when trade was bad and money was virtually non-existent.

A few hours after dinner, tea would be served, probably centred around cold meats and a raised pork pie with pickles. Slices of Christmas loaf or cake would follow, always eaten with cheese in the true Yorkshire fashion. It would most probably be a piece of Lancashire or Cheshire, for Wensleydale at this time was the finest of all English blue cheeses, considered to be far superior to Stilton.

---

490 Bill o' th' Hoylus End, *Revised edition of poems*, p.57.

491 Bill o' th' Hoylus End, *Haworth, Cowanhead & Bogthorn Almanac*, 1875, January.

Figure 53. Yorkshire goose giblet pie was considered a great delicacy. When the local poet Bill o' th' Hoylus End was invited to share one in 1863, he celebrated the event in verse.

Today Christmas dinners are predominantly family affairs, but in the Victorian period they might also be large, social events arranged for members of particular organisations. In 1855, for example, 240 members of the 6th West Yorkshire Militia met in its Riding School in Halifax to share 340 lb of prime beef, 1½ loads of potatoes and 36 large plain puddings. 190 gallons of strong foaming brown ale helped to wash these down, 6½ pt a man to his 1¼ lb of beef. Hopefully the 2nd West Yorkshire Regiment dined more modestly before commencing their ball at 10 p.m. and dancing through the night till 4.30 a.m.![492]

In the same week Edward Akroyd provided a Christmas dinner for 300 of his aged workers, while James Akroyd & Son did the same for 200 old combers and weavers. This private generosity was mirrored in the rates-funded Halifax Union Workhouse, where paupers were served 171 lb beef, 176 lb of pudding and 90 lb of bread. The Poor Law Guardians were always keen to let the public know that they had given the inmates a good time on Christmas Day, a great

---

[492] Lonsdale Collection, *Newspaper cuttings*, vol.17, p.60.

contrast to the usual meagre fare. In 1908 they published the following details in the local newspaper:

> 700 lb best English beef, which was most juicy, satisfying, tender, and cooked in eleven large rounds.
>
> Turnips, carrots and potatoes in great quantity to eat with the beef.
>
> 84 lb sultana raisins, 112 lb currants, 36 lb mixed peel, 167 lb sugar, 75 lb suet, 56 lb lard, 50 eggs and 3 lb yeast to make 53 plum puddings and spice bread.
>
> 2 barrels of apples, 2 boxes of oranges, 14 lb nuts, 2 lb almonds, 7 lb dessert raisins for dessert.
>
> 80 lb mixed sweets
>
> 700 paper bags for sharing out sweets and fruit for children and elderly women
>
> 26 lb tobacco, 288 clay pipes and 2 lb snuff
>
> Coloured paper for decorations.[493]

Christmas Day and the informal meals and parties that took place shortly afterwards marked the end of the year's cycle of culinary customs. In just six day's time, however, it was New Year's Eve, when the whole process would start over again in its never-ending, but constantly evolving, progress.

Figure 54. Mid-nineteenth-century Christmas puddings were much plainer than those of today, and still boiled in a cloth rather than a basin.

---

[493] Ibid., vol.17, p.120.

Figure 55. *Local wedding parties commenced the day with a hot ale and rum posset before setting off on the long walk to the church. It was handed round in a communal posset pot, into which the bride dropped the wedding ring. Each person then tried to fish it out using a large tablespoon.*

CHAPTER 13

FROM CRADLE TO GRAVE

As in all communities, births, marriages and deaths, also described as 'hatches, matches and despatches', were marked here by their own particular practices and foods. In the small settlements of the Pennines this never-ending sequence concerned far more than the immediate family, each individual event involving a much larger group of friends and neighbours.

Births

Today the progression through pregnancy, on to childbirth and beyond is closely monitored by well-trained health professionals backed up with modern medical facilities. As a result of these improvements, coupled with much-improved diets and living conditions, the former unbelievably high death rates of both mothers and babies has become a thing of the past. Back in the 1840s, Robert Howard found starving women going through labour either standing with their arms supported on the necks of a couple of their neighbours, or else kneeling on a cushion to lean on a pillow placed across the seat of a chair.[494] Since the child was particularly at risk, it was usually baptised as soon as possible, the formal christening taking place either at the church, or in the home, about a month later. If all had gone well, the arrival of the new baby was celebrated by a drinking session known as 'wetting the child's head'.[495]

Shortly afterwards came 'the child's first visit', the first time it was taken to visit a relation, friend or neighbour. In 1821, for example, when Hannah Ayton and her baby went to tea at Miss Wadsworth's house in Elland, 'it being the little stranger's first visit, she had [to take] home sixpence, an egg, bread and salt' to ensure its future good fortune. Sometimes a match might be added to this list, probably to provide light and heat too.[496]

Birthdays

Birthdays, with their cakes, cards and presents, are rarely, if ever, recorded locally until the opening years of the twentieth century in most homes, being introduced mainly by confectioners and stationers for commercial reasons.

---

[494] Howard, *A history of the typhus of Heptonstall Slack*, p.58.

[495] Wright, *English dialect dictionary*, under 'Child (2)'.

[496] Hamerton, *Olde Eland*, p.98.

219

Weddings

Weddings usually took place at the parish church even after civil ceremonies were allowed in 1836. In this rural area the church might be many miles away, before the huge medieval parishes were divided up in the mid-nineteenth century. In Haworth, for example, everyone had to go to Bradford parish church until the village's chapelry became independent in 1864, while those in Todmorden had to go to Rochdale up to 1866. The majority of the population had to walk to make these sixteen-mile round trips. For their 'walking weddings', as many as twelve couples would set off together, sometimes led by a fiddler on horseback.[497] As John Wood remembered at Denholme:

> The whole of the wedding party met at the residence of the bridegroom. Before breakfast proper commenced, or rather it ought to be called the first course at breakfast, a large pot that would hold two or three quarts, with two, three and sometimes four handles, called a posset pot, filled with hot ale and rum posset, would be handed round the party from one to another. Into the posset the bride would drop a wedding ring, and it was the object of each one of the party, by taking three or four tablespoonful of the posset at a time, to fish up the wedding ring, for it was firmly believed that the one who fished it up, whether male of female, would be the next of that party to be married. Then followed tea with liberal proportion of rum in it.[498]

A number of the posset pots made either in one of the Halifax potteries, or in those over towards Burnley at Cliviger, still survive. The earliest has a lion, a unicorn and a crown painted on one side and flowers on the other, the initials 'C.I.A.' and date '1737' commemorating the wedding for which it was made. Later ones, probably dating from around 1850 when less exuberant weddings came into fashion, were often initialled or named and dated in slip-trailed white clay. Their contents would be made to a recipe similar to this one, which should start by measuring the capacity of the posset pot. A good Halifax example holds 8 pints and weighs about 17 lb when full!

Hot ale & rum posset

for each person take:
½ pt/300 ml strong brown ale
1 tsp ground ginger
2 tbs, or to taste, brown sugar
2 tbs rum

---

[497] Craven, *A Brontë moorland village*, p.123; Hamerton, *Olde Eland*, p.98.

[498] J. Wood, *The autobiography of John Wood*, Bradford, 1877, p.23.

1 pinch each ground cinnamon & cloves

Bring all except the rum to the boil, stir until the sugar has dissolved, pour into a warmed pot and stir in the rum just before serving.

Figure 56. *Local potters made large communal drinking vessels for serving hot ale and rum possets to wedding parties before they set off on their long walks to the parish church. These examples comprise a rare painted example of 1737 (1), one of 1825 for a couple with a G as their surname (2), one for Bethiah Sharp dated January 1849 (3), and another with S for the surname (4).*

By the time the breakfast was over the company got quite lively and their faces, normally quite rosy from living in the bracing atmosphere of the hills 1,200 feet above sea level, became glowing red, the perspiration standing out in drops. Breakfast over, the party would prepare for a journey of six or seven miles to the [Bradford] parish church, headed by the indispensable fiddler.[499]

---

[499] Ibid.

In contrast, those who were 'above the rank of labourer' would organise a 'riding wedding' as described by 'a Yorkshire Gentleman';

> [At Haworth] A levy was made on the horses of the neighbourhood, and a merry cavalcade of mounted men and women, single and double, traversed the way to Bradford church.[500]

Others, less well off, would ride on donkeys, those from Blackley wearing hats made in the local pottery as they proceeded to their parish church in Elland.[501] It came as a relief to Todmorden folk when local proprietors began to hire six– or eight–seater jaunt carriages to carry them over the hills to Rochdale and back.[502]

Immediately after the ceremony, this usually being held for a number of couples just before the Sunday service, everyone retired to an adjacent public house for a rest and refreshment before making the long return journey. 'The inn and church appeared to be in natural connection, and as the labours of the Temperance Society had then to begin, the interests of sobriety were not always consulted'.[503] Hopefully the day would be fine, otherwise the bride in her blue and white cotton print bedgown, along with the rest of the party, would be soaked to the skin and chilled to the bone. The return might take the form of a race, riders from Bradford:

> on remounting their steeds, commenced with a race, and not infrequently an inebriate or unskilled horseman was put *'hors de combat.'* A race also was frequent at the end of the wedding expeditions, from the bridge to the toll-bar at Haworth [that is] anything but level.[504]

The climb up through the village to West Lane rises around 200 ft in its first half mile. In Haworth, the wedding party then went to their favourite inn. Each man already had a ribbon in his hat, but now, standing outside the door, the groom held a long ribbon to be run for. Five or six would then remove their coats, vests, hats, shoes, stockings, and probably even more of their clothing for this 'rough amusement … where the half-naked runners were a scandal to all decent strangers.'[505] The ribbon was then stretched across the road by a couple of men, ready to give to the winner. Then followed a 'hen-drinking', an entirely

---

[500] Gaskell, *The life of Charlotte Brontë*, p.568.

[501] Hamerton, *Olde Eland*, p.99.

[502] Travis, *Notes: (historical and biographical)*, p.183.

[503] Gaskell, *The life of Charlotte Brontë*, p.568.

[504] Ibid.

[505] Ibid., p.70.

male celebration, at which the groom paid for the first rounds, after which a hat was passed round to collect funds for further drinks.[506]

If it could be afforded, a good dinner was then provided at a local inn, probably with a plum pudding followed by roast beef and vegetables, then fruit pies and tarts. Otherwise, guests would contribute beforehand to pay for all the food and drinks, as well as a fiddler. In return for this custom, the landlord might present the newly-weds with a useful present, such as a copper kettle. Around Todmorden this 'spree' was often postponed to the Monday evening, after work, when everyone had recovered from their long walk.[507]

So far there has been no mention of the wedding cakes that form such a great part of modern wedding receptions. Most people found them unnecessary, only the wealthier families providing richly fruited and elaborately iced cakes from the early to mid-nineteenth century. Since they included large quantities of expensive ingredients, required well controlled ovens and great skill in their making and decorating, they were usually ordered from a professional confectioner. Their advertisements for 'Bride cakes' appear in directories, almanacs and similar publications. Only towards the end of the century did they become popular throughout all levels of society, but even then only the most confident of bakers trusted themselves to make a cake large and fine enough to impress the wedding party.

Funerals

Today numerous and early deaths are fortunately rare experiences. As a result, what our ancestors considered to be a major part of life-experience is now seen as an unnaturally morbid obsession. In mid-nineteenth century Halifax, for example, the average age of death for labourers and millworkers was a mere twenty-two years, tradesmen and shopkeepers made it to twenty-four, while gentry and mill-owners could expect more than double, at fifty-five.[508] Much of this was due to high infant mortality, those who managed to survive into adulthood often living beyond their sixties and seventies. A further change reflects where we die, today usually in a hospital or hospice with medical care, not in the home after home-nursed illness or fatal accident, as in the past. Whenever a person died, the initial laying-out was often performed by an

---

[506] Craven, *A Brontë moorland village*, p.134; Wright, *English dialect dictionary*, under 'Hen'.

[507] Travis, *Notes: (historical and biographical)*, p.183.

[508] H. Whone, *The essential West Riding: its character in words and pictures*, Wakefield, EP Publishing, 1975, p.92.

elderly lady who had a well-earned local reputation for her work, only the wealthy employing an undertaker for much more than providing the coffin. The deceased would then be displayed in an open coffin in the parlour if there was one, or if not in the sole living room, so that mourners could come and say their last farewells. During this period curtains would be pulled close to keep out the light, and pictures and mirrors turned to face the wall.

To prepare for the funeral, the first task was to draw up a 'bidding sheet' to list everyone to be invited. Up to the Edwardian period invitations were delivered personally by the undertaker in funeral dress, who went to the houses of those whom the family wish to attend, saying 'You are respectfully bidden to the funeral of … to be at the house of … .'[509] He then gave the date and time at which the cortège would leave the house of the deceased and follow the coffin to the church. Those who were a little better-off would provide the bidder with a number of professionally made sponge finger biscuits called:

Funeral biscuits: West Family[510]

4 oz/100 g eggs
4 oz/100 g sugar
5 oz/125 g flour
¼ tsp baking powder
3 drops lemon essence

Whisk the eggs, add the sugar, and whisk for 30 minutes before adding the essence. Sift the flour with the baking powder and fold this into the egg mixture little by little. (This was traditionally done with the hand, rather than a spoon.) Put into a forcing bag with a ½ in/1 cm diameter nozzle and pipe in 5 in/13 cm lengths onto a piece of greased greaseproof paper laid on a baking tray, allowing space for them to spread. Bake at 200ºC/400ºF gas mark 6 for 8-10 minutes and leave to cool before removing them from the paper and storing in an airtight container.

Pairs of these were then enclosed within paper wrappers with those for the well-to-do being specially printed by firms such as Jacobs of Halifax. Their designs featured appropriate lines of the burial service from the Book of

---

[509] Travis, *Notes: (historical and biographical)*, p.183; H.L. Roth, *The Yorkshire coiners and notes on old and prehistoric Halifax*, Halifax, F. King & Sons, 1906, p.18.
[510] West family, *Manuscript recipe book*, p.40.

Common Prayer, verses such as this 1790s example:

> When ghastly Death with unrelenting hand,
> Cuts down a father! Brother! Or a friend!
> The still small voice should make you understand
> How frail you are – how near your final end.

and an advertisement:

FUNERAL BISCUITS
BY
BRAMLEY
CONFECTIONER, TEA DEALER, AND
MILLINER
HALIFAX.[511]

As mourners gathered at the house, they were usually received by a family member, offered some basic refreshment if they had travelled from a distance, and invited in to view the deceased. At James Potterton's funeral at Ogden in June 1833, mourners also found a pair of stewards from his Friendly Society flanking the door, each with his six- or seven-foot staff of office draped in black crepe tied with black ribbons, these men acting as ceremonial 'mutes' for the funeral. Passing into the house, a woman standing at one side of the door offered a 'cutting cake' (currant cake) to each person, while a man at the other side provided home-brewed beer either hot or cold, or plain or sweetened, according to the nature of the weather and personal preferences. Once everyone had arrived and paid their respects, the coffin was closed and moved out into the middle of the road, where a chapter of the scripture was read out, two or three hymns sung, and prayers said. It took three teams of bearers to carry him down to the church at Illingworth.[512]

Similar proceedings took place in Stanbury, where mourners were received with a glass of port wine, a funeral card and a funeral biscuit. As the cortège crossed the Sladen valley to Haworth, friends walked in front singing:

> And am I born to die,
> To lay this body down,
> And must my trembling spirit fly
> Into a world unknown ...[513]

Having been met at the church gate, and conducted into the church for the

---

[511] Roth, *The Yorkshire coiners*, p.18.

[512] Lonsdale Collection, *Newspaper cuttings*, vol.31, p.139.

[513] Craven, *A Brontë moorland village*, p.131.

service, everyone assembled around the open grave for the final commitment. Here the bareheaded sexton invited all to the 'burying drinking' in the nearby inn. At Illingworth two 'burying cakes', each the size of a large hot-cross bun, were laid out on the table before each person, with cheese placed on dishes down the centre. Half-gallon jugs of warm or cold sweetened ale were then used to fill the pint-pots that were shared between each pair of mourners. After these refreshments and socializing everyone finally went home, carrying what was left of their cakes tied up in their handkerchiefs. In Stanbury it was customary for each person to give a shilling towards the family's expenses just before leaving, for the provision of even a simple funeral was extremely expensive, as shown by the bill from Thomas Potterton's undertaker, dated 19 August 1821:

a bidding sheet [and bidding?]	£3 5 6
cake	£1 8 6
cheese, sugar, spices	£1 12 6
[other expenses?]	<u>£1 12 0</u>
	£7 18 6[514]

So far, the surviving evidence has suggested that these early to mid-nineteenth century funerals were quite dignified affairs such as we might experience today, but this was not the case. Having gathered evidence from around Haworth, Mrs. Gaskell discovered the much more revealing truth:

> The old custom of 'arvills', or funeral feasts, led to such frequent pitched battles between the drunken mourners … The sexton, standing at the foot of the open grave, announced that the 'arvill' would be held at the Black Bull, or whatever public-house might be fixed upon by the friends of the dead; and thither the mourners and their acquaintances repaired. The origin of the custom had been the necessity of furnishing some refreshment for those who came from a distance, to pay the last mark of respect to a friend … But the arvills at Haworth were often far more jovial doings. Among the poor, the mourners were only expected to provide a kind of special roll for each person; and the expense of the liquors – rum, or ale, or a mixture of both called 'dog's nose' – were generally defrayed by each guest putting some money on a plate set in the middle of the table … As few 'shirked their liquor', there were very frequently 'up-and-down-fights' before the close of the day; sometimes with the horrid additions of 'pawsing' [kicking] and 'gouging' [the eyes] and biting.[515]

---

[514] Lonsdale Collection, *Newspaper cuttings*, vol.31, p.139.

[515] Gaskell, *The life of Charlotte Brontë*, pp.70-72.

In later years, when church, chapel, education and the teetotal movement had reformed the boisterous manners of some parts of the local community, these hard drinking sessions began to be replaced by the more sedate 'Funeral Teas'. Some were still held in public houses, the Bay Horse at Cross Stones offering 'Funeral Dinners and Teas Prepared in the best possible style and on the most reasonable terms.'[516] Since some now considered inns to be vendors of the demon drink, professional confectioners began to cater for meals served in other venues, such as church halls. In 1866 John Crossley was supplying:

> Funerals with Bread, Biscuits, Wine &c. Breakfasts and Teas Supplied for the same ... PLAIN TEA 6d., MEAT DO. 8d. No extra charge for distance within ten miles. One day's notice required.[517]

while in Todmorden it was an undertaker, Mrs Fielden, who decided to extend her business into catering, offering a complete package of services 'on the most reasonable terms.'[518]

The food provided at these teas usually comprised cold meats, sandwiches, salads, pickles and pastries, but had always to include one absolutely essential element, roasted or boiled ham. To omit this would bring unfavourable comment. In contrast, one wife announced at her third wedding that she had already buried two husbands "ansomely, with 'am!'[519] Great family pride went into the provision of a good send-off for one of their own, even if the final bill was beyond their means and might take years to recover from the accumulated debts.

Figure 57. In late Victorian Calderdale, great pride was taken in providing ham sandwiches at funeral teas.

[516] Rudman, *Todmorden old pub trail*, p.60.

[517] Savage, *Sam Banks: his life and times*, p.14.

[518] Ibid., p.74.

[519] Turner, *A spring-time saunter*, p.5.

Figure 58. After funerals at Illingworth, the sexton invited the mourners to a 'burying drinking' at a nearby inn. The tables were laid with two 'burying cakes' for each person and a pint mug for each pair, ready to be filled with warm or cold sweetened ale.

BIBLIOGRAPHY

Archives

Antiquarian, *Sketches of old Hebden Bridge and its people.* 1882. Hebden Bridge Local History Society Archive MISC 50/4 S.

Bedford, H., *Manuscript notebooks*, Leeds University, Brotherton Library Special Collections MS 432/4.

Grimshaw, D., *Manuscript recipe book written at Todmorden National School*, 1933, Private collection.

Lister family of Shibden Hall, *Family and estate records*, West Yorkshire Archive Service (Calderdale), SH/3.

Lonsdale Collection, *Newspaper cuttings*, Calderdale Libraries, Sowerby Bridge.

West Family. *Manuscript recipe book.* Private collection.

Books and articles

Anon., *159 recipes from good kitchens*, Sowerby Bridge, 1914.

Anon., *Halifax Historical Almanack*, Halifax, W. Stephenson, 1861.

Arnold, N., *Edwardian Cornholme*, Cornholme, Workers Educational Association, 1981.

Ashton, M.H., Fletcher, C.A. & Ingham, M. & F., *The St Michael's recipe and quotation book*, Mytholmroyd, 1908.

Bailey, I., Cant, D., Petford, A. & Smith, N., *Pennine perspectives: aspects of the history of Midgley*, Midgley, Midgley Books, 2007.

Baumber, M., *A history of Haworth from the earliest times*, Lancaster, Carnegie, 2009.

Beddoe, J. and Rowe, J.H., 'The ethnology of West Yorkshire', *Yorkshire Archaeological Journal*, 1907, 19, pp.31-60 & Table 3.

Bill o' th' Hoylus End [W. Wright], *Haworth, Cowanhead & Bogthorn Almanac*, Keighley, 1875.

Bill o' th' Hoylus End [W. Wright], *Random rhymes & rambles*, Keighley, 1876.

Bill o' th' Hoylus End [W. Wright], *Revised edition of poems*, Keighley, John Overend, 1891.

Billingsley, J., 'Families, friends and neighbours: folklore and cultural tradition in Midgley' in I. Bailey, D. Cant, A. Petford, & N. Smith, *Pennine perspectives: aspects of the history of Midgley*, Midgley, Midgley Books, 2007.

Binns, A., *Valley of a hundred chapels*, Heptonstall, Grace Judson Press, 2013.

Blinman, A., *Sowerby Bridge: our memories, our history*, Sowerby Bridge, Workers Educational Association, 1988.

Brears, P., 'John Harper at Shibden – a Gothick lady and her architect', *York Historian*, 1978, 2, pp.56-64.

Brears, P., *The gentlewoman's kitchen,* Wakefield, Wakefield Historical Publications, 1965.

Brears, P., *The old Devon farmhouse,* Tiverton, Devon Books, 1998.

Brears, P., *Traditional food in Cumbria,* Carlisle, Bookcase, 2017.

Brears, P., *Traditional food in Yorkshire,* Totnes, Prospect Books, 2014.

Brighouse & District Local History Society, *What was happening in Brighouse 100 years ago,* Brighouse, 1992.

Brontë, C., *Shirley,* 1849. Reprinted London, Everyman's Library, 2008

Brontë, E., *Wuthering Heights,* 1847. Reprinted London, Everyman's Library, 1991.

Calderdale Libraries, *Memory lane: recollections of Brighouse, Rastrick & Hipperholme,* Halifax, Calderdale Leisure Services, 1992.

Calderdale Libraries, *Memory lane: recollections of Elland,* Halifax, Calderdale Leisure Services, 1987.

Calderdale Libraries, *Memory lane: recollections of Sowerby Bridge,* Halifax, Calderdale Leisure Services, 1990.

Calderdale Libraries, *Memory lane: recollections of Todmorden,* Halifax, Calderdale Leisure Services, 1988.

Cobbett, W., *Rural rides,* Vol.2, London, Dent, 1967.

Crabtree, J., *A concise history of the parish and vicarage of Halifax,* Halifax, Hartley and Walker, 1836.

Craven, J., *A Brontë moorland village,* Keighley, Rydal Press, 1907.

Crawford, M. & Richardson, S., *Erringden, Langfield and Stansfield probate records, 1688-1700,* Hebden Bridge, Hebden Bridge Local History Society, 2015.

Crump, W.B., 'Halifax Visitors Book, Vol.1', *Transactions of the Halifax Antiquarian Society,* 1937, pp.21-124.

Crump, W.B., *The little hill farm: Calder Valley,* London, Scrivener Press, 1949.

Cudworth, W., *Round about Bradford,* Bradford, Thomas Brear, 1876.

Davids, S., *Oxenhope in times past,* Chorley, Countryside Publications, 1986.

Davies, R., Petford, A. & Senior, J., *The Diaries of Cornelius Ashworth 1782-1816,* Hebden Bridge, Hebden Bridge Local History Society, 2011.

Dixon, J.H., *Folklore with old things of the Brontës, of Bronte land and of 'thrums,* Harrogate, 1906.

Dugdale, D., *Todmorden market: a 200 year snapshot of Todmorden life,* Todmorden, 2011.

Ellwood, S. *At the foot of the Lud: a history of Luddenden Foot,* Hebden Bridge, Royd Press, 2010.

Garrett, T. *The encyclopedia of practical cookery,* London, L. Upcott Gill, 1894,

Gaskell, E., *The life of Charlotte Brontë,* Originally published 1857, Harmondsworth, Penguin, 1975. The pages referred to are in chapter 2 of the Haworth edition.

Giles, C., *Rural houses of West Yorkshire 1400-1830,* London, HMSO, 1986

Greenwood, E., *Life on a Pennine farm,* Burnley, 1998.

Haliday, W.J. and Umpleby, A.S., *The white rose garland of Yorkshire dialect verse and local and folk-lore rhymes,* London, J.M. Dent, 1949.

Halifax Historical Almanac 1861

Hamerton, L., *Olde Eland,* Elland, Gledhill, 1901.

Hanson, T.W., *The story of old Halifax,* Halifax, 1920.

Hartley, J., *The Halifax Original Illuminated Clock Almanack,* Halifax, 1869, 1895.

Hartley, M. & Ingilby, J., *Life and tradition in West Yorkshire,* London, J.M. Dent, 1976.

Harwood, H.W., 'As things were: a social study of Upper Calder Valley', *Transactions of the Halifax Antiquarian Society,* 1968, 15-26

Harwood, H.W. and Marsden F.H. (eds.), *The Pace-Egg: the Midgley version. With an introductory study.* Originally published 1935. Reprinted Halifax: David Bland, 1977.

Haslehurst, P., *The family friend and young woman's companion,* Sheffield, [1814].

Hawksbridge Baptist Church, *A useful recipe book,* Oxenhope, [n.d.].

Heaton, H., *The Yorkshire woollen and worsted industries,* 2nd ed., Oxford, Clarendon Press, 1965.

Heaton, M., *Recollections and history of Oxenhope,* Oxenhope, 2006.

Heywood, M. & F. and Jennings, B., *A history of Todmorden,* Otley, Smith Settle, 1996.

Holden, J., *A short history of Todmorden,* Manchester, Manchester University Press, 1912.

Hotchops, N., 'Keighley Pudding Eaters', *Keighley Visitor and General Advertiser,* Temperance Society, October 1858; January 1859.

Howard, R., *A history of the typhus of Heptonstall Slack,* Hebden Bridge, 1844.

Jennings, B. (ed.), *Pennine valley: a history of Upper Calderdale,* Otley, Smith Settle, 1994.

Kaye, S., *Yorkshire cooking,* Halifax, Halifax Courier, 1969.

Kendall, H.P., 'Quickstavers in Sowerby', *Transactions of the Halifax Antiquarian Society,* 1914, 173-196.

King Cross [Wesleyan] Circuit, *Recipes and quotations: souvenir of the British Empire bazaar,* Halifax, 1913.

Kitchener, W., *The cook's oracle: containing receipts for plain cookery,* London, A. Constable & Co, 1822.

Leigh, B., *Book of golden recipes,* Leeds, 1913.

Lister, J., *Poems by Tom Halifax,* 3 vols, Halifax, [n.d.].

Long, W.H., *A survey of the agriculture of Yorkshire,* London, Royal Agricultural Society of England, 1969.

Mellor, S. (ed.), *Biographies, sketches, & rhymes by the Calder Valley Poets*, Halifax, Edward Mortimer, 1916.

Mitchell, W.R., *By gum, life were sparse: memories of northern mill towns*, Originally published 1991, London, Warner, 1993.

Newell, A., *History of Vale Baptist Church Todmorden 1851-1901*, Todmorden, [n.d.].

Ogden, J.H., 'Burlees and Old Town', *Transactions of the Halifax Antiquarian Society*, 1904, 73-92.

Oxenhope Church School Rebuilding Fund, *Recipe book*, Oxenhope, 1926.

Parker, J., *Illustrated rambles from Hipperholme to Tong*, Bradford, Percy, Lund Humphries, 1904.

Pickles, W., *Between you and me: the autobiography of Wilfred Pickles*, London, Werner Laurie, 1949.

Porritt, A., *It happened here: third series*, Halifax, Weardale Press, 1969.

Reach, A.B., *The Yorkshire textile districts in 1849*, Helmshore, Helmshore Local History Society, 1974.

Roth, H.L., *The Yorkshire coiners and notes on old and prehistoric Halifax*, Halifax, F. King & Sons, 1906.

Rudman, B., *Todmorden old pub trail*, Littleborough, George Kelsall, 1989.

Savage, E. (ed.), *Sam Banks: his life and times*, Todmorden, Todmorden Antiquarian Society, 1985.

Siddal: our memories, our history, Halifax, Workers Educational Association, 1989.

Slyman, S., *T' story o' th' pudding macking un eiting: a defence for Haworth*, Cullingworth, 1867.

Southwart, E., *Brontë moors & villages from Thornton to Haworth*, London, John Lane, 1923.

St John's Church, *Good recipes: a souvenir*, Hebden Bridge, 1933.

Stringfellow, G., *The Sowerby Bridge rush bearing*, Halifax, Metropolitan Borough of Calderdale, 1980.

Sutcliffe, H., *By moor and fell: landscapes and lang-settle lore from West Yorkshire*, London, T.F. Unwin, 1899.

The Commercial Directory for 1818-19-20, Manchester, James Pigot, 1818.

Thomas, P., *Hardship and hope: Hebden Royd and Todmorden during the First World War (1914-1918)*, [Hebden Bridge], 2016.

Thompson, D., *Stanbury: a Pennine country village*, Calgary, Two Margaret's Publications, 2002.

Todmorden & Hebden Bridge Historical Almanack, Todmorden, 1861, 1867, 1869, 1875, 1876, 1895.

Travis, J., *Local historical notes and personal reminiscences*, Todmorden, Frederick Lee & Co, 1905.

Travis, J., *Notes: (historical and biographical) mainly of Todmorden and district,*

Rochdale, 1896.

Trigg, W.B., 'Excursion to Ovenden', *Transactions of the Halifax Antiquarian Society*, 1925, 81-104.

Trigg, W.B., 'The Halifax coalfield: Parts 1-2', *Transactions of the Halifax Antiquarian Society*, 1930, 117-158.

Trigg, W.B., 'The Halifax coalfield: Parts 3-4', *Transactions of the Halifax Antiquarian Society*, 1931, 73-111.

Trigg, W.B., 'The Halifax coalfield: Part 5', *Transactions of the Halifax Antiquarian Society*, 1932, 261-292.

Turner, J.H., *Haworth past and present: a history of Haworth, Stanbury & Oxenhope*, Brighouse, J.S. Jowett, 1879.

Turner, J.H., *The Rev. Oliver Heywood, 1630-1702: his autobiography, diaries, anecdote and event books*, vol.4, Bingley, 1835.

Turner, W., *A spring-time saunter: round and about Bronte land*, Halifax, Halifax Courier, 1913 (First edition).

Walton, J.K., *Fish and chips and the British working class 1870-1940*, Leicester, Leicester University Press, 1992.

Watson, J., *The history and antiquities of the parish of Halifax*, London, T. Lowndes, 1775. Republished Manchester, E.J. Morten, 1973.

Webster, E., 'Some Dean Clough archives', *Transactions of the Halifax Antiquarian Society*, 1988, 41-56.

White, F. (ed.), *Good things in England: a practical cookery book for everyday use*, Originally published 1932, London, Futura, 1974.

Whone, H., *The essential West Riding: its character in words and pictures*, Wakefield, EP Publishing, 1975.

Wilson, C.A. (ed.), *Food for the community: special diets for special groups*, Edinburgh, Edinburgh University Press, 1993.

Wood, J., *The autobiography of John Wood*, Bradford, 1877.

Wood, S. & Brears, P., *The real Wuthering Heights: the story of the Withins farms*, Stroud, Amberley, 2016

Wood, S., *Haworth, Oxenhope & Stanbury from old photographs*, Stroud, Amberley, 2011.

Wright, J. (ed.), *The English dialect dictionary*, 6 vols, Oxford, Oxford University Press, 1923.

SUBJECT INDEX

PEOPLE INDEX

LOCATION INDEX

RECIPE INDEX

248

249